Revit® Architecture 2022 for Designers

Revit® Architecture 2022 for Designers

Douglas R. Seidler

ASID, IIDA, LEED AP, IDEC
Marymount University

FAIRCHILD BOOKS

NEW YORK • LONDON • OXFORD • NEW DELHI • SYDNEY

FAIRCHILD BOOKS

Bloomsbury Publishing Inc

1385 Broadway, New York, NY 10018, USA

50 Bedford Square, London, WC1B 3DP, UK

29 Earlsfort Terrace, Dublin 2, Ireland

BLOOMSBURY, FAIRCHILD BOOKS and the Fairchild Books logo are trademarks of Bloomsbury Publishing Plc

Second Edition published 2016

Third Edition published 2018

Fourth edition published 2020

This edition first published 2022

Reprinted 2022, 2023

Library of Congress Cataloging-in-Publication Data

Names: Seidler, Douglas R., author.

Title: Revit architecture 2022 for designers / Douglas R. Seidler, ASID, IIDA, LEED AP, IDEC, Marymount University.

Description: Fifth edition. | New York : Fairchild Books, 2022. | Includes index. |

Identifiers: LCCN 2021035745 (print) | LCCN 2021035746 (ebook) | ISBN 9781501385568 (paperback) | ISBN 9781501385551 (pdf)

Subjects: LCSH: Architectural drawing--Data processing. | Architecture--Computer-aided design. | Autodesk Revit.

Classification: LCC NA2728 .S45 2022 (print) | LCC NA2728 (ebook) | DDC 720.22/2--dc23

LC record available at https://lccn.loc.gov/2021035745

LC ebook record available at https://lccn.loc.gov/2021035746

ISBN: PB: 978-1-5013-8556-8

ePDF: 978-1-5013-8555-1

eBook: 978-1-5013-8554-4

Printed and bound in Great Britain

To find out more about our authors and books visit www.fairchildbooks.com and sign up for our newsletter.

for Patrícia, Maya, and André

CONTENTS

EXTENDED CONTENTS

EXTENDED CONTENTS (continued)

PREFACE

I believe any interested student can learn a new skill with clear, organized instruction. Complex skills require more focus and clearer instruction. *Revit is no different.*

I teach and write about complex software like Revit and AutoCAD by limiting instruction to the most relevant topics. Each topic is presented with custom graphics and easy-to-read text. The instruction creates strong connections to architectural graphic standards, the design studio, and the design profession. Guided discovery exercises reinforce the newly attained knowledge, while application exercises provide an opportunity to apply the skill to something new.

Now in its fifth edition, Revit Architecture 2022 for Designers provides focused, clear, and relevant instruction for both interior design and architecture students. This edition fully integrates instruction to draw, dimension, annotate, and print using the International System of Units (SI) which is commonly referred to as the metric system.

Audience and Prerequisite Knowledge

Revit is rapidly replacing AutoCAD as the digital drawing tool of choice for architects and interior designers. This book aims to help design students master Revit as a tool in the design studio and in practice.

You can broadly sort the numerous Revit books into two categories—"guides for dummies" and "exhaustive references"—neither of which specifically addresses how professional designers use Revit. *Revit Architecture 2022 for Designers* sits between these two categories, providing both a thorough primer for new learners and expanded conceptual discussion for design professionals. The progressive introduction of concepts (chapters build on previous chapters), digital exercises, and professional examples make this book easy to follow for learners new to Revit.

The only prerequisites for the book are a fundamental knowledge of computers, manual drafting techniques, and architectural drawing types.

Revit Version Compatibility

The instruction in this book is written for Revit 2022. While many of the concepts and features discussed are backwards compatible with prior versions of Revit, the text introduces many features new to Revit 2022. While most universities teach and use the latest version of Revit, many professional offices do not update their software annually due to hardware requirements and professional education costs. I have written this book to help students switch between versions of Revit as they transition from the classroom to the office.

Content Overview

We learn best when we can create connections between the new information we are learning and information that we already know. Chapter 1 introduces Revit and Building Information Modeling (BIM) through comparisons to AutoCAD and hand drawing. Chapters 2–3 introduce you to drawing tools in Revit. Understanding how to use each of the tools keeps you in control of your drawing and allows you to "ask of the computer" rather than let Revit dictate how your drawings will look. Each chapter begins with a basic introduction of Revit's features for the drawing convention and gradually moves through intermediate and more advanced drawing techniques.

Chapters 4–10 emphasize drawing for design presentations. Floor plans, finish plans, reflected ceiling plans, elevations, and perspectives are reviewed throughout this section of the textbook. By combining these presentation drawings skills with the foundation drawing skills acquired earlier in the book, you will be prepared to create drawings that visually communicate your design ideas.

Chapters 11–14 cover construction documents in Revit, ending with organized sheet sets. Construction drawing types include construction plans, demolition plans, furniture plans, finish plans, and reflected ceiling plans. Additional topics include schedules, enlarged plans, and construction details. By combining these construction document skills with a strong foundation for drawing in Revit, you will be prepared to work on or create any Revit project.

Companion Download

The textbook instruction is supplemented with a digital companion download. The download includes guided discover exercises, custom title sheets, example drawings, and project templates.

Learn more about the companion download at **WWW.RAFDBOOK.COM/DOWNLOADS**.

ACKNOWLEDGMENTS

I would like to thank the interior design students at Marymount University for challenging the way I think about teaching every day. Your frowns, blank stares, and awe-inspiring projects are my barometer. Special thanks are due to Lisa Corrado, Kirsten Ederer, and Kurt Seip for contributing their drawings to this book.

Tran Truong was kind enough to share her senior capstone project which I am honored to include on the cover of this textbook. Thank you, Tran.

Architectural Resources Cambridge/ARC graciously supplied construction drawings shown as examples throughout this book. These drawings anchor the instruction with concrete examples from practice. Thank you.

During the revision process, I received critical feedback from my peers at many institutions. I am grateful to each of you for taking time from your busy schedule to help shape this text.

Richard Bettini	Kean University
George Fares	Kansas State University
Kim Rich Meister	University of Georgia
Kristine Winner	Northern Virginia Community College

I also greatly appreciate the enthusiasm, guidance, and collaboration of the team at Fairchild Books. Thank you Emily Samulski, Joseph Miranda, Jenna Lefkowitz, Edie Weinberg, Louise Dugdale, Ken Bruce, and Deborah Maloney for your critical feedback and support.

As always, I must thank my mother for allowing me to take things apart, my father for (mostly) teaching me to put things back together, and my sister for unwillingly donating her toys to this noble cause.

To my amazing wife, daughter, and son, thank you for your unconditional love and support.

INTRODUCTION

chapter 1

INTRODUCING REVIT ARCHITECTURE

IN THIS CHAPTER

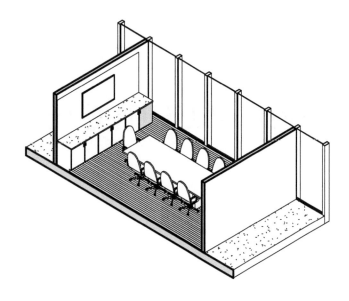

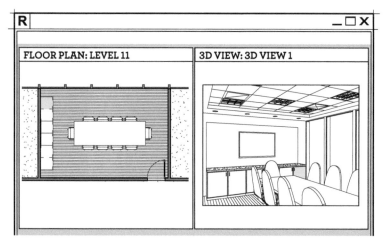

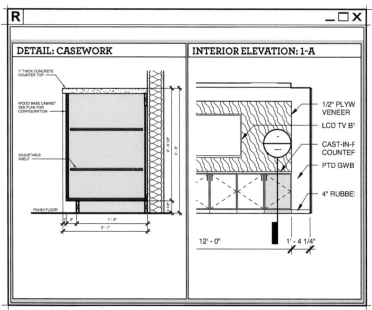

What Is BIM and Why Should I Use It?

Autodesk's Revit Architecture 2022 is a revolutionary modeling program for the architectural industry. Revit is in a class of programs that utilize Building Information Modeling (BIM for short) to organize and present large data sets that describe every aspect of a building.

Architectural design, by its nature, requires us to solve complex three-dimensional problems. BIM projects hold huge amounts of project data in a single file. Because of this single database, BIM creates efficiencies during design and documentation phases by quickly presenting and updating objects in multiple views.

Some of these views take the form of architectural drawings like plan, elevation, section, and perspective. Other views take the form of tables and spreadsheets.

The light blue built-in cabinet shown in these views is a single BIM object visually represented in plan view, perspective view, elevation view, and detail section view. Because each view is displaying the same BIM object, any modifications to that object are automatically updated in each view.

In BIM, this principle applies to many other objects like doors, windows, furniture, and stairs. BIM also dynamically builds schedules that accurately reflect the location and quantity of items (like furniture and doors) in a project.

The bottom line is that when an entire project is organized in a single database, you can spend more time focusing on design and less time coordinating information across multiple sheets in a drawing set.

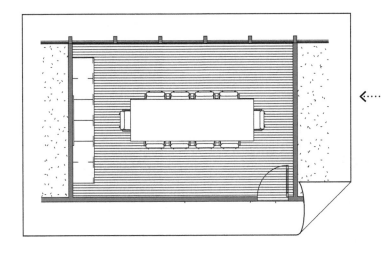

How Is BIM Different from CAD?

Computer-aided Design (CAD) software provided a huge leap forward in building documentation from hand drawing.

- CAD drawings are essentially digital sheets of paper. Like many digital tools, CAD improves productivity and accuracy by allowing users to copy and paste between drawings. CAD also allows users to quickly edit drawings.
- CAD drawings are most commonly organized with multiple layers that host digital lines.

Revit models are organized broadly into three types of elements: Datum elements, Model elements, and View-Specific elements.

DATUM ELEMENTS are the foundation of the Revit model by which everything is referenced.

- Levels are the most commonly used datum element. Levels define the location of level-hosted elements in the model. Level-hosted elements include Walls, Floors, Ceilings, and Furniture.
- Reference Planes are two-dimensional planes used to build three-dimensional objects in Revit.
- Grids are used to define the location of structural elements like columns and walls.

MODEL ELEMENTS are subdivided into host elements and model components.

- Common host elements include walls, floors, ceilings, and roofs.
- Model components often require a compatible host element. For example, a door (model component) can only be inserted into a wall (host element), which is placed on a level (datum element).

VIEW-SPECIFIC ELEMENTS are visible only in the view they are placed. Annotation text, room labels, and dimensions are common view-specific elements.

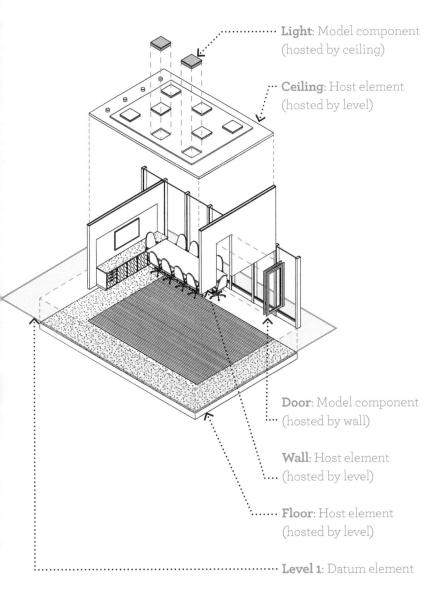

Light: Model component (hosted by ceiling)

Ceiling: Host element (hosted by level)

Door: Model component (hosted by wall)

Wall: Host element (hosted by level)

Floor: Host element (hosted by level)

Level 1: Datum element

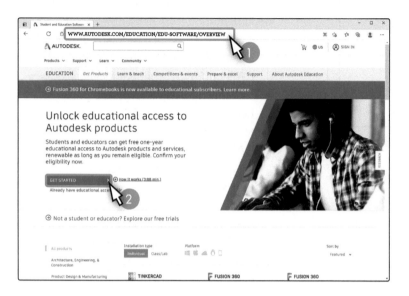

Autodesk Educational Community

Historically, Autodesk has been very generous in providing free software to students. At the time of publication, students can download a one-year Educational license of Revit Architecture 2022.

While the Revit educational software incorporates all the functionality of the professional software, it may not be used for commercial or for-profit purposes.

Register with Autodesk

- *Step 1*: **OPEN** the website **WWW.AUTODESK.COM/EDUCATION/EDU-SOFTWARE/OVERVIEW** in your Web browser.
- *Step 2*: **CLICK** the **GET STARTED** button.

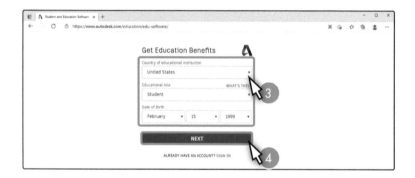

- *Step 3*: **COMPLETE** the requested education benefits information.
- *Step 4*: **CLICK** the **NEXT** button.

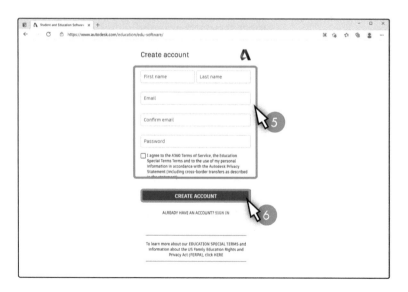

- *Step 5*: **COMPLETE** the requested registration information. It is recommended that you use your school email address in the email field.
- *Step 6*: **CLICK** the **CREATE ACCOUNT** button.

- *Step 7 (not shown)*: Autodesk requires that you activate your account before you can download Revit. Check your email for additional instructions provided by Autodesk to activate your account.

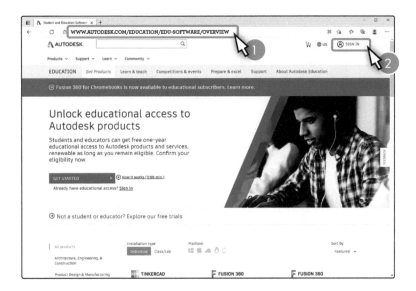

Download Revit

- *Step 1*: **OPEN** the Autodesk website:
  WWW.AUTODESK.COM/EDUCATION/EDU-SOFTWARE/OVERVIEW in your Web browser.
- *Step 2*: **CLICK** the **SIGN IN** button.

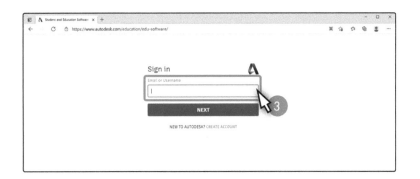

- *Step 3*: **SIGN IN** to Autodesk's student website with the **AUTODESK ID** created during the registration process.

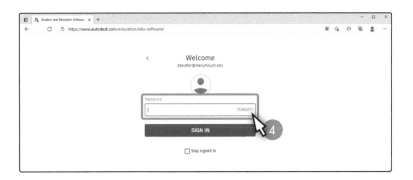

- *Step 4*: **SIGN IN** to Autodesk's student website with the **PASSWORD** created during the registration process.

Tip: Make sure your computer meets the minimum requirements for Revit 2022 listed at **WWW.RAFDBOOK.COM/DOWNLOADS**.

INSTALLING REVIT (continued)

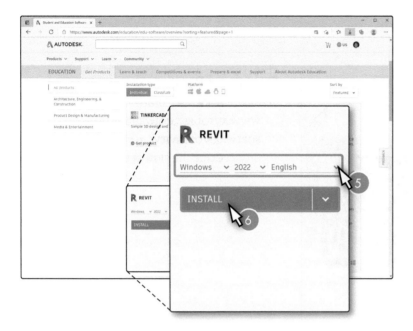

Download Revit (continued)

Once you have signed into your Autodesk Education account, you can download your free version of Revit.

- *Step 5:* **SELECT** the **WINDOWS OPERATING** system, the **2022** version, and the **ENGLISH** language.

- *Step 6:* **CLICK** the **INSTALL** button.

- *Step 7:* Once the download is complete, double-click the **REVIT_2022** setup file located in your Web browser or your downloads folder.

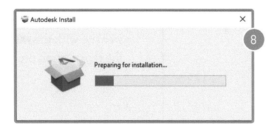

- *Step 8:* The **AUTODESK INSTALL** dialog box shows the progress preparing the **REVIT_2022** setup file for installation.

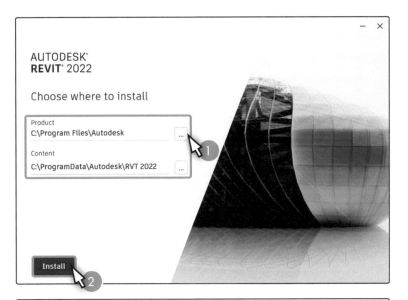

Install Revit

The installation process involves both downloading and installing Revit 2022 on your computer. The entire process will vary based on the speed of your Internet connection.

- *Step 1 (optional)*: Tell the Autodesk Installer where to install Revit on your computer. Most users will use the default install locations as show in this example.

- *Step 2*: **CLICK** the **INSTALL** button.

- *Step 3*: The installation percentage allows you to follow the progress. You should keep your computer connected to a reliable Internet connection until installation is complete.

- *Step 4*: **CLICK** the **RESTART** button when the installation is complete.

Activating Revit 2022

The first time you open Revit, Autodesk will request you register the software. You must be connected to the Internet to activate Revit.

- *Step 1*: **OPEN REVIT** and **CLICK** the **SIGN IN WITH YOUR AUTODESK ID** button.
- If you have a network license or serial number (not common), click the appropriate button in the other license types section of the activation dialog box.

The Autodesk Licensing dialog box prompts you to sign in with your Autodesk account. This is the same email address and password used on page 7 to download Revit.

- *Step 2*: Follow the prompts to sign into your Autodesk account.

- *Step 3*: If you have setup 2 Step Verification on your Autodesk account, Autodesk will send you a SMS message with a 6-digit security code. **TYPE** the **6-DIGIT CODE** in the dialog box.
- *Step 4*: **CLICK** the **ENTER CODE** button to verify your sign in and activate your Revit 2022 software license.

Installing Family Content Packs

Beginning in Revit 2021, Autodesk changed how library content is installed. This change installs a minimal set of content with Revit. Other content libraries must be downloaded and installed separately from the main installation of the software.

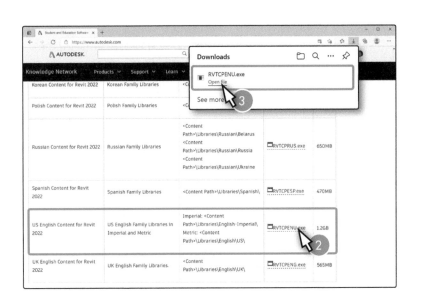

- *Step 1 (not shown)*: **VISIT** and **WWW. RAFDBOOK.COM/DOWNLOAD** to locate the appropriate family content pack for your Revit version.
- *Step 2*: **DOWNLOAD** the appropriate content pack. In this example, we downloaded **RVTCPENU.EXE** which contains US English Family Libraries in both Imperial and Metric.
- *Step 3*: **LAUNCH** the installer file downloaded in the previous step.

- *Step 4*: The **AUTODESK INSTALL** dialog box shows the progress preparing the **CONTENT PACK** setup file for installation.

Once the installation completes, both Imperial and SI libraries of Revit families are available for use on your computer.

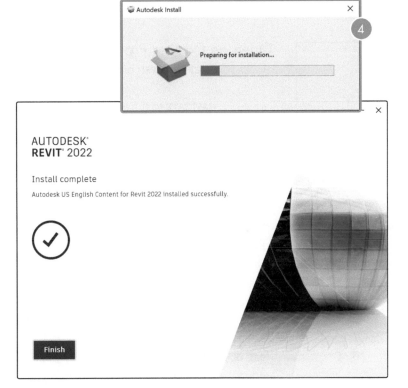

A Revit project file (.RVT) holds all of the information for a building.

Revit
Architecture
2022

Create a New Project

- *Step 1*: **OPEN** Revit Architecture 2022 by double-clicking on the desktop icon.

- *Step 2*: **CLICK** the **NEW PROJECT** link on the Revit welcome screen.

> **Tip:** Interior Designers and Architects should change **NEW PROJECT TEMPLATE** from **CONSTRUCTION** to **ARCHITECTURE** as illustrated in the following steps.

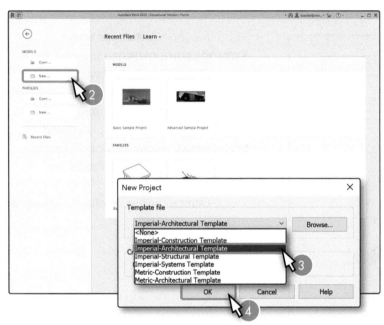

Revit prompts you to select a template file for the new project.

- *Step 3*: **SELECT** the **IMPERIAL-ARCHITECTURAL TEMPLATE**.
- *Step 4*: **CLICK** the **OK** button to start the new project.

Open an Existing Project

- *Step 1*: **CLICK** the **OPEN** button.

- *Step 2*: **NAVIGATE** to the folder with your Revit files. **CLICK ONCE** on the **FILE** you want to open.
- *Step 3*: **CLICK** the **OPEN** button.

> **Version Compatibility Tip:**
> Revit models are complex databases. Because of these complexities, Revit files are not backwards compatible. To say it another way, Revit 2022 files will not open in earlier versions of the software, including Revit 2019 and Revit 2018. That said, you can upgrade an older Revit model by opening it in a newer version of Revit.

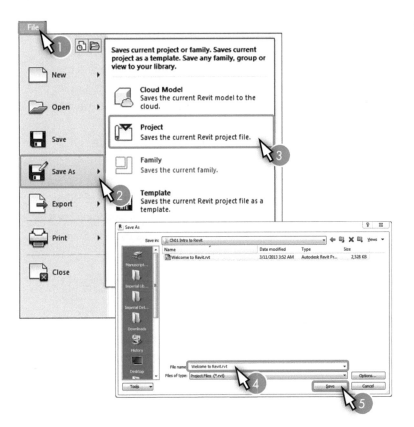

Saving Projects
- *Step 1*: **CLICK** the **FILE MENU** button.
- *Step 2*: **CLICK** the **SAVE AS** button.
- *Step 3*: **CLICK** the **PROJECT** button.

- *Step 4*: **NAVIGATE** to the folder or portable drive where you want to save the Revit project. **TYPE** the **FILENAME** in the **SAVE AS** dialog box.
- *Step 5*: **CLICK** the **SAVE** button.

Active and Backup Project Files
- Every time you save a project, Revit creates a backup project file from the most recent version.
- By default, Revit keeps three backup project files in the same folder with the active project file.

- The **ACTIVE PROJECT NAME** contains the file name and the **.RVT** extension.

- **BACKUP PROJECT NAMES** are appended with a four-digit number that increases with every new backup. In this example, the **0003.rvt** file is the most recent backup.

Tip: Keep the **BACKUP PROJECT FILES** on your computer or portable drive in case the active Revit project becomes corrupt or fails to open.

Graphical User Interface

Revit user interface contains multiple elements that you use to create and modify the Revit model. The interface is similar to AutoCAD and other Autodesk software.

Parts of the User Interface

- **FILE TAB:** First introduced in Revit 2018, the File tab replaces the Application Menu present in previous versions of Revit.

- The **QUICK ACCESS TOOLBAR** contains a list of commonly used tools such as Save, Undo, and Aligned Dimension.

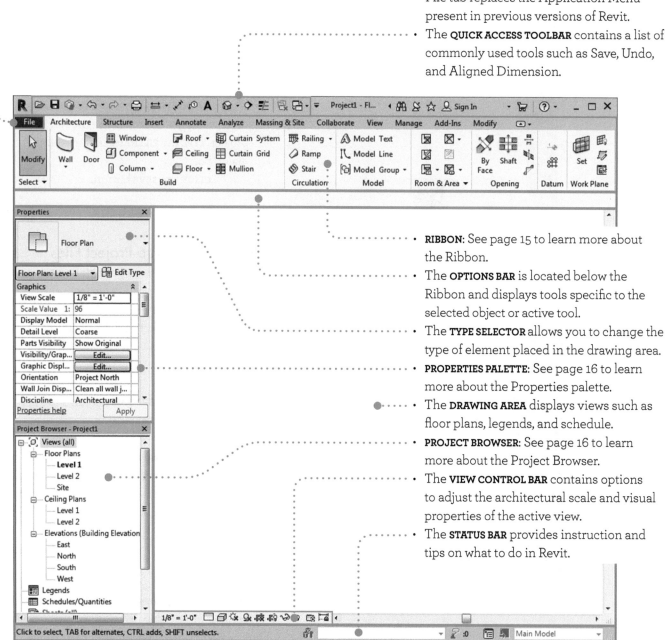

- **RIBBON:** See page 15 to learn more about the Ribbon.

- The **OPTIONS BAR** is located below the Ribbon and displays tools specific to the selected object or active tool.

- The **TYPE SELECTOR** allows you to change the type of element placed in the drawing area.

- **PROPERTIES PALETTE:** See page 16 to learn more about the Properties palette.

- The **DRAWING AREA** displays views such as floor plans, legends, and schedule.

- **PROJECT BROWSER:** See page 16 to learn more about the Project Browser.

- The **VIEW CONTROL BAR** contains options to adjust the architectural scale and visual properties of the active view.

- The **STATUS BAR** provides instruction and tips on what to do in Revit.

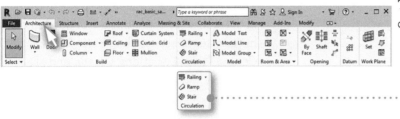

Ribbon

The **RIBBON** is divided into several tabs, which contain Revit's core functionality.

- The **ARCHITECTURE** tab (shown here) is subdivided into six panels.

- The **CIRCULATION** panel contains the **RAILING**, **RAMP**, and **STAIR** buttons, all of which are related to building circulation.

Full Ribbon State

The **FULL RIBBON** state is the default layout. Each panel is expanded to show buttons related to the panel.

- **CLICK** the **MINIMIZE TO PANEL** button to cycle through four different panel states.

Panel Tiles Ribbon State

The **PANEL TILES** ribbon collapses each panel into a large tile with a single icon.

- Reveal each panel's buttons by hovering the mouse over the panel's icon.
- **CLICK** the **MINIMIZE TO PANEL** button to cycle to the next panel state.

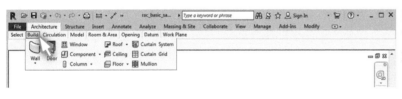

Panel Buttons Ribbon State

The **PANEL BUTTONS** ribbon collapses each panel into small text icons.

- Reveal each panel's buttons by hovering the mouse over the panel's name.
- **CLICK** the **MINIMIZE TO PANEL** button to cycle to the next panel state.

Panel Tabs Ribbon State

The **PANEL TABS** ribbon completely collapses each tab.

- Click on the tab name to reveal its panels and buttons. The tab will autohide after several seconds of inactivity.
- **CLICK** the **MINIMIZE TO PANEL** button to cycle to the next panel state.

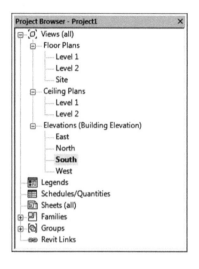

Project Browser

The Project Browser displays all of the views in the active project. Views are divided into major categories including Floor Plans, Ceiling Plans, Elevations, Details, and 3D Views.

This browser shows the default views in a new architectural project. You'll notice the views are limited to **FLOOR PLANS**, **CEILING PLANS**, and **BUILDING ELEVATIONS**. As you add views to the project, Revit will place them in the appropriate category. In addition to the architectural views, the Project Browser contains **LEGEND**, **SCHEDULE/QUANTITY**, and **SHEET** categories.

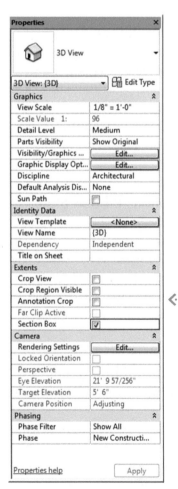

Properties Palette

The Properties palette displays all available information for the selected object in the model.

- For **FURNITURE**, like this task chair, the Properties palette provides access to the floor level, fabric and finish, comments, and construction phase.

- When nothing is selected, the Properties palette provides information about the **CURRENT VIEW**.
- In this example, the 3D view's properties can be reviewed and updated in the Properties palette.

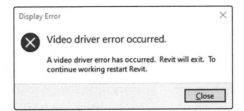

Revit relies on your computer's graphics card to create a sophisticated graphics experience. If you receive graphics errors similar to this example when switching to 3D views, your graphics card may not be compatible with Revit's graphics requirements.

Disabling Graphics Hardware Acceleration

Disabling Graphics Hardware Acceleration in Revit often eliminates software crashes. Follow these steps to disable hardware acceleration.

- *Step 1*: In the File tab, **CLICK** the **OPTIONS** button at the bottom of the menu.

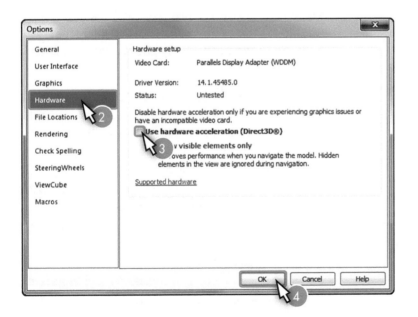

- *Step 2*: **CLICK** the **HARDWARE** section in the options dialog box.
- *Step 3*: **UNCHECK** the **USE HARDWARE ACCELERATION** box.

- *Step 4*: **CLICK** the **OK** button to save the changes.

- *Step 5 (not shown)*: You will need to save, close, and re-open your Revit Projects for this change to take effect. Only documents opened after this change will be affected by the video card change.

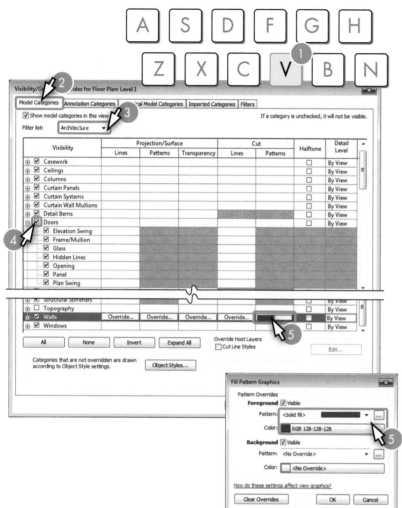

The Visibility/Graphic Overrides dialog box is used to control the display categories in the active view. Categories in Revit are often compared to Layer in AutoCAD. The primary difference is that elements in Revit are automatically associated with the correct category while lines in AutoCAD need to be manually assigned to layers.

Controlling Model Categories

- *Step 1 (not shown)*: **OPEN VISIBILITY/GRAPHICS** by **TYPING** the letters **VV** on the keyboard. (Type **V** twice.)
- *Step 2*: The two most commonly used categories groupings are **MODEL CATEGORIES** and **ANNOTATION CATEGORIES.**
- *Step 3*: **FILTER** the lists of categories under the **MODEL CATEGORIES** tab by selecting **ARCHITECTURE.**
- *Step 4*: The **VISIBILITY CHECK BOX** turns the category **ON** or **OFF** in the active view. In this example, the **DOORS** will be **HIDDEN** in plan view when the **DOOR CATEGORY VISIBILITY** is changed to **OFF.**
- *Step 5*: The **LINE** and **PATTERN** overrides allow you to adjust how the category is graphically displayed in the active view. In this example, the **CUT PATTERN** for the **WALLS CATEGORY** was changed to **GRAY/SOLID FILL.**

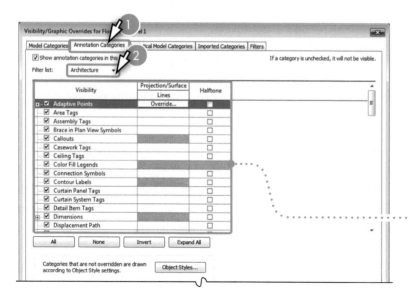

Controlling Annotation Categories

Annotative categories contain most elements in a view that contain text including dimensions, room tags, and symbols.

- *Step 1*: The two most commonly used categories groupings are **MODEL CATEGORIES** and **ANNOTATION CATEGORIES.**
- *Step 2*: **FILTER** the lists of categories under the **MODEL CATEGORIES** tab by selecting **ARCHITECTURE.**
- *Step 3*: Adjust the **VISIBILITY** and **LINE STYLE** for each annotative category in the active view.

Working simultaneously with multiple views in Revit allows you to see design changes in both two and three dimensions.

Tab Open Views

- *Steps 1–2*: On the keyboard, **TYPE** the letter **T** and then **W** to create a **TAB** for all open views.
- **T W** is short for **TAB WINDOWS**.

Each open view is presented as a tab as seen in this example. The view name for each window is visible at the top of the window.

- *Step 3*: **CLOSE** any unwanted views by **CLICKING** the **X**.

Tiling Open Views

Tiling windows is more frequently used when you want to work on multiple views at the same time.

- *Steps 1–2*: On the keyboard, **TYPE** the letter **W** and then **T** to **TILE** all open views in Revit.
- **W T** is short for **WINDOW TILE**.

Each open view is arranged beside other views as seen in this example.

- *Step 3*: **CLOSE** any unwanted views by **CLICKING** the red **X**.
- *Step 4 (not shown)*: **TYPE** the letter **W** and then **T** to re-tile the open views.

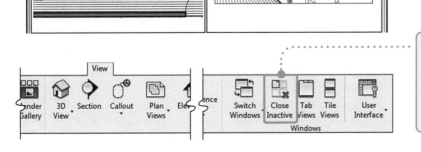

Tip: The **CLOSE INACTIVE VIEWS** button in the **VIEW** tab closes all open views except for the current view. This is helpful when you have multiple views open and do not want to close them one at a time.

TEXTBOOK LEARNING EXERCISES

Companion Downloads

Several chapters contain additional files that support the instructions presented in the chapter. Download these support files at **WWW.RAFDBOOK.COM/DOWNLOADS.**

Guided Discovery Exercises

Each chapter contains a set of companion support files. These files are intended to guide you through the instructions presented in the chapter. To complete the guided discovery exercises, download support files at **WWW.RAFDBOOK.COM/DOWNLOADS.**

Application Exercises

Once you've mastered each chapter's content, it is time to start applying your Revit knowledge to something new. In each of the application exercises, you are asked to work with an assignment from your instructor or on a previously completed project.

Checklists

Many of the chapters include checklists to help you remember important tips related to the content discussed in the chapter. Checklists are divided into **GENERAL REVIT TIPS, ANNOTATION TIPS,** and **DIMENSION TIPS.**

chapter 2

FLOOR PLAN BASICS

loor plans are at the heart of any strong design presentation. A good plan visually communicates the spatial conditions in a building or project, including the relationship between adjacent spaces. Revit can help create strong drawings by simplifying the drafting process. For example, walls, doors, windows, and furniture are automatically represented with appropriate line weight. Because these objects also contain three-dimensional properties, Revit can use information in the plan view to generate elevation and perspective views.

IN THIS CHAPTER

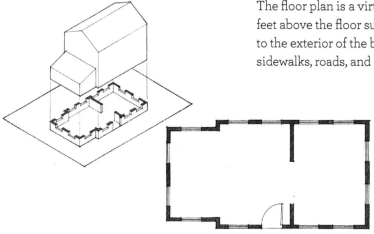

The floor plan is a virtual slice through an entire building, usually four feet above the floor surface. This slice, called the "cut plane," may extend to the exterior of the building in ground floor plans to include exterior sidewalks, roads, and landscaping.

Floor plans are two-dimensional drawings that visually communicate the spatial conditions in a building or project, including the relationship between adjacent spaces.

Elements drawn in Revit's plan view (e.g., walls, doors, windows, and furniture) are graphically represented with appropriate line weight.

Because these same elements contain three-dimensional properties, Revit can also use information added to the plan view in elevation and perspective views.

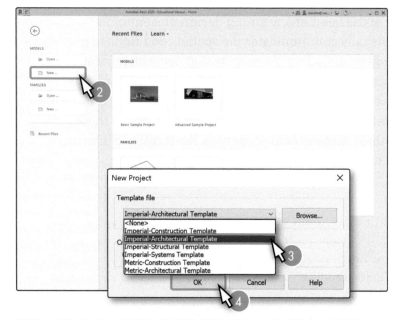

Starting a New Revit Project

Before you can draw in Revit, you need to create a new project.

- *Step 1 (not shown)*: **OPEN** Revit.
- *Step 2*: **CLICK** the **NEW PROJECT** link on the Revit welcome screen.

Revit prompts you to select a template file for the new project.

- *Step 3*: **SELECT** the **IMPERIAL-ARCHITECTURAL TEMPLATE**.

  The SI template for this step is **METRIC-ARCHITECTURAL TEMPLATE**.

- *Step 4*: **CLICK** the **OK** button to start the new project.
- *Step 5*: In the **PROJECT BROWSER**, you will see **LEVEL 1** in bold font face. This indicates the current view is **FLOOR PLAN: LEVEL 1**.

Unlike AutoCAD, every drawing for a Revit project is held in a single file. These files have a **.RVT** extension.

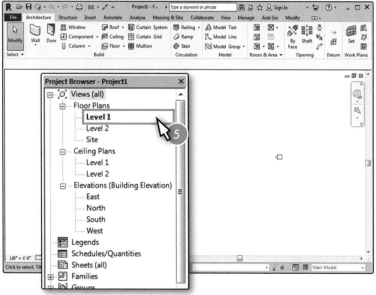

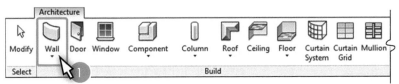

Walls in Revit are intelligent three-dimensional objects that automatically connect to other walls. Walls are drawn in the plan view.

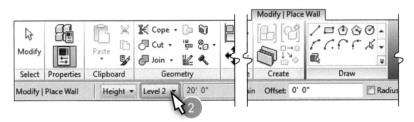

- *Step 1*: From any plan view, **CLICK** the **WALL** button in the **ARCHITECTURE** tab.

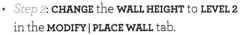

- *Step 2*: **CHANGE** the **WALL HEIGHT** to **LEVEL 2** in the **MODIFY | PLACE WALL** tab.
- Because walls in Revit are three-dimensional, it is important to connect them to the level above. In this example, we are adding walls to Level 1 so we want to constrain the wall's height to Level 2.

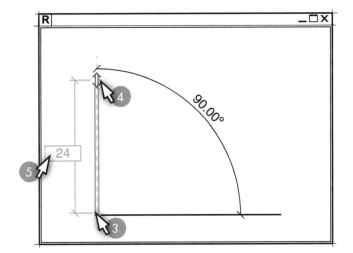

- *Step 3*: **CLICK ONCE** in the lower left of the plan view.
- *Step 4*: **DRAG** the cursor upward on the screen, keeping the vertical angle to 90°.
- *Step 5*: **TYPE 24** on the keyboard and press **ENTER**. This sets the length of the wall to 24′.

> The SI measurement for this step is **6000**.

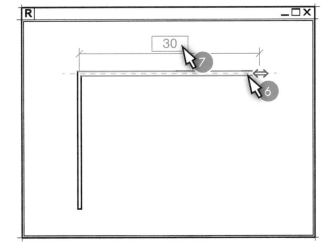

- *Step 6*: **DRAG** the cursor to the right on the screen.
- *Step 7*: **TYPE 30** on the keyboard and press **ENTER**. This sets the length of the wall to 30′.

> The SI measurement for this step is **9000**.

> **Tip**: Because Revit's default **Imperial** unit of length is feet, you do not need to include the foot symbol when typing dimensions.
>
> Revit's default **SI** unit length is millimeters. You do not need to include the mm symbol when typing SI dimensions.

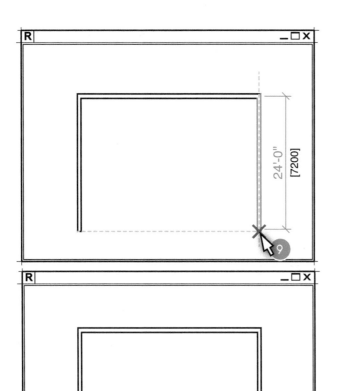

- *Step 8 (not shown)*: **DRAG** the cursor in the down direction. As the wall approaches the length of the first wall (24'), Revit creates a dashed horizontal reference line. The cursor will also show the intersection object snap icon, which is an "x."

  The SI measurement for this step is **7200**.

- *Step 9*: **CLICK ONCE** when you see the **INTERSECTION OBJECT SNAP** icon.

- *Step 10 (not shown)*: **DRAG** the cursor to the **LEFT** until you see the **ENDPOINT OBJECT SNAP** icon, which is a square.

  The SI measurement for this step is **9000**.

- *Step 11*: **CLICK ONCE** to draw the fourth and final wall.
- *Step 12 (not shown)*: **PRESS** the **ESC** key on the keyboard to end the Wall command.

Copying Walls

- *Step 1*: **CLICK ONCE** on the left wall as shown in the example. Clicking on any wall activates the **MODIFY WALL** tab in the ribbon.
- *Step 2*: **CLICK** the **COPY** button in the **MODIFY WALL** tab.

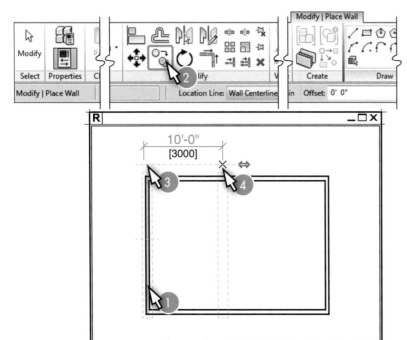

- *Step 3*: **CLICK ONCE** above the selected wall and move the cursor to the right.
- *Step 4*: **CLICK ONCE** when the temporary dimension shows a copy distance of **10'-0"**.

  The SI measurement for this step is **3000**.

- *Step 5 (not shown)*: **PRESS** the **ESC** key on the keyboard to end the Wall command.

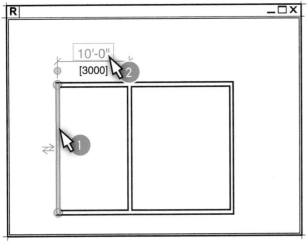

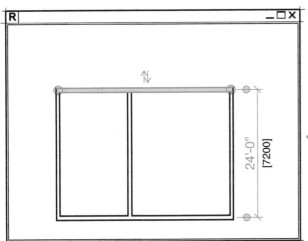

Moving Walls

Revit allows you to move walls by modifying the distance between two walls in the plan. In this example, increasing the distance will move the wall to the left. Decreasing the distance will move the wall to the right.

- *Step 1*: **CLICK ONCE** on the wall you want to move. Revit will highlight the wall and show temporary dimensions to the nearest wall. In this example, the wall is located **10'-0"** from the nearest wall.
- *Step 2*: **CLICK ONCE** on the **10'-0"** temporary dimension and type the new distance. In this example, **TYPE 12** and press **ENTER** to move the wall **12'-0"** from the adjacent wall.

  The SI measurement for this step is **6000**.

- *Step 3 (not shown)*: **PRESS CTRL+Z** on the keyboard to **UNDO** the last move.

- This second example shows the temporary dimension that appears when you click on the top wall in your project. In this example, increasing the distance greater than 24'-0" will move the wall up. Decreasing the distance less than 24'-0" will move the selected wall down.

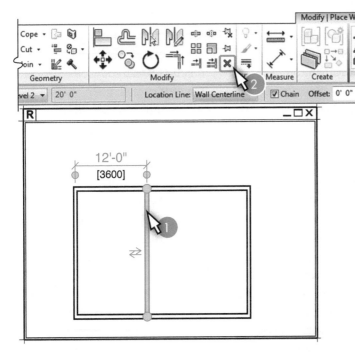

Deleting Walls

- *Step 1*: **CLICK ONCE** on the **WALL** you want to delete.
- *Step 2*: **CLICK** the **DELETE** button in the **MODIFY | WALLS** tab or **PRESS DELETE** on the keyboard.

Repeat these steps to delete additional walls in the floor plan.

DRAWING WALLS (continued)

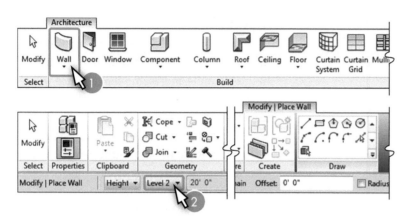

Rectangle and Polygon Walls

In addition to straight wall segments, the Build Wall command can also create rectangular and polygon-shaped walls.

- *Step 1*: **CLICK** the **WALL** button in the **ARCHITECTURE** tab.
- *Step 2*: In the **MODIFY | PLACE WALL** tab, connect the **WALL HEIGHT** to **LEVEL 2**.

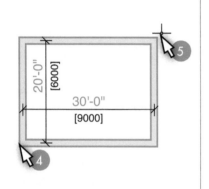

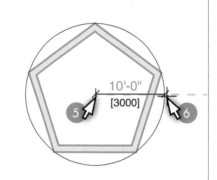

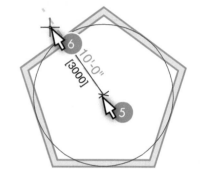

Rectangle Walls

- *Step 3*: **CLICK ONCE** on the **RECTANGLE** button in the draw panel.
- *Step 4*: **CLICK ONCE** in the lower-left-hand corner of the plan view.
- *Step 5*: As you **DRAG** the cursor up and to the right, Revit indicates the size of the rectangle with temporary dimensions. **CLICK ONCE** to locate the upper-right corner of the rectangle walls.
- *Step 6 (not shown)*: **PRESS** the **ESC** key to end the Wall command.

Inscribed Polygon Walls

- *Step 3*: **CLICK ONCE** on the **INSCRIBED POLYGON** button in the **DRAW** panel.
- *Step 4*: Indicate the number of sides for the polygon in the Options bar.
- *Step 5*: **CLICK ONCE** in the plan view to locate the center of the polygon.
- *Step 6*: As you **MOVE** the cursor away from the center, Revit indicates the radius of the polygon with temporary dimensions. **CLICK ONCE** to set the radius of the polygon walls or **TYPE** the radius and press **ENTER**.
- *Step 7 (not shown)*: **PRESS** the **ESC** key to end the Wall command.

Circumscribed Polygon Walls

- *Step 3*: **CLICK ONCE** on the **CIRCUMSCRIBED POLYGON** button in the **DRAW** panel.
- *Step 4*: Indicate the number of sides for the polygon in the Options bar.
- *Step 5*: **CLICK ONCE** in the plan view to locate the center of the polygon.
- *Step 6*: As you **MOVE** the cursor away from the center, Revit indicates the radius of the polygon with temporary dimensions. **CLICK ONCE** to set the radius of the polygon walls or **TYPE** the radius and press **ENTER**.
- *Step 7 (not shown)*: **PRESS** the **ESC** key to end the Wall command.

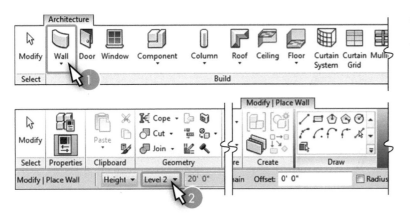

Circle and Arc Walls

Add curved walls to your project with the circle and arc draw commands.

- *Step 1*: **CLICK** the **WALL** button in the **ARCHITECTURE** tab.
- *Step 2*: In the **MODIFY | PLACE WALL** tab, connect the **WALL HEIGHT** to **LEVEL 2**.

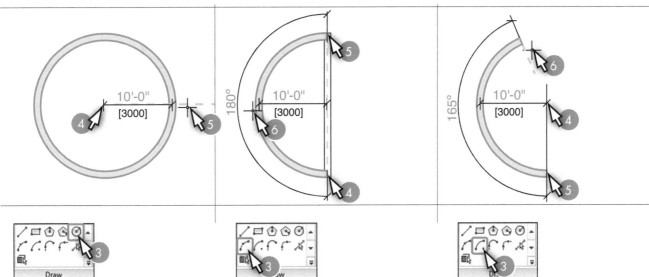

Circle Wall

- *Step 3*: **CLICK ONCE** on the **CIRCLE** button in the draw panel.
- *Step 4*: **CLICK ONCE** in the plan view to indicate the center of the circle wall.
- *Step 5*: As you **DRAG** the cursor away from the center, Revit indicates the radius of the circle with temporary dimensions. **CLICK ONCE** to set the radius of the circle wall or **TYPE** the radius and press **ENTER**.
- *Step 6 (not shown)*: **PRESS** the **ESC** key to end the Wall command.

Arc Wall (start-end-radius)

- *Step 3*: **CLICK ONCE** on the **START-END-RADIUS ARC** button in the draw panel.
- *Step 4*: **CLICK ONCE** in the plan view to indicate the first point of the arc wall.
- *Step 5*: **CLICK ONCE** in the plan view to indicate the second point of the arc wall.
- *Step 6*: **DRAG** the cursor away from the wall. **CLICK ONCE** to set the radius or **TYPE** the radius and press **ENTER**.
- *Step 7 (not shown)*: **PRESS** the **ESC** key to end the Wall command.

Arc Wall (center-ends)

- *Step 3*: **CLICK ONCE** on the **CENTER-ENDS ARC** button in the draw panel.
- *Step 4*: **CLICK ONCE** in the plan view to indicate the center of the arc wall.
- *Step 5*: **DRAG** the cursor away from the first click. **CLICK ONCE** to set the radius or **TYPE** the radius and press **ENTER**. This click also marks one end of the arc wall.
- *Step 6*: **DRAG** the cursor and **CLICK ONCE** to mark the second end of the arc wall.
- *Step 7 (not shown)*: **PRESS** the **ESC** key to end the Wall command.

DRAWING WALLS (continued)

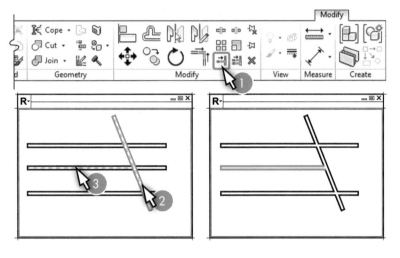

Trimming One Wall

- *Step 1*: **CLICK** the **TRIM/EXTEND SINGLE ELEMENT** button in the **MODIFY** tab.

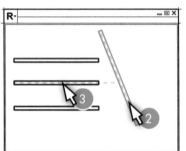 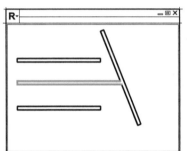

- *Step 2*: **CLICK ONCE** on the wall that is the trim boundary (or cutting edge).
- *Step 3*: **CLICK ONCE** on the portion of the wall that you want to keep.

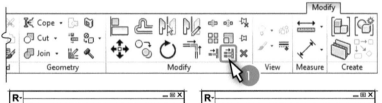

Extending One Wall

- *Step 1*: **CLICK** the **TRIM/EXTEND SINGLE ELEMENT** button in the **MODIFY** tab.
- *Step 2*: **CLICK ONCE** on the wall that is the extension boundary.
- *Step 3*: **CLICK ONCE** on the wall that you want to extend.

Trimming Multiple Walls

- *Step 1*: **CLICK** the **TRIM/EXTEND MULTIPLE ELEMENTS** button in the **MODIFY** tab.

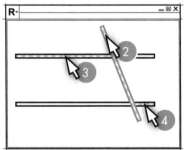 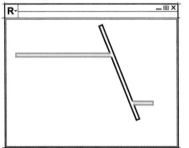

- *Step 2*: **CLICK ONCE** on the wall that is the trim boundary.
- *Step 3*: **CLICK ONCE** on the first wall that you want to trim.
- *Step 4*: **CLICK ONCE** on the second wall that you want to trim.

Extending Multiple Walls

- *Step 1*: **CLICK** the **TRIM/EXTEND MULTIPLE ELEMENTS** button in the **MODIFY** tab.
- *Step 2*: **CLICK ONCE** on the wall that is the extension boundary.
- *Step 3*: **CLICK ONCE** on the first wall that you want to extend.
- *Step 4*: **CLICK ONCE** on the second wall that you want to extend.

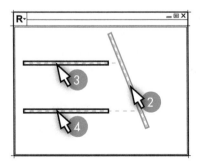 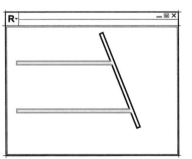

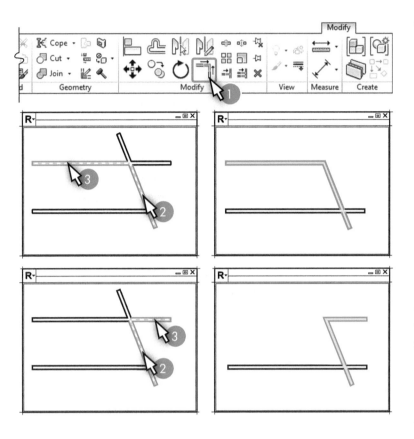

Trim/Extend to Corner

The Trim/Extend to Corner command is similar to the Fillet command in AutoCAD.

- *Step 1*: **CLICK** the **TRIM/EXTEND TO CORNER** button in the **MODIFY** tab.

- *Step 2*: **CLICK ONCE** on the first wall that you want to connect.
- *Step 3*: As you **HOVER** the **CURSOR** over other walls, Revit indicates the corner location with a dashed blue line. **CLICK ONCE** on the second wall to trim the two selected walls to their corner.

In this example, *Step 2* and *Step 3* are repeated, clicking on different portions of the same walls. Note the differences between the resulting corner in these two examples.

Fillet Arc/Radius Wall Corners

The Fillet Arc command draws a new curved wall between two existing walls in a plan view.

- *Step 1*: **CLICK** the **WALL** button in the **ARCHITECTURE** tab.

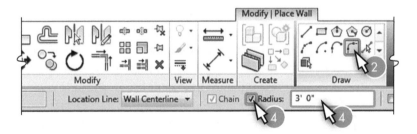

- *Step 2*: **CLICK ONCE** on the **FILLET ARC** button in the **DRAW** panel.
- *Step 3 (not shown)*: **CONNECT** the **WALL HEIGHT** to **LEVEL 2** in the **MODIFY | PLACE WALL** tab.
- *Step 4*: **CHECK** the radius option and set the radius value. In this example, the radius is set to **3'-0"**.

> The SI measurement for this step is **900.**

- *Step 5*: **CLICK ONCE** on the **FIRST EXISTING WALL** that you want to connect.
- *Step 6*: **CLICK ONCE** on the **SECOND EXISTING WALL** that you want to connect. Revit connects to two walls with a new arc wall.

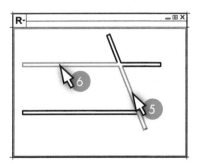
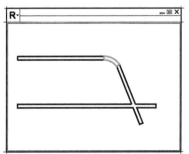

DRAWING DOORS AND WINDOWS

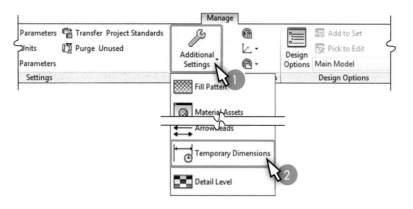

Temporary Dimensions

By default, Revit's temporary dimensions provide dimensional information to the center lines of walls, doors, and windows. Many designers prefer to locate walls and doors from the edge of the opening to the closest wall face.

- *Step 1*: **CLICK** the **ADDITIONAL SETTINGS** button in the **MANAGE** tab.
- *Step 2*: **CLICK** the **TEMPORARY DIMENSIONS** button in the Drop-down menu. This opens the **TEMPORARY DIMENSION PROPERTIES** dialog box.
- *Step 3*: **CLICK** the **FACES** option for temporary dimensions from walls.
- *Step 4*: **CLICK** the **OPENINGS** option for temporary dimensions from doors and windows.
- *Step 5*: **CLICK** the **OK** button to close the dialog box and save the new settings.

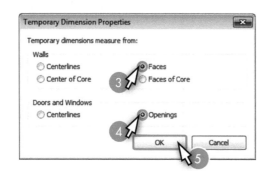

Loading Door Families (Adding New Doors)

Revit allows you to load new door families as you add new doors to the floor plan.

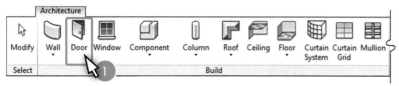

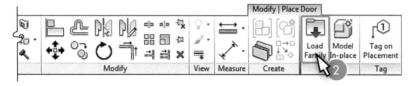

- *Step 1*: **CLICK** the **DOOR** button in the **ARCHITECTURE** tab.
- *Step 2*: **CLICK** the **LOAD FAMILY** button in the **MODIFY | PLACE DOOR** tab.
- *Step 3*: The **LOAD FAMILY** file browser opens with the **US IMPERIAL** folder visible. If this folder is not visible, **CLICK** the **IMPERIAL LIBRARY** shortcut icon in the file browser.
- *Step 4 (not shown)*: **DOUBLE-CLICK** on the **DOOR** folder.
- *Step 5*: **CLICK ONCE** on the **DOOR-SINGLE-PANEL** door family.
- *Step 6*: **CLICK ONCE** on the **OPEN** button.
- *Step 7 (not shown)*: You will be prompted to specify which door family types to load. **CLICK ONCE** on the **72" X 84"** type. **CLICK** the **OK** button in the Specify Type dialog box.

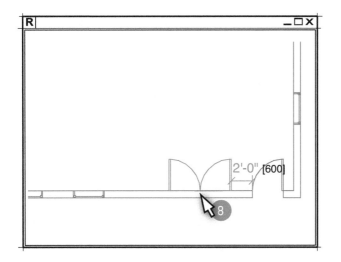

Loading Door Families (continued)

As you move the cursor over walls in the floor plan view, Revit shows the double-flush door and temporary dimensions to the closest wall or opening.

- *Step 8*: **CLICK ONCE** to insert the Door-Double-Flush_Panel door into a wall.

> **Tip:** Beginning with Revit 2020, there was a change in how the library content is installed and only a minimal set of content is installed with Revit. If you do not see the door families shown in these examples, reference page 11 to learn how to install this library content on your computer.

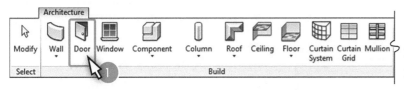

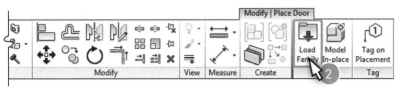

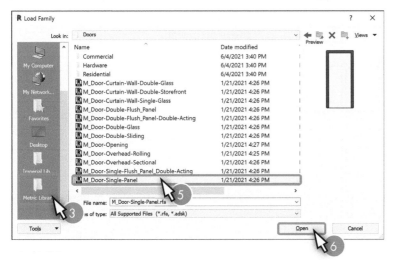

Loading Metric Door Families (Adding New Doors)

Revit allows you to load new door families as you add new doors to the floor plan.

- *Step 1*: **CLICK** the **DOOR** button in the **ARCHITECTURE** tab.
- *Step 2*: **CLICK** the **LOAD FAMILY** button in the **MODIFY | PLACE DOOR** tab.
- *Step 3*: **CLICK** the **METRIC LIBRARY** shortcut icon in the file browser.
- *Step 4 (not shown)*: **DOUBLE-CLICK** on the **US** folder and then the **DOORS** folder.
- *Step 5*: **CLICK ONCE** on the **M_DOOR-SINGLE-PANEL** door family.
- *Step 6*: **CLICK ONCE** on the **OPEN** button.

- *Step 7 (not shown)*: You will be prompted to specify which door family types to load. **CLICK ONCE** on the **900 X 2100MM** type. **CLICK** the **OK** button in the Specify Type dialog box.

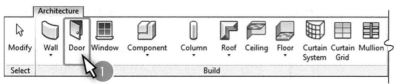

Adding Doors to the Floor Plan

- *Step 1*: **CLICK** the **DOOR** button in the **ARCHITECTURE** tab.
- *Step 2 (not shown)*: **MOVE** the **CURSOR** over walls in the plan view to see the door and temporary dimensions to the closest wall.
- *Step 3 (not shown)*: **PRESS** the **SPACE BAR** to flip the door's swing.
- *Step 4*: **CLICK ONCE** to insert the door into a wall.

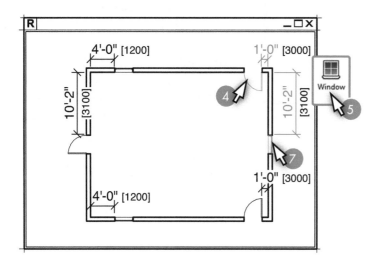

Adding Windows to the Floor Plan

- *Step 5*: **CLICK** the **WINDOW** button in the **ARCHITECTURE** tab.
- *Step 6 (not shown)*: **MOVE** the **CURSOR** over walls in the floor plan view to see window and temporary dimensions to the closest wall.
- *Step 7*: **CLICK ONCE** to insert the window into a wall.

> **Guided Discovery 2.1:** Following the exercise to the left, **ADD** doors and windows to the floor plan. The support file is at **WWW.RAFDBOOK.COM/DOWNLOADS.**

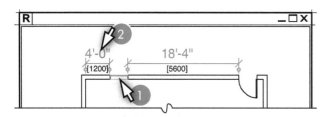

Moving Doors and Windows

Revit allows you to move doors and windows along the wall where they were initially placed.

- *Step 1*: **CLICK ONCE** on the window or door you want to move. Revit will highlight the object and show temporary dimensions to the nearest opening or wall. In this example, the window is located 4'-0" from the nearest wall.
- *Step 2*: **CLICK ONCE** on the **4'-0"** temporary dimension between the window and the wall.

> The SI measurement for this step is **1200.**

- *Step 3*: **TYPE 2** and **PRESS ENTER** to move the window 2'-0" from the adjacent wall.

> The SI measurement for this step is **600.**

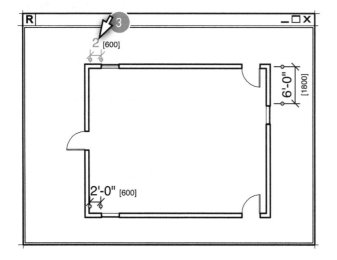

Copying Doors and Windows

- *Step 1*: **CLICK ONCE** on the **WINDOW**. Clicking on any window activates the **MODIFY | WINDOWS** tab.
- *Step 2*: **CLICK** the **COPY** button in the **MODIFY | WINDOWS** tab.
- *Step 3*: **CLICK ONCE** above the selected window (or door) and **MOVE** the cursor to the right.
- *Step 4*: **CLICK ONCE** when the temporary dimension shows a copy distance of 6'-0".

  The SI measurement for this step is **1800**.

- *Step 5 (not shown)*: **PRESS** the **ESC** key to end the Copy command.

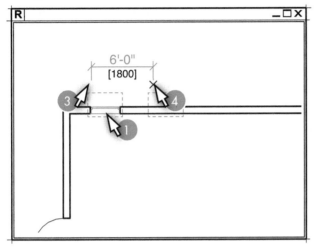

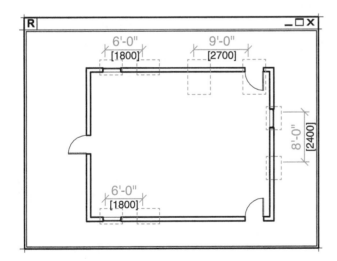

Guided Discovery 2.1 (continued): Following the exercise to the left, **COPY** both doors and windows using the indicated dimensions.

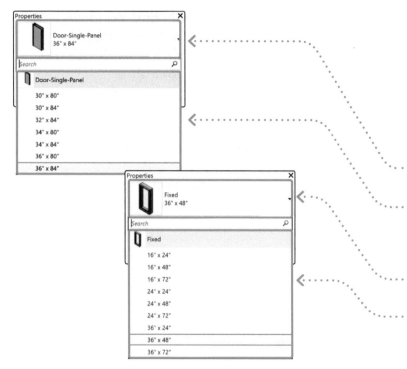

Door and Window Families

In Revit, objects such as doors and windows are members of larger groups called families. New projects in Revit contain default families. Additional families can be loaded into a project from the Revit library or from manufacturer websites.

- The default door family is a Single-Flush door.
- The Single-Flush door family contains multiple types of Single-Flush doors that vary in dimension.

- The default window family is a Fixed window.
- The Fixed window family contains multiple types of fixed windows that vary in dimension.

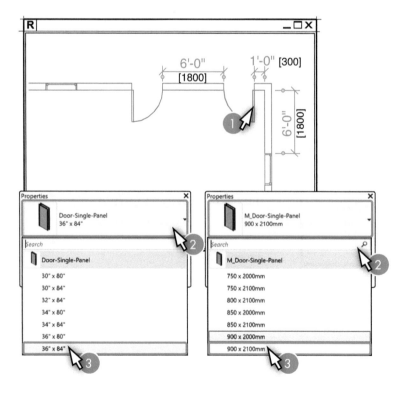

Changing Door Types

- *Step 1*: **CLICK ONCE** on a **DOOR** in the floor plan view. The **PROPERTIES** palette updates to show the current door family (**SINGLE-FLUSH**) and type (**36" X 84"**).

- *Step 2*: **CLICK ONCE** on the down arrow in the **PROPERTIES** palette to show available family types for the **SINGLE-FLUSH** family.
- *Step 3*: **CLICK** on the **32" X 84"** family type to change the size of the door. The door in plan view will update to reflect the new door size.

> The SI equivalent door family is **900 X 2100MM**.

> **Guided Discovery 2.1 (continued)**: Repeat the steps above to change all doors in the floor plan from to **32" X 84"**.

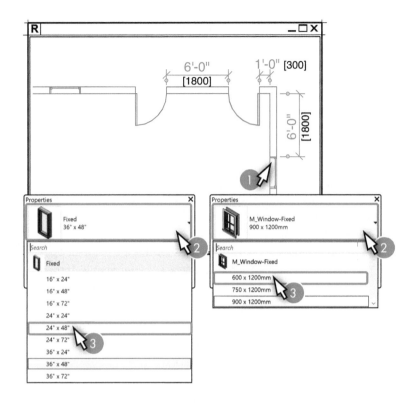

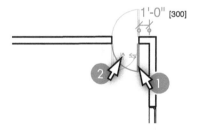

Changing Window Types

- *Step 1*: **CLICK ONCE** on a **WINDOW** in the floor plan view. The **PROPERTIES** palette updates to show the current window family (**FIXED**) and type (**36″ X 48″**).

  > The SI equivalent window family type is **900 X 1200MM.**

- *Step 2*: **CLICK ONCE** on the down arrow in the **PROPERTIES** palette to show available family types for the **FIXED** window family.
- *Step 3*: **CLICK** on the **24″ X 48″** family type to change the size of the window. The window in plan view will update to reflect the new size.

  > The SI equivalent window family is **600 X 1200MM.**

> **Guided Discovery 2.1 (continued):** Repeat the steps above to change all windows in the floor plan to **24″ X 48″**.

Flipping Doors and Windows

Revit allows you to change the orientation of doors and windows after they are placed in a wall.

- *Step 1*: **CLICK ONCE** on the **DOOR** you want to flip. Revit will highlight the door and two flip controls.
- *Step 2*: **CLICK ONCE** on the vertical flip controls to control whether the door swings in or out.
- *Step 3 (not shown):* **CLICK ONCE** on the horizontal flip controls to control whether the door swings left or right.

Deleting Doors and Windows

- *Step 1 (not shown):* **CLICK ONCE** on the window you want to delete.
- *Step 2*: **CLICK** the **DELETE** button in the **MODIFY | DOORS** tab or **PRESS DELETE** on the keyboard.

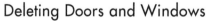

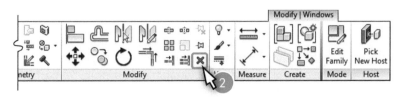

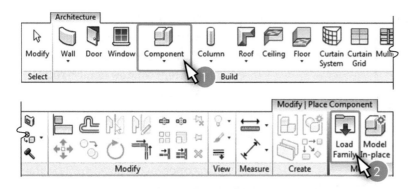

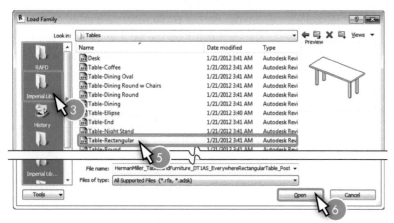

Adding Tables

Similar to door and window families, Revit contains a limited list of furniture families.

- *Step 1*: From any plan view, **CLICK** the **COMPONENT** button in the **ARCHITECTURE** tab.

- *Step 2*: **CLICK** the **LOAD FAMILY** button in the **MODIFY | PLACE COMPONENT** tab.

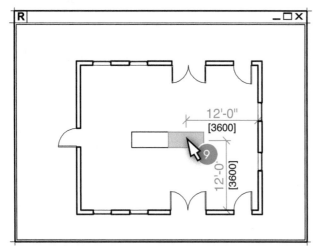

- *Step 3*: The **LOAD FAMILY** file browser opens with the **US IMPERIAL** folder visible. If this folder is not visible, **CLICK** the **IMPERIAL LIBRARY** shortcut icon in the file browser.

- *Step 4 (not shown)*: **NAVIGATE** to the following folder: **US IMPERIAL> FURNITURE>TABLES**.

- *Step 5*: **CLICK ONCE** on the **TABLE-RECTANGULAR** furniture family.

- *Step 6*: **CLICK** the **OPEN** button.

- *Step 7 (not shown)*: **MOVE** the **CURSOR** over the floor plan view. Revit shows the table and temporary dimensions to the closest wall.

- *Step 8 (not shown)*: **PRESS** the **SPACEBAR** to rotate the furniture in the plan view.

- *Step 9*: **CLICK ONCE** to insert the table in the room.

- *Step 10 (not shown)*: **PRESS** the **ESCAPE** key twice to end the Place command.

> **Guided Discovery 2.2:** Insert two tables in the room to match the furniture in this example. The support file for this exercise is at **WWW.RAFDBOOK.COM/DOWNLOADS**.

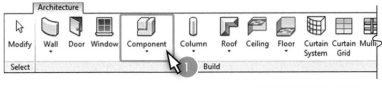

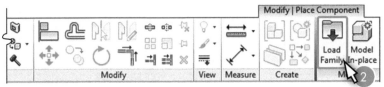

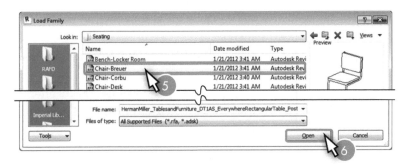

Adding Seating

- *Step 1*: From any plan view, **CLICK** the **COMPONENT** button in the **ARCHITECTURE** tab.

- *Step 2*: **CLICK** the **LOAD FAMILY** button in the **MODIFY | PLACE COMPONENT** tab.

- *Step 3 (not shown)*: The **LOAD FAMILY** file browser opens with the **US IMPERIAL** folder visible. If this folder is not visible, **CLICK** the **IMPERIAL LIBRARY** shortcut icon in the file browser.
- *Step 4 (not shown)*: **NAVIGATE** to the following folder: **US IMPERIAL> FURNITURE>SEATING**.
- *Step 5*: **CLICK ONCE** on the **CHAIR-BREUER** furniture family.
- *Step 6*: **CLICK ONCE** on the **OPEN** button.

- *Step 7 (not shown)*: **MOVE** the **CURSOR** over the floor plan view. Revit shows the chair and temporary dimensions to the closest wall.
- *Step 8 (not shown)*: **PRESS** the **SPACEBAR** to rotate the furniture in the plan view.
- *Step 9*: **CLICK ONCE** to insert the table in the room. (Try inserting a chair to match the furniture in this example.)
- *Step 10 (not shown)*: **PRESS** the **ESCAPE** key twice to end the Place command.

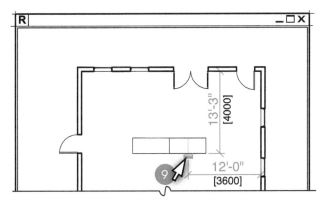

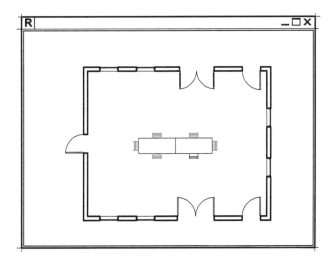

> **Guided Discovery 2.2 (continued):** Insert six chairs in the room to match the furniture in this example.

DRAWING FURNITURE (continued)

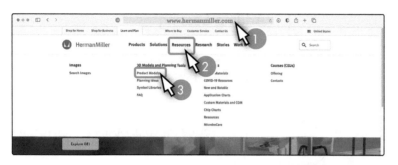

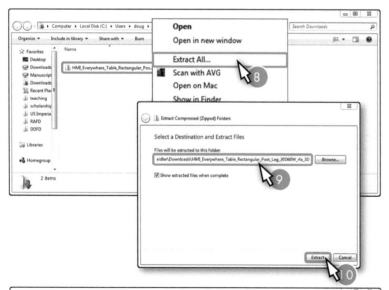

Downloading Furniture Families

Many furniture manufacturers provide Revit families for their furniture collections. In this example, you will download and insert a Herman Miller table into the floor plan. Furniture families are also available for download at BIMOBJECT.com.

- *Step 1*: **OPEN** a **WEB BROWSER** and navigate to **WWW.HERMANMILLER.COM**.
- *Step 2*: **CLICK** the **RESOURCES** navigation menu.
- *Step 3*: **CLICK** the **PRODUCT MODELS** link.

- *Steps 4-5*: **CLICK** the **TRAINING TABLES** filter in the **PRODUCT CATEGORY** menu and then click the **APPLY** button.

- *Steps 6-7*: **CLICK** the **REVIT FILE** download link for the **EVERYWHERE TABLE RECTANGULAR POST LEG** training table.

Most browsers will store this file in the downloads folder on your computer.
- *Step 8*: In this example, Herman Miller has compressed the family as a zipped folder. To uncompress the folder, **RIGHT-CLICK** on the zipped folder and **SELECT EXTRACT ALL**
- *Step 9*: In the **EXTRACT COMPRESSED FOLDERS** dialog box, use the default folder.
- *Step 10*: **CLICK** the **EXTRACT** button.

The download folder will now contain both the original zipped folder and the uncompressed folder.

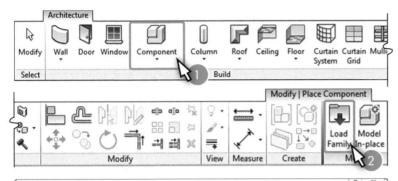

Adding Furniture Families

- *Step 1*: From any plan view, **CLICK** the **COMPONENT** button in the **ARCHITECTURE** tab.

- *Step 2*: **CLICK** the **LOAD FAMILY** button in the **MODIFY | PLACE COMPONENT** tab.

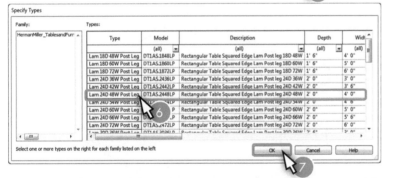

- *Step 3 (not shown)*: **NAVIGATE** to the following folder: **DOWNLOADS> HMI_EVERYWHERE_TABLE**
- *Step 4*: **CLICK ONCE** on the furniture family.
- *Step 5*: **CLICK** the **OPEN** button.

Many manufacturer families will prompt you to select the specific furniture types to load for the selected family.

- *Step 6*: **CLICK ONCE** on the **LAM 24D 48W POST LEG** type.
- *Step 7*: **CLICK** the **OK** button.

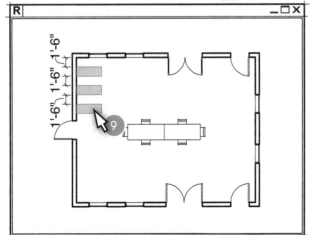

- *Step 8 (not shown)*: **MOVE** the **CURSOR** over the floor plan view. Revit shows the table and temporary dimensions to the closest wall.
- *Step 9*: **CLICK ONCE** to insert the Herman Miller table in the room.

> **Guided Discovery 2.2 (continued):** Insert three tables in the room to match the furniture shown in this floor plan.

STOREFRONT WALLS

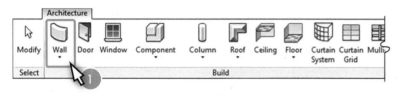

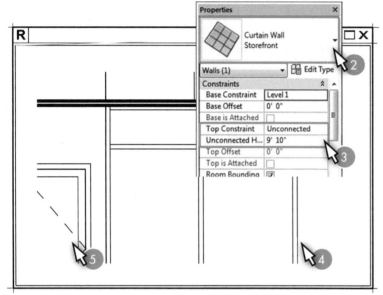

Adding Interior Storefront Walls

Storefront walls are panel systems made of glass and mullions. In Revit, the mullion placement in storefronts is limited to equal spacing between mullions.

- *Step 1*: From a plan view, **CLICK** the **WALL** button in the **ARCHITECTURE** tab.
- *Step 2*: **SELECT** the **CURTAIN WALL STOREFRONT** family type in the **PROPERTIES** box.
- *Step 3*: **SET** the wall's **TOP CONSTRAINT** to **UNCONNECTED. SET** the **UNCONNECTED HEIGHT** to the **CEILING HEIGHT** in the space. In this example, the unconnected height is set to **9′ 10″**.

  The SI measurement for this step is **3000.**

- *Step 4*: **CLICK ONCE** in the plan view to locate the first edge of the storefront wall.
- *Step 5*: **CLICK ONCE** in the plan view to locate the second edge of the storefront wall.
- *Step 6* (*not shown*): **PRESS** the **ESC** key **TWICE** to end the Wall command.

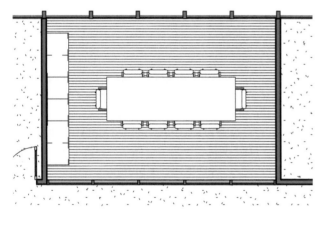

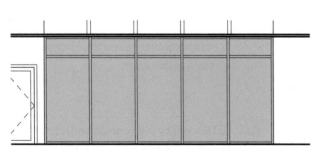

These views illustrate the storefront system created on this page.

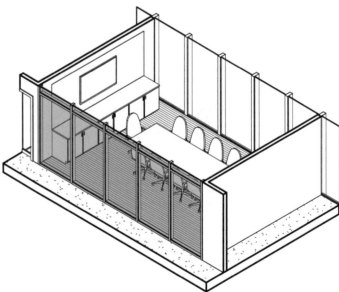

Guided Discovery 2.3: To complete this exercise, follow the steps on these pages along with the instructions on page 52. The support file for this exercise is at **WWW.RAFDBOOK.COM/DOWNLOADS.**

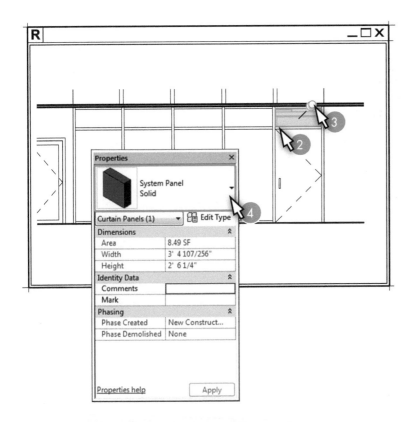

Adding Solid Panels to Storefronts

- *Step 1 (not shown):* **OPEN** an **ELEVATION** view of the storefront wall.
- *Step 2:* **PLACE** the **CURSOR** over the **EDGE OF THE GLASS PANEL** you want to change. **PRESS** the **TAB** key multiple times until the panel is outlined in blue. **CLICK ONCE** to select the panel.
- *Step 3:* **CLICK** the **PIN** to unlock the panel.
- *Step 4:* **CHANGE** the **PANEL TYPE** to **SYSTEM PANEL SOLID** in the **PROPERTIES** box.

> **Tip:** You can adjust the vertical and horizontal mullion spacing in a Storefront system in the **TYPE PROPERTIES** dialog box for the Storefront.
> **CLICK ONCE** on the **STOREFRONT** and then click the **EDIT TYPE** button in the **PROPERTIES** dialog box.

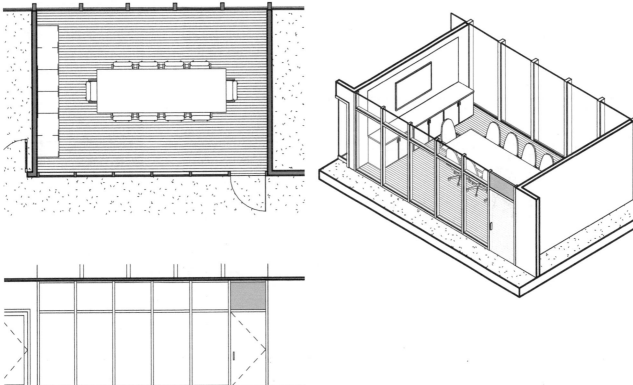

These views illustrate the solid panel added to the storefront system.

STOREFRONT WALLS (continued)

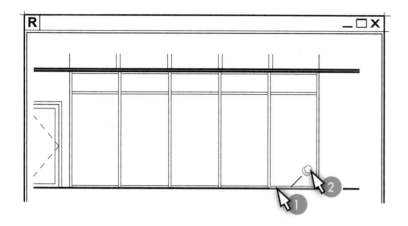

Adding Doors to Storefronts

- *Step 1*: **CLICK ONCE** on the **MULLION** at the bottom of the door location in the storefront.
- *Step 2*: **CLICK** the **PIN** to unlock the mullion.
- *Step 3 (not shown)*: **PRESS** the **DELETE** key to remove the mullion from the wall system.

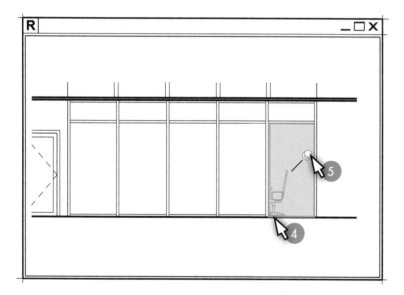

- *Step 4*: **PLACE** the **CURSOR** over the **EDGE OF THE GLASS PANEL** you want to change to a door. **PRESS** the **TAB** key multiple times until the panel is outlined in blue. **CLICK ONCE** to select the panel.
- *Step 5*: **CLICK** the **PIN** to unlock the panel.

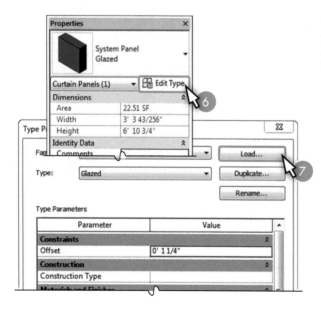

Curtain Wall Doors are not loaded in new Revit projects. The next few steps involve loading the door into the Revit project.

- *Step 6*: **CLICK** the **EDIT TYPE** button in the **PROPERTIES** box. This opens the **TYPE PROPERTIES** dialog box.
- *Step 7*: **CLICK** the **LOAD** button in the **TYPE PROPERTIES** dialog box.

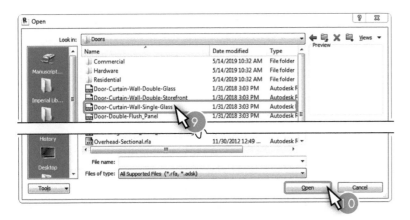

Adding Doors to Storefronts (continued)

- *Step 8 (not shown)*: **BROWSE** to the **US IMPERIAL>DOORS** folder in the **LOAD FAMILY** dialog box.
- *Step 9*: **SELECT** the **DOOR-CURTAIN-WALL-SINGLE-GLASS.RFA** panel family in the **LOAD FAMILY** dialog box.

- *Step 10*: **CLICK** the **OK** button to load the family into the current Revit project.

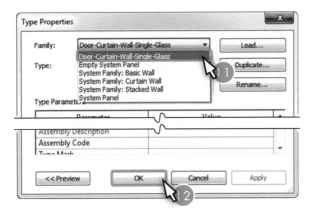

- *Step 11*: **SELECT** the **DOOR-CURTAIN-WALL-SINGLE-GLASS** family in the **TYPE PROPERTIES** dialog box.

- *Step 12*: **CLICK** the **OK** button to replace the glass panel with a door panel in the Revit project.

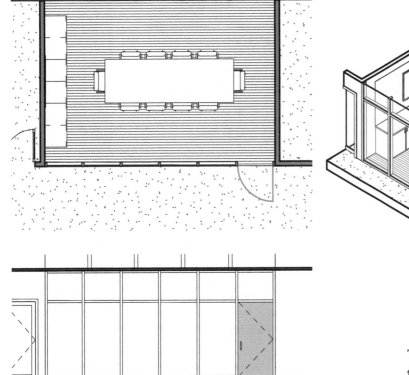

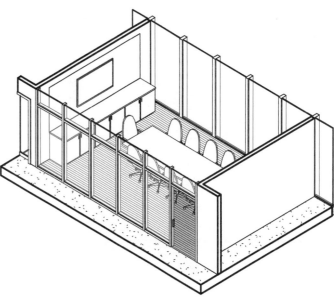

These views illustrate the door panel added to the storefront system.

CURTAIN WALLS

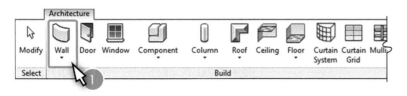

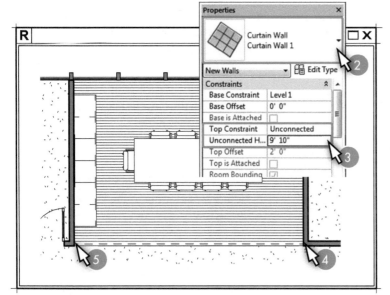

Adding Interior Curtain Walls

Curtain walls are more versatile than storefront panel systems because you have greater flexibility in the placement of mullions.

- *Step 1:* From a plan view, **CLICK** the **WALL** button in the **ARCHITECTURE** tab.
- *Step 2:* **SELECT** the **CURTAIN WALL CURTAIN WALL 1** family type in the **PROPERTIES** box.
- *Step 3:* **SET** the wall's **TOP CONSTRAINT** to **UNCONNECTED. SET** the **UNCONNECTED HEIGHT** to the **CEILING HEIGHT** in the space. In this example, the unconnected height is set to **9′ 10″**.

  The SI measurement for this step is **3000**.

- *Step 4:* **CLICK ONCE** in the plan view to locate the first edge of the curtain wall.
- *Step 5:* **CLICK ONCE** in the plan view to locate the second edge of the curtain wall. The system at this point consists of one large sheet of glass.
- *Step 6 (not shown):* **PRESS** the **ESC** key **TWICE** to end the Wall command.

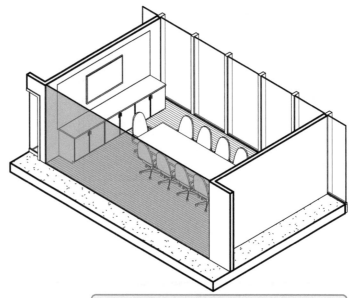

These views illustrate the curtain wall system created on this page.

Guided Discovery 2.4: To complete this exercise, follow the steps on these pages along with the instructions on page 52. The support file for this exercise is at **WWW.RAFDBOOK.COM/DOWNLOADS**.

Adding Curtain Grids

Curtain grids divide the curtain wall system into panels. The curtain grid lines also become the location for mullions or glass joints in the curtain wall system.

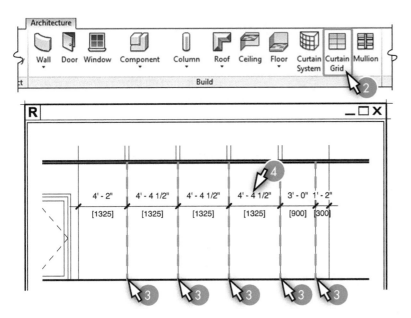

- *Step 1 (not shown)*: **OPEN** an **ELEVATION** view of the storefront wall.
- *Step 2*: **CLICK** the **CURTAIN GRID** button in the **ARCHITECTURE** tab.

- *Step 3*: **CLICK** on the **LOWER** or **UPPER EDGE** of the curtain wall to add vertical grid lines as shown in this example.
- *Step 4*: **CLICK** on the **TEMPORARY DIMENSIONS** to accurately place the curtain grids.

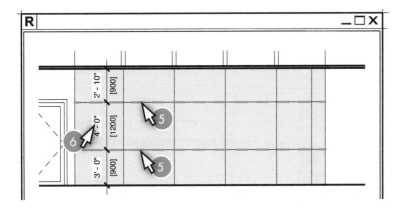

- *Step 5*: **CLICK** on any vertical curtain grid line to add horizontal grid lines as shown in this example.
- *Step 6*: **CLICK** on the **TEMPORARY DIMENSIONS** to accurately place the curtain grids.

Joining Panels

Join two adjacent panels into a larger panel by removing the grid segment between the panels. In this example, two panels are joined together where the door will be placed in the curtain wall system.

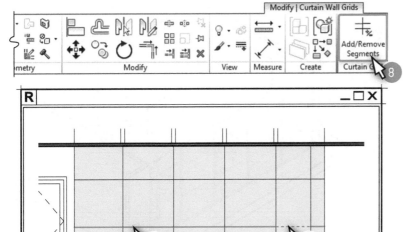

- *Step 7*: **CLICK ONCE** anywhere along the **GRID** between the panels to be joined.
- *Step 8*: **CLICK** the **ADD/REMOVE SEGMENTS** button in the **MODIFY | CURTAIN WALL GRIDS** tab.
- *Step 9*: **CLICK ONCE** on the **GRID SEGMENT** you want to remove. This joins the panels on either side of the removed grid segment.

CURTAIN WALLS (continued)

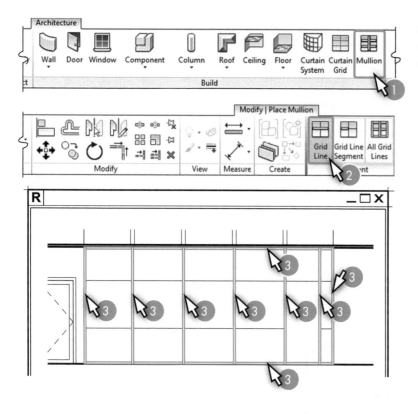

Adding Mullions

Curtain mullions are the structural supports for the glass in curtain wall systems.

- *Step 1*: **CLICK** the **MULLION** button in the **ARCHITECTURE** tab.

- *Step 2*: **CLICK** the **GRID LINE** button in the **MODIFY | PLACE MULLION** tab.

- *Step 3*: **CLICK** on each **GRID LINE** where you want a continuous mullion.

- *Step 4*: **CLICK** the **GRID LINE SEGMENT** button in the **MODIFY | PLACE MULLION** tab.

- *Step 5*: **CLICK** on the **GRID LINE SEGMENT** above the door to add a single mullion.

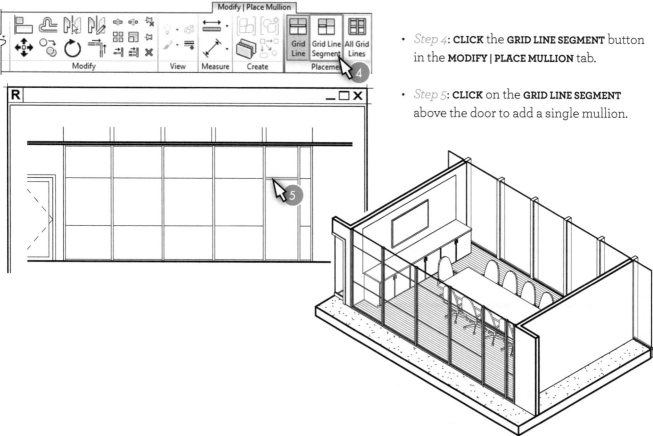

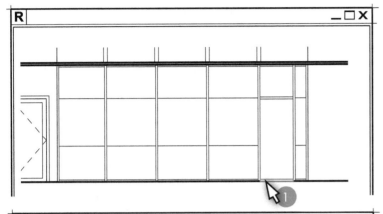

Adding Doors

- *Step 1*: **CLICK ONCE** on the **MULLION** at the bottom of the door location in the curtain wall.
- *Step 2 (not shown)*: **PRESS** the **DELETE** key to remove the mullion from the wall system.

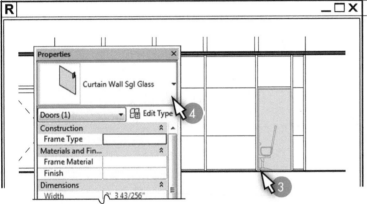
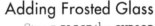
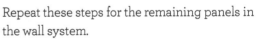

- *Step 3*: **PLACE** the **CURSOR** over the **EDGE OF THE GLASS PANEL** you want to change to a door. **PRESS** the **TAB** key multiple times until the panel is outlined in blue. **CLICK ONCE** to select the panel.
- *Step 4*: **SELECT** the **CURTAIN WALL SGL GLASS** family in the **PROPERTIES** box.

Adding Frosted Glass

- *Step 5*: **PLACE** the **CURSOR** over the **EDGE OF THE GLASS PANEL** you want to change to a frosted panel. **PRESS** the **TAB** key multiple times until the panel is outlined in blue. **CLICK ONCE** to select the panel.
- *Step 6*: **SELECT** the **SYSTEM PANEL FROSTED** family in the **PROPERTIES** box.

Repeat these steps for the remaining panels in the wall system.

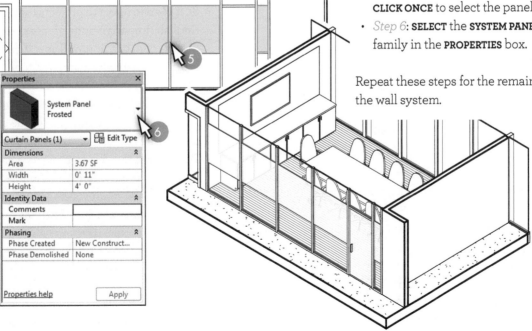

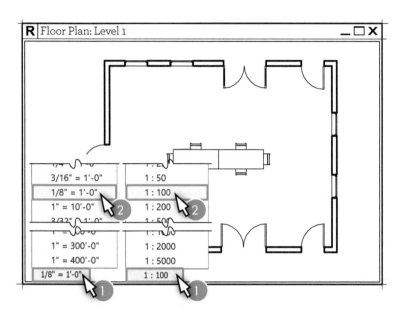

Architectural Drawing Scale

Every view in Revit (with the exception of perspective views) contains an architectural scale parameter. Any changes made to the scale of a view are saved with the project. Changing the scale of a drawing will change the size of annotation elements (text, dimensions, symbols) relative to the building.

- *Step 1:* **CLICK** on the **ARCHITECTURAL SCALE** in the status bar.
- *Step 2:* **SELECT** the **PREFERRED SCALE** from the list of possible architectural scales.

Drawing in Metric (SI)

The International System of Units (SI) is commonly referred to as the metric system. There are multiple terms that describe the use of SI in the design industry.

- **Hard Metric** refers to projects that use metric measurements in design, construction, and specifications. For example, a Hard Metric door (specified in India) is 800mm [31.5"] or 1000mm [39.4"] wide and 2045mm [80.5"] tall.
- **Soft Metric** refers to projects that use English (imperial) units of measure for design, construction, and specification that are mathematically converted to metric. For example, a Soft Metric door (specified in the United States of America) measures 762mm [30"] or 915mm [36"] wide and 2032mm [80"] tall.
- **Dual systems** refers to projects designed in English units where both English units and soft metric units are included in dimensions and specifications for comparison purposes.

Imperial Architectural Scale	Imperial Scale Factor	SI Architectural Scale	SI Scale Factor
3" = 1'-0"	4	1:5	5
1 1/2" = 1'-0"	8		
1" = 1'-0"	12	1:10	10
3/4" = 1'-0"	16		
1/2" = 1'-0"	24	1:20	20
3/8" = 1'-0"	32		
1/4" = 1'-0"	48	1:50	50
3/16" = 1'-0"	64		
1/8" = 1'-0"	96	1:100	100
3/32" = 1'-0"	128		
1/16" = 1'-0"	192	1:200	200
1/32" = 1'-0"	384		
		1:500	500
		1:1000	1000

A comparative list of Imperial and SI equivalent architectural scales is provided above. Note how close the scale factors are when comparing SI and Imperial scales across rows in this table.

For example, **1/8" = 1'-0"** and **1:100** are essentially the same architectural scale.

Companion Download 2.1:
A list of standard Imperial and SI architectural scales is located on page 302 and at **WWW.RAFDBOOK.COM/DOWNLOADS.**

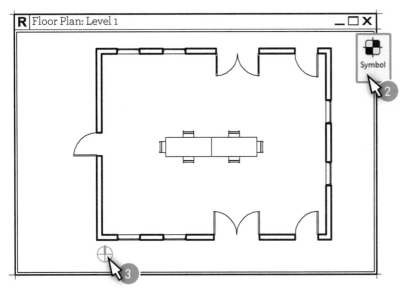

Adding a North Arrow

- *Step 1 (not shown)*: **OPEN** a **PLAN VIEW**.
- *Step 2*: **CLICK** the **SYMBOL** button in the **ANNOTATION** tab.
- *Step 3*: **CLICK** in the **PLAN VIEW** to place the north arrow.
- *Step 4 (not shown)*: Use the **MODIFY** panel to move and rotate the north arrow in the view.

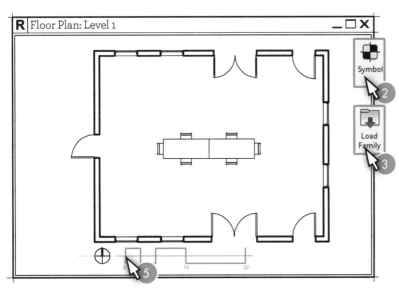

Adding a Graphic Scale

- *Step 1 (not shown)*: **OPEN** a **PLAN VIEW**.
- *Step 2*: **CLICK** the **SYMBOL** button in the **ANNOTATION** tab.
- *Step 3*: **CLICK** the **LOAD FAMILY** button in the **MODIFY | PLACE SYMBOL** tab.
- *Step 4 (not shown)*: In the **LOAD FAMILY** file window, **BROWSE** to **US IMPERIAL> ANNOTATIONS>GRAPHIC SCALE 1-8.RFA** and **CLICK OPEN**.
- *Step 5*: **CLICK** in the **PLAN VIEW** to place the graphic scale. In this example, the scale is aligned with the north arrow.
- *Step 6 (not shown)*: Use the **MODIFY** panel to move and rotate the north arrow in the view.

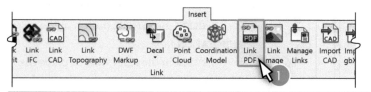

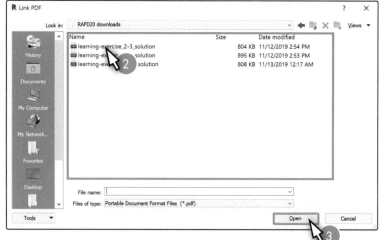

Linking PDF Drawings

Revit provides the ability to link PDF drawings. For complex building shells, a linked PDF drawing allows you to trace the geometry of the building.

- *Step 1*: **CLICK** the **LINK PDF** button in the **INSERT** tab. This opens the **LINK PDF FORMATS** dialog box.

- *Step 2*: **LOCATE** the PDF drawing you wish to link using the file browser.

- *Step 3*: **CLICK** the **OPEN** button. This opens the **IMPORT PDF** dialog box.

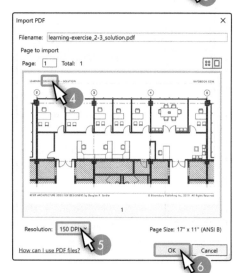

- *Step 4 (optional)*: If you are linking a multi-page PDF, select the page you want to link.
- *Step 5*: **SET** the **RESOLUTION**.
- *Step 6*: **CLICK** the **OK** button. The linked PDF is shown in the drawing area and moves with the cursor.
- *Step 7 (not shown)*: **CLICK** the **ONCE** to place the PDF in the current view.

Scaling PDF Drawings

After linking a PDF drawing, you need to scale the PDF so that the lines and dimensions match the drawing units in Revit.

- *Step 1*: **SELECT** the **PDF** image in the plan view.
- *Step 2*: In the **MODIFY | RASTER IMAGES** tab, **CLICK** the **ENABLE SNAPS** button.
- *Step 3*: In the **MODIFY | RASTER IMAGES** tab, **CLICK** the **SCALE** button.
- *Steps 4-5*: **CLICK** on each endpoint of a known distance (like a door opening).
- *Steps 6*: On the keyboard, **TYPE** the known **DISTANCE** and **PRESS ENTER**.

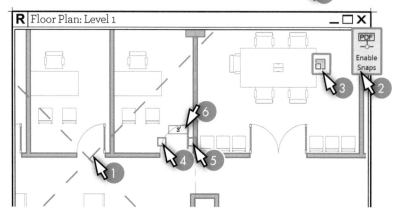

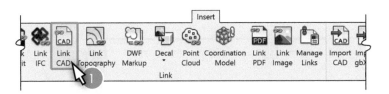

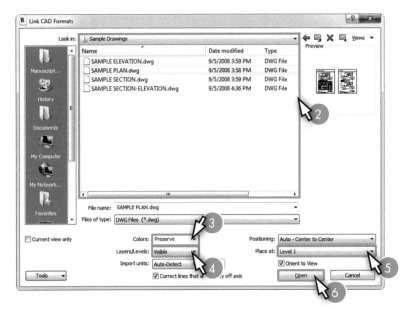

Linking AutoCAD Drawings

Revit provides the ability to link CAD drawings created in AutoCAD or other software. For complex building shells, a linked CAD drawing allows you to trace the geometry of the building.

- *Step 1:* **CLICK** the **LINK CAD** button in the **INSERT** tab. This opens the **LINK CAD FORMATS** dialog box.
- *Step 2:* **LOCATE** the CAD drawing you wish to link using the file browser.
- *Step 3:* **SET** the **COLORS** Drop-down menu to **PRESERVE** or **BLACK AND WHITE**. The **PRESERVE** option displays CAD lines with the colors selected in the CAD software. The **BLACK AND WHITE** option converts all CAD lines to black.
- *Step 4:* **SET** the **LAYERS/LEVELS** Drop-down menu to **VISIBLE**.
- *Step 5:* **SET** the **PLACE AT** Drop-down menu to match the level of the CAD drawing.
- *Step 6:* **CLICK** the **OPEN** button to link the CAD drawing to your Revit project.

Managing AutoCAD Links

You can load, unload, and remove CAD links using the Manage Links dialog box.

- *Step 1:* **CLICK** the **MANAGE LINKS** button in the **INSERT** tab. This opens the **MANAGE LINKS** dialog box.
- *Step 2:* **CLICK** the **CAD FORMATS** tab in the **MANAGE LINKS** dialog box to see all CAD drawings linked to the current project.
- *Step 3:* **SELECT** the CAD file you want to modify.
- *Step 4:* The **UNLOAD** button visibly removes a CAD file from Revit.
- *Step 5:* The **RELOAD** button loads the most recent version of a CAD file into Revit. This is useful if the CAD file has changed since you opened the Revit project. The **RELOAD** button will also turn on any unloaded CAD files.
- *Step 6:* The **REMOVE** button detaches the CAD file from the Revit project.

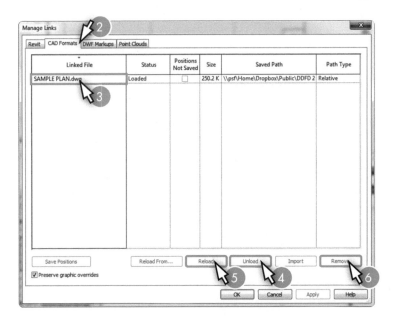

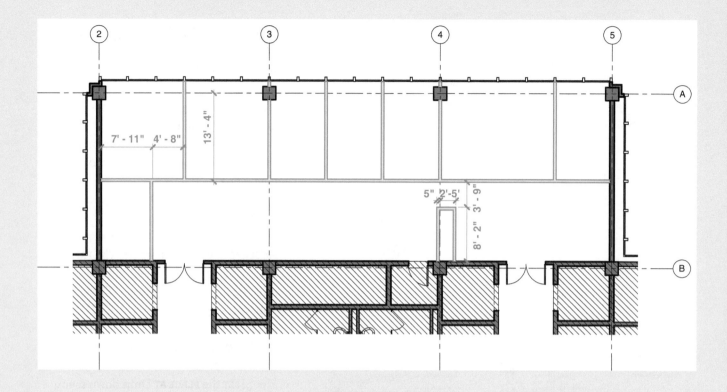

Guided Discovery Exercises

Guided Discovery 2.3 Storefront Walls

- To begin this exercise download the support files at **WWW.RAFDBOOK.COM/DOWNLOADS.**
- Follow the step-by-step exercises on page 40 to add **STOREFRONT** to the companion Revit project.
- Add **DOORS** and **SOLID PANELS** to the storefront system.
- Add **FROSTED GLASS PANELS** to the storefront system.

Guided Discovery 2.4 Curtain Walls

- To begin this exercise download the support files at **WWW.RAFDBOOK.COM/DOWNLOADS.**

> **SI Exercise Example:**
> You can also download a SI version of this drawing at **WWW.RAFDBOOK.COM/DOWNLOADS.**

- Follow the step-by-step exercises on page 44 to add **CURTAIN WALL** to the companion Revit project.
- Add **DOORS** and **SOLID PANELS** to the curtain wall system.
- Add **FROSTED GLASS PANELS** to the curtain wall system.

Learning Exercises

These exercises are intended to help you improve your understanding of adding walls, doors, and furniture to a Revit project. The Revit project you begin in this learning exercise will continue in future chapters.

To begin this exercise, download and open **LEARNING_EXERCISE_2-1.RVT** from **WWW.RAFDBOOK.COM/DOWNLOADS.**

Learning Exercise 2.1: Adding Walls

- Open the **LEVEL 11 TENANT SPACE** plan view in the **PROJECT BROWSER.**
- Add **5″ GENERIC WALLS** to match the blue walls in the example above. If dimensions are not provided, align the walls with the center of existing mullions.
- **SAVE** the project to your computer or a portable drive.

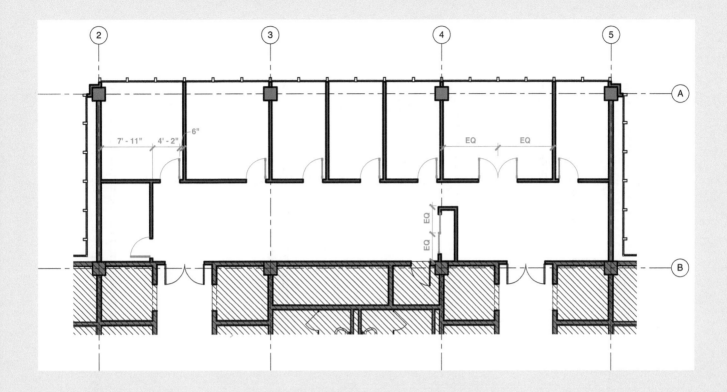

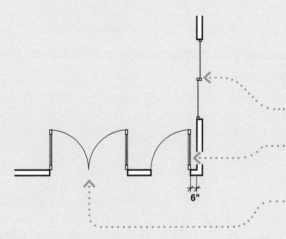

Learning Exercises (continued)

Learning Exercise 2.2: Adding Doors

- Open the **LEVEL 11 TENANT SPACE** plan view in the **PROJECT BROWSER**.
- Add **SLIDING-2 PANEL (72″ X 84″)** to match sliding doors in the example above.
- Add **SINGLE-GLASS 1 (36″ X 84″)** to match similar doors in the example above. Unless noted otherwise, all doors are to be placed 6″ from the adjacent wall.
- Add **DOUBLE-GLASS 1 (72″ X 84″)** to match the similar double doors in the example above.
- **SAVE** the project to your computer or a portable drive.

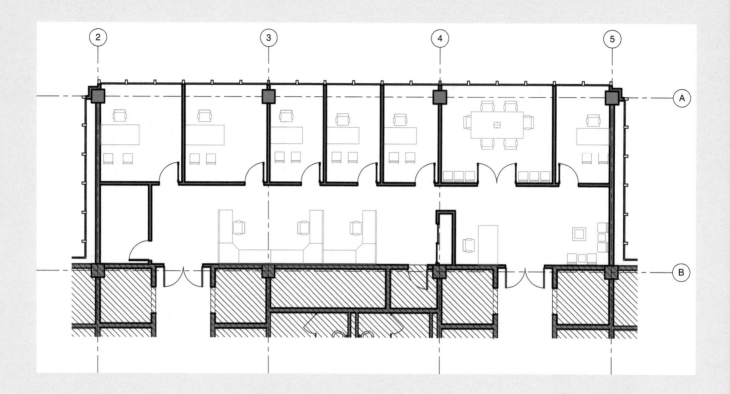

Learning Exercises (continued)

Learning Exercise 2.3: Adding Furniture

- Open the **LEVEL 11 TENANT SPACE** plan view in the **PROJECT BROWSER**.
- Add furniture to the floor plan using furniture from the
  US IMPERIAL LIBRARY, FURNITURE MANUFACTURER'S WEBSITES, or
  furniture from **BIMOBJECT.COM.** You can use the furniture below
  as a guide. (Reference page 36 for more information.)
- **SAVE** the project to your computer or a portable drive.

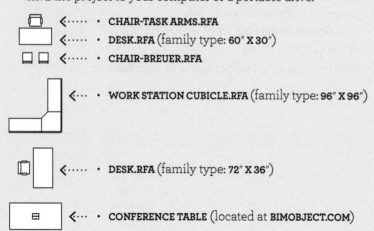

- **CHAIR-TASK ARMS.RFA**
- **DESK.RFA** (family type: **60" X 30"**)
- **CHAIR-BREUER.RFA**

- **WORK STATION CUBICLE.RFA** (family type: **96" X 96"**)

- **DESK.RFA** (family type: **72" X 36"**)

- **CONFERENCE TABLE** (located at **BIMOBJECT.COM**)

chapter 3

MULTI-LEVEL BUILDINGS

The previous chapter introduced basic tools to create and modify a floor plan in Revit. Now that you have mastered the basics, it is time to explore the advanced skills you need to start a new multi-level Revit project.

IN THIS CHAPTER

This drawing explains how model elements in Revit relate to each other in a multi-level building.

DATUM ELEMENTS are the foundation of the Revit model by which everything is referenced. Levels are the most commonly used datum element.

HOST ELEMENTS in this diagram include walls, floors, ceilings (not shown), stairs, and roofs. These elements are all constrained to a specific level.

HOSTED ELEMENTS in this diagram include the doors and railings. These elements are all hosted by model elements.

Floor Slabs

Floor slabs are typically sketched by tracing the perimeter of the building. In Revit, slabs are most visible in 3-D views, sections, and details. Slab openings are created for staircases. Learn more about floor slabs and slab openings on page 66.

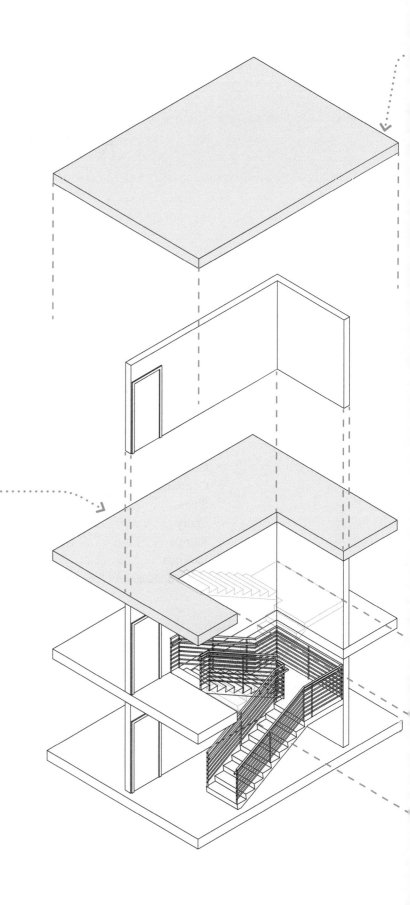

Flat Roofs

Flat roofs are common in commercial construction. In Revit, this type of roof can be constructed with a floor slab.

- Learn more about roofs in Chapter 9.
- Learn more about slabs on page 66.

Railings

Railings are automatically added to the interior and exterior edge of a stair run. Railings can also be manually added to a balcony or stair landing. Learn more about adding railings on page 56

Levels

Building Elevations and Section drawings are the best views to add and modify Levels in the project. Learn more about adding Levels to your project on page 58.

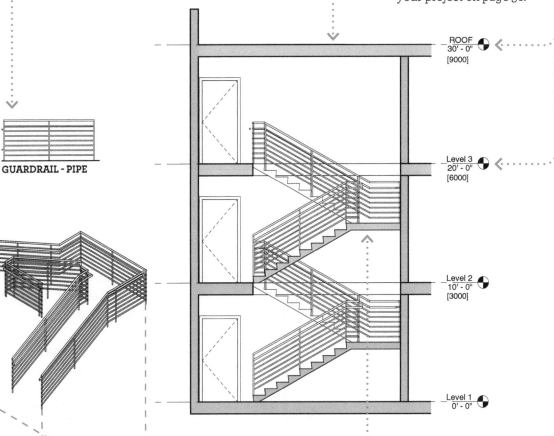

GUARDRAIL - PIPE

ROOF
30' - 0"
[9000]

Level 3
20' - 0"
[6000]

Level 2
10' - 0"
[3000]

Level 1
0' - 0"

Stairs

Revit uses calculation rules to determine the number of treads and risers needed for the stair based on the distance between the top and bottom stair constraint. The stair in this example has a Base Level Constraint of Level 2 and ends Top Level Constraint of Level 3.

- Learn more about stairs on page 68.

BUILDING LEVELS

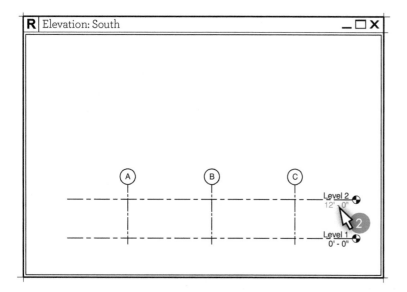

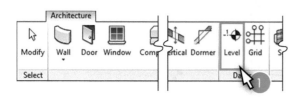

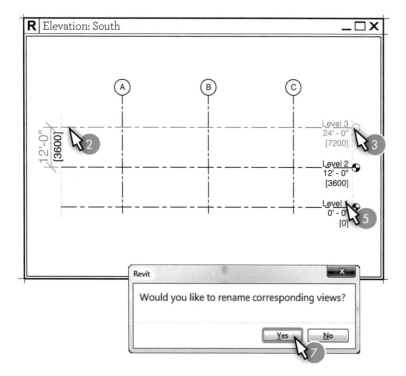

Introducing Levels

Levels are datum elements that host building elements like floors, ceilings, and furniture. When you add furniture to the Revit project, the furniture is associated with a level. Other objects, like walls and columns, are constrained to levels. For example, walls often start at one level and end at the next level.

- *Step 1 (not shown)*: To view the levels in a Revit project **OPEN** a **BUILDING ELEVATION** view. In this example, the **SOUTH ELEVATION** is visible.
- *Step 2*: **DOUBLE-CLICK** on the level's **ELEVATION** to adjust its height.

In this example, Level 2 was moved from **10'-0"** to **12'-0"**.

> **SI:** Level 2 was moved from **3000** to **3600**.

Adding Levels

When you begin a multi-level project in Revit, you need to know the floor-to-floor height for each level.

- *Step 1*: From the **SOUTH ELEVATION** view, **CLICK** the **LEVEL** button in the **ARCHITECTURE** tab.
- *Step 2*: **MOVE** the **CURSOR** above the left side of **LEVEL 2** as shown in this example. When you see both the blue alignment constraint and a temporary dimension of 12'-0", **CLICK ONCE** to locate the left position of the new level.
- *Step 3*: **MOVE** the **CURSOR** to the **RIGHT** as shown in this example. **CLICK ONCE** when you see the blue alignment constraint.
- *Step 4 (not shown)*: **PRESS** the **ESC** key twice on the keyboard to end the Level command.

Renaming Levels

- *Step 5*: **DOUBLE-CLICK** on **LEVEL 1** in the elevation view to edit the level's name.
- *Step 6 (not shown)*: **PRESS ENTER** on the keyboard to rename the level.
- *Step 7*: Revit displays the following confirmation dialog box. **CLICK YES** to rename the plan and ceiling levels in the **PROJECT BROWSER** to match the new level name.

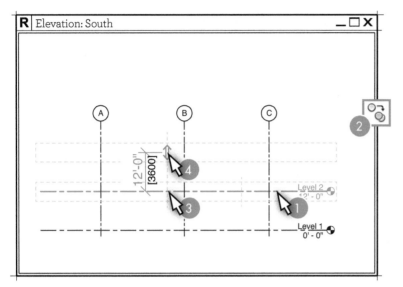

Copying Levels

You can also add new levels by copying existing levels.

- *Step 1*: **CLICK ONCE** on an existing **LEVEL** as shown in the example.
- *Step 2*: **CLICK** the **COPY** button in the **MODIFY LEVELS** ribbon.
- *Step 3*: **CLICK ONCE** on the selected **LEVEL** and **MOVE** the cursor **UP**.
- *Step 4*: **CLICK ONCE** when the temporary dimension shows a copy distance of **12'-0"**.

> The SI measurement for this step is **3600**.

- *Step 5 (not shown)*: **PRESS** the **ESC** key on the keyboard to end the Copy command.

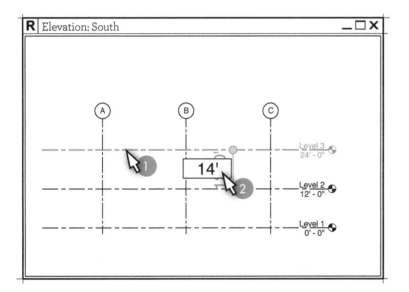

Moving Levels

Similar to walls, Revit allows you to move levels by modifying the distance between two levels in an elevation view.

- *Step 1*: **CLICK ONCE** on the **LEVEL** you want to move. Revit will show temporary dimensions to the nearest level.
- *Step 2*: **CLICK ONCE** on the **12'-0"** temporary dimension and type the new distance. In this example, the dimension was changed to **14'**.

> The SI measurement for this step is **4300**.

- *Step 3 (not shown)*: **PRESS** the **ESC** key on the keyboard to end the Move command.

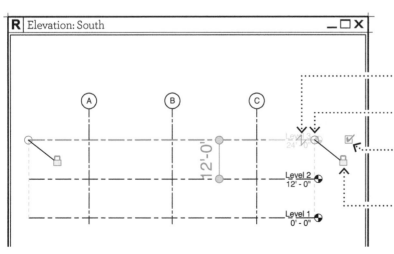

Adjusting Level Graphics

Click once on a grid line to adjust its visual properties.

- **CLICK** the **ELBOW** symbol to add an elbow in the level near the level's name and height.
- **CLICK AND DRAG** the **MODEL END** to adjust the length of the level line.
- **CLICK** the **CHECK BOX** to show the **LEVEL NAME** and **LEVEL ELEVATION** at the end of the level line.
- **CLICK** the **CONSTRAINT LOCK** to remove the **ALIGNMENT CONSTRAINT** with the adjacent level lines.

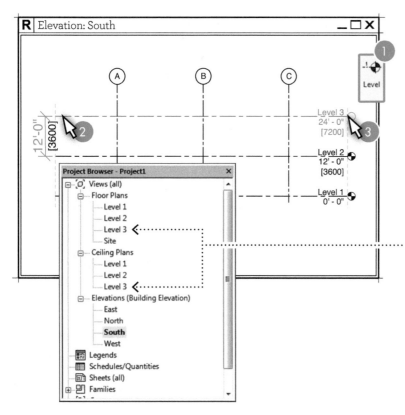

Floor Plan and Ceiling Plan Views

The method you choose to add levels to the Revit project will determine whether Revit automatically adds a floor plan view and ceiling plan view to the Project Browser.

Level Button Method

When you add levels using the Level button, Revit automatically adds the floor plan view and ceiling plan view to the Project Browser.

- *Steps 1–3*: In this example, **LEVEL 3** was added in the **SOUTH ELEVATION** view.
- After adding the level, the **PROJECT BROWSER** shows **LEVEL 3** in the floor plan and ceiling plan views.

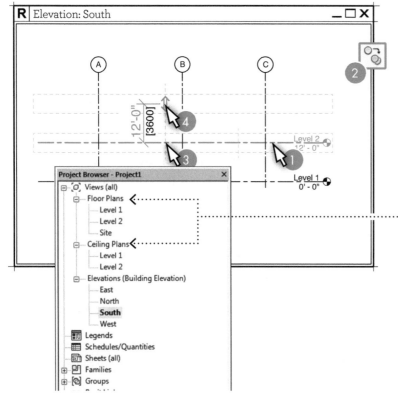

Level Copy Method

When you add levels using the Copy button, Revit will not automatically add the corresponding floor plan view or ceiling plan view to the Project Browser.

- *Steps 1–4*: In this example, **LEVEL 3** was added in the **SOUTH ELEVATION** view using the **COPY** button.

- After adding the level, the **PROJECT BROWSER** does not show **LEVEL 3** in either the floor plan or ceiling plan view.

Add **LEVEL 3** views to the **PROJECT BROWSER** using the instructions on the next page.

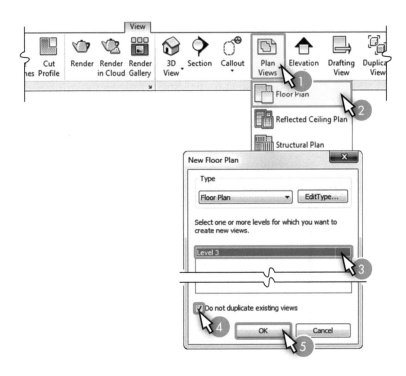

Adding Floor Plan Views

You can add a floor plan view for any level defined in the Revit project.

- *Step 1*: **CLICK** the **PLAN VIEWS DOWN ARROW** in the **VIEW** tab.
- *Step 2*: In the Drop-down menu, **CLICK** the **FLOOR PLAN** button. This will open the **NEW FLOOR PLAN** dialog box.

- *Step 3*: **CLICK ONCE** on the **FLOOR PLAN LEVEL** you want to add to the **PROJECT BROWSER**. To add multiple levels at once, **HOLD** the **SHIFT** key while clicking each level name.
- *Step 4 (optional)*: Revit hides floor plan levels that exist in the **PROJECT BROWSER**. **UNCHECK** this box to show all available levels in the project. Adding levels that already exist will create duplicate level views in the **PROJECT BROWSER**.

- *Step 5*: **CLICK** the **OK** button to add plan views of the selected levels to the **PROJECT BROWSER**.

Adding Reflected Ceiling Plan (RCP) Views

You can add a reflected ceiling plan view for any level defined in the Revit project.

- *Step 1*: **CLICK** the **PLAN VIEW DOWN ARROW** in the **VIEW** tab.
- *Step 2*: In the Drop-down menu, **CLICK** the **REFLECTED CEILING PLAN** button. This opens the **NEW RCP** dialog box.

- *Step 3*: **CLICK ONCE** on the **RCP LEVEL** you want to add to the **PROJECT BROWSER**. To add multiple levels at once, **HOLD** the **SHIFT** key while clicking each level name.

- *Step 4*: **CLICK** the **OK** button to add ceiling views of the selected levels to the **PROJECT BROWSER**.

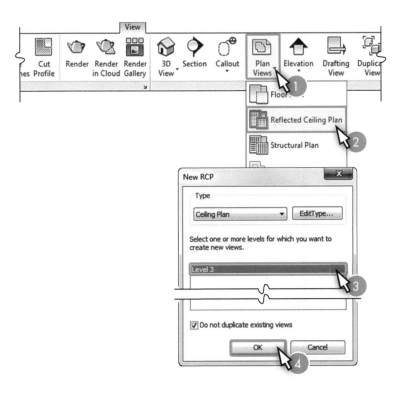

COLUMN GRID LINES

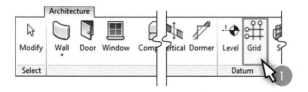

Adding Column Grid Lines

After defining a project's levels, structural grids are the next datum element added to a new Revit model. Structural column grid lines are visible in most plan views.

- *Step 1:* From the **LEVEL 1** plan view, **CLICK** the **GRID** button in the **ARCHITECTURE** tab.

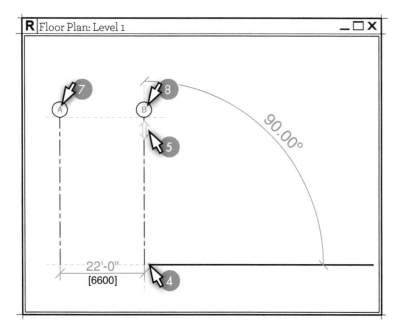

- *Step 2:* **CLICK ONCE** in the floor plan to locate the bottom position of the grid line as shown in this example.
- *Step 3:* **CLICK ONCE** in the floor plan to locate the top position of the grid line.

- *Step 4:* **MOVE** the **CURSOR** to the right of the first grid line as shown in this example. Revit indicates the distance between the grid lines with a temporary dimension. When you are **22′-0″** from the first grid line, **CLICK ONCE** to locate the bottom position of the second grid line.

  The SI measurement for this step is **6600**.

- *Step 5:* **CLICK ONCE** in the floor plan to locate the top position of the second grid line.
- *Step 6 (not shown):* **PRESS** the **ESC** key twice on the keyboard to end the Grid command.
- *Steps 7–8:* **CLICK ONCE** on the grid line number **1** and change it to the letter **A**. **CLICK ONCE** on the grid line number **2** and change it to the letter **B**.

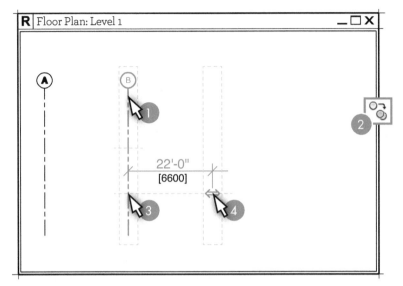

Copying Column Grid Lines

In addition to the Grid command, you can add new grid lines by copying existing grid lines.

- *Step 1*: **CLICK ONCE** on an existing **GRID LINE** as shown in the example.
- *Step 2*: **CLICK** the **COPY** button in the **MODIFY GRIDS** ribbon.
- *Step 3*: **CLICK ONCE** on the selected **GRID LINE** and **MOVE** the cursor to the **RIGHT**.
- *Step 4*: **CLICK ONCE** when the temporary dimension shows a copy distance of **22'-0"**.

> The SI measurement for this step is **6600**.

- *Step 5 (not shown)*: **PRESS** the **ESC** key on the keyboard to end the Copy command.

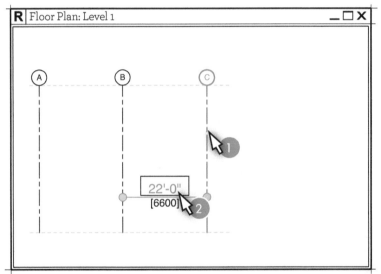

Moving Column Grid Lines

Similar to walls, Revit allows you to move grid lines by modifying the distance between two grid lines in the plan.

- *Step 1*: **CLICK ONCE** on the **GRID LINE** you want to move. Revit displays temporary dimensions to the nearest grid line.
- *Step 2*: **CLICK ONCE** on the **TEMPORARY DIMENSION** and type the new distance.

- *Step 3 (not shown)*: **PRESS** the **ESC** key on the keyboard to end the Move command.

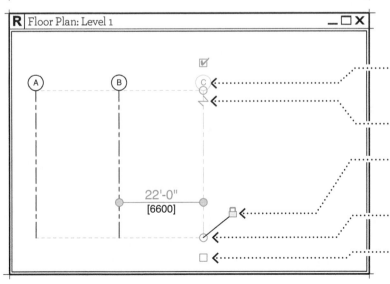

Adjusting Grid Line Graphics

Click once on a grid line to adjust its visual properties.

- **DOUBLE-CLICK** on the **GRID NUMBER** or **LETTER** to change its value to another number or letter.
- **CLICK** the **ELBOW** symbol to add an elbow in the grid line.
- **CLICK** the **CONSTRAINT LOCK** to remove the **ALIGNMENT CONSTRAINT** with the adjacent grid lines.
- **CLICK AND DRAG** the **MODEL END** to adjust the length of the **GRID LINE**.
- **CLICK** the **CHECK BOX** to show the **GRID BUBBLE** at the bottom of the grid line.

COLUMNS

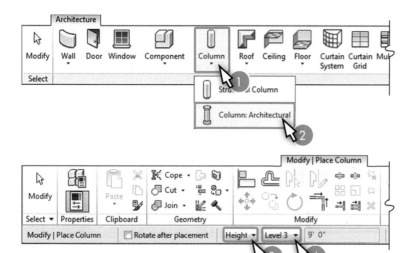

Adding Columns

You can add columns to any grid line intersection in the plan view.

- *Step 1*: **CLICK** the **COLUMN DOWN ARROW** in the **ARCHITECTURE** tab.
- *Step 2*: In the Drop-down menu, **CLICK** the **COLUMN: ARCHITECTURAL** button.

- *Step 3*: In the options bar, set the column placement constraint to **HEIGHT**.
- *Step 4*: **CONNECT** the **COLUMN HEIGHT** to the **NEXT LEVEL**. In this example, the column height is constrained to **LEVEL 3**.

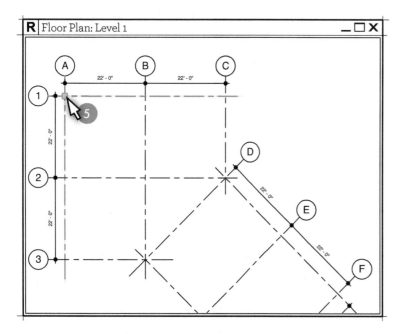

As you move the cursor over the plan view, column grid lines highlight in blue. At the intersection of two column grids, you will see both grid lines highlighted.

- *Step 5*: **CLICK ONCE** at the intersection of **GRID LINE A** and **GRID LINE 1** to add the column.

Column Families

CLICK the **LOAD FAMILY** button to add additional column families to Revit.

- **ARCHITECTURAL** columns are located in the **US IMPERIAL > COLUMN** folder.
- **STRUCTURAL** columns are located in the **US IMPERIAL > STRUCTURAL COLUMNS** folder.

Architectural columns

- Rectangular Column.rfa
- Chamfered Column.rfa
- Round Column.rfa
- Wood Timber Column.rfa

Structural columns

- Concrete
  Concrete-Rectangular-Column.rfa
- Steel
  W-Wide Flange-Column.rfa

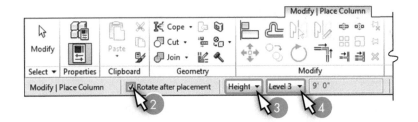

Adding Rotated Columns

- *Step 1 (not shown)*: **CLICK** the **COLUMN DOWN ARROW** in the **ARCHITECTURE** tab. In the Drop-down menu, **CLICK** the **COLUMN: ARCHITECTURAL** button.
- *Step 2*: In the options bar, **CHECK** the **ROTATE AFTER PLACEMENT** option.
- *Step 3*: In the options bar, set the column placement constraint to **HEIGHT**.
- *Step 4*: **CONNECT** the **COLUMN HEIGHT** to the **NEXT LEVEL**. In this example, the column height is constrained to **LEVEL 3**.

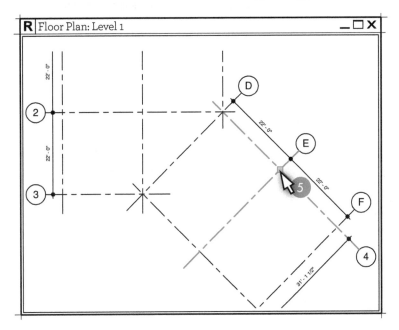

- *Step 5*: **CLICK ONCE** at the intersection of **GRID LINE E** and **GRID LINE 4** to add the column as shown in this example.

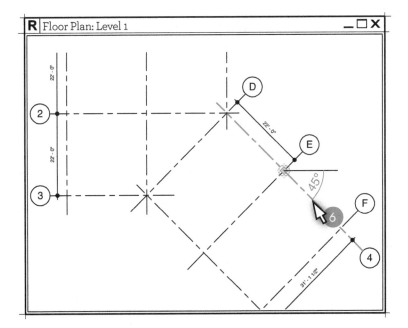

As you move the cursor, Revit rotates the column using the grid line intersection as a pivot point.

- *Step 6*: **CLICK ONCE** on **GRID LINE 4** to rotate the column to match the angle of the column grid line.

SLABS

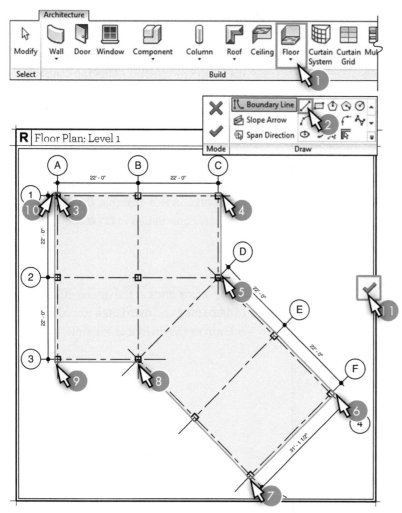

Adding Floor Slabs

- *Step 1*: **CLICK** the **FLOOR** button in the **ARCHITECTURE** tab.

- *Step 2*: **CLICK** the **DRAW LINE** button in the **MODIFY | CREATE FLOOR BOUNDARY** tab.

- *Steps 3-10*: Following the example, **CLICK** on each corner of the building.

- *Step 11*: **CLICK** the **FINISH SKETCH** button in the **MODIFY | CREATE FLOOR BOUNDARY** tab to finish the slab sketch.

Copying Floors Slabs

Once you have drawn a floor slab, you can copy it to other levels in the Revit project.

- *Step 1*: **OPEN** any view where you can see the existing floor and **CLICK ONCE** on the **FLOOR**.
- *Step 2*: **CLICK** the **COPY TO CLIPBOARD** button in the **MODIFY SLABS** ribbon.
- *Steps 3-4*: **CLICK** the **PASTE FROM CLIPBOARD** down arrow. **SELECT** the **ALIGNED TO SELECTED LEVELS** option.
- *Step 5*: **SELECT** the **LEVEL 2** in the Select Levels dialog box.
- *Step 6*: **CLICK** the **OK** button to copy the existing floor slab to each additional level.

> **Tip**: You can also use **PASTE ALIGNED TO SELECTED LEVELS** to copy furniture, windows, and doors between levels.

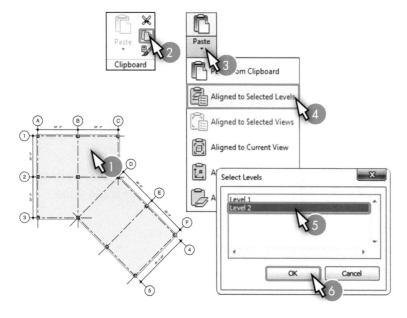

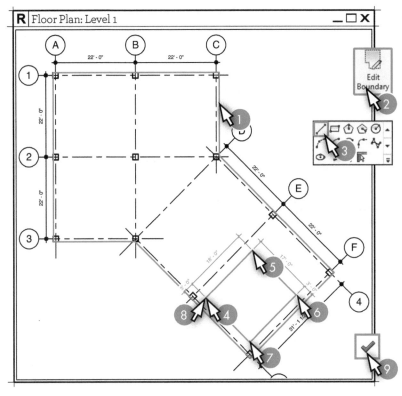

Adding Slab Openings

- *Step 1*: In the **FLOOR PLAN** view, **CLICK** on the floor slab edge as shown in this example.
- *Step 2*: **CLICK** the **EDIT BOUNDARY** button in the **MODIFY | FLOOR BOUNDARY** tab.
- *Step 3*: **CLICK** the **DRAW LINE** button in the **MODIFY | FLOOR BOUNDARY** tab.

- *Steps 4–8*: Following the example, **CLICK** to draw each edge of the new slab opening. Use the temporary dimensions to modify the opening and to match the dimensions in this example.
- *Step 9*: **CLICK** the **FINISH SKETCH** button in the **MODIFY | FLOOR BOUNDARY** tab to finish the slab sketch.

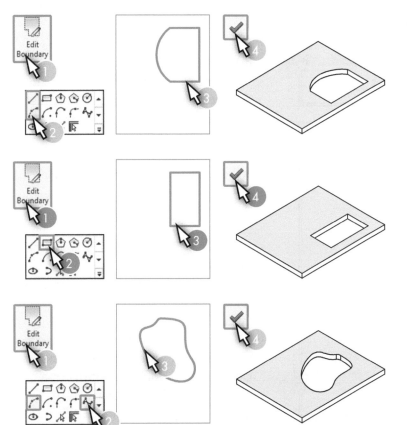

Curved Slab Openings

Slabs and slab openings can vary in shape and size as required by the design parameters. The examples to the left show different slab openings. Each example also indicates which **DRAW TOOLS** were used to create the shapes.

- *Step 1*: In the **FLOOR PLAN** view, **SELECT** the floor slab (*not shown*) and **CLICK** the **EDIT BOUNDARY** button in the **MODIFY | FLOOR BOUNDARY** tab.
- *Step 2*: **CLICK** the **DRAW TOOL** button.
- *Step 3*: Draw the shape that represents the slab opening.
- *Step 4*: **CLICK** the **FINISH SKETCH** button.

Slab openings are used to create floor-to-floor connections, which can include stairs, elevators, and balconies. Except for rare instances, slab openings should not cross over column lines.

STAIRS

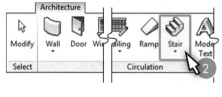

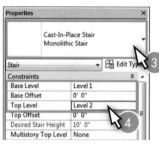

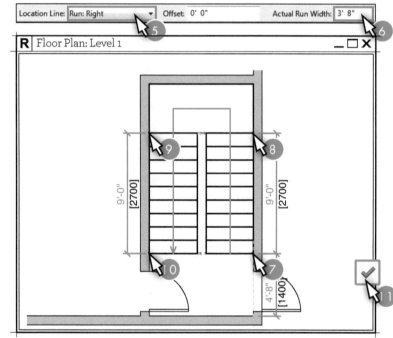

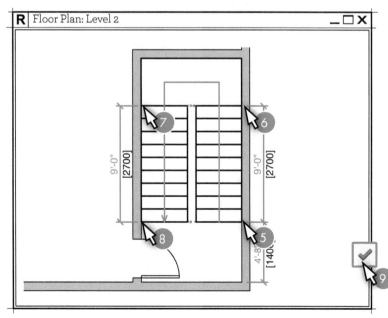

Adding Straight Stairs

- *Step 1 (not shown)*: **OPEN** the **LEVEL 1** view in the **PROJECT BROWSER**.
- *Step 2*: **CLICK** the **STAIR** button in the **ARCHITECTURE** tab.
- *Step 3*: **CHANGE** the **STAIR TYPE** to **CAST-IN-PLACE STAIR** in the stair **PROPERTIES** box.
- *Step 4*: For this example, verify the **BASE LEVEL** is set to **LEVEL 1** and that the **TOP LEVEL** is set to **LEVEL 2**. When drawing stairs, set the **BASE LEVEL** and **TOP LEVEL** to match the start and end levels in your project.
- *Step 5*: In the **MODIFY | CREATE STAIR** tab, **SET** the **LOCATION LINE** to **RUN: RIGHT**.
- *Step 6*: **SET** the **ACTUAL RUN WIDTH** to **3'-8"**.

> The SI measurement for this step is **1100**.

In the Level 1 plan view, sketch the stair following these steps:

- *Step 7*: **CLICK ONCE** on the **PERIMETER WALL** with a **TEMPORARY DIMENSION** of **4'-8"** from the bottom of the stairwell.

> The SI measurement for this step is **1400**.

- *Steps 8–10*: **CLICK ONCE** at each point to match the example.
- *Step 11*: **CLICK** the **FINISH SKETCH** button in the **MODIFY | CREATE STAIR** tab to finish the stair sketch. Revit will complete the stair and add handrails.

OPEN the **LEVEL 2** view and sketch the stair following these steps:

- *Step 1 (not shown)*: **CLICK** the **STAIR** button in the **ARCHITECTURE** tab.
- *Step 2 (not shown)*: **CHANGE** the **STAIR TYPE** to **CAST-IN-PLACE STAIR**.
- *Step 3 (not shown)*: Verify the **BASE LEVEL** is set to **LEVEL 2** and that the **TOP LEVEL** is set to **LEVEL 3**.
- *Step 4 (not shown)*: In the **MODIFY | CREATE STAIR** tab, **SET** the **LOCATION LINE** to **RUN: RIGHT** and the **ACTUAL RUN WIDTH** to **3'-8"**.
- *Steps 5–8*: **CLICK ONCE** at each point to match the example.
- *Step 9*: **CLICK** the **FINISH SKETCH** button.

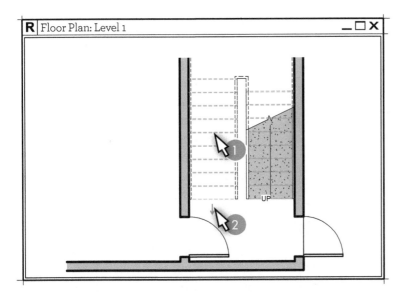

Changing a Stair's Up Direction

A stair's up direction is determined when you initially sketch it in plan view. Follow these steps to flip a stair's up direction:

- *Step 1*: **CLICK** the **STAIR** you want to modify.
- *Step 2*: **CLICK** the **FLIP STAIR ARROW**.

Use this method to change the direction of any Revit stair including straight, curved, and spiral stairs.

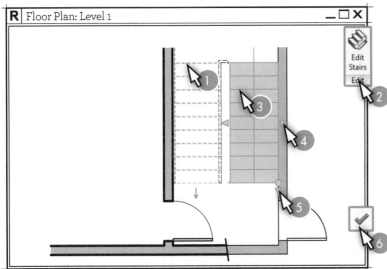

Modifying Stairs

You can change the width or length of an existing stair with the edit stairs button.

- *Step 1*: **CLICK** the **STAIR** you want to modify.
- *Step 2*: **CLICK** the **EDIT STAIRS** button in the **MODIFY | STAIRS** tab.
- *Step 3*: **CLICK** the stair run or landing you want to modify.
- *Step 4*: Use the **SHAPE HANDLE** on either side of the stair to change the stair's width.
- *Step 5*: The **SHAPE HANDLE** at the end of a run adds or removes treads from the run.
- *Step 6*: **CLICK** the **FINISH SKETCH** button to finish the stair sketch.

Changing a Stair's Shape

- Repeat *Steps 1-2* in the modifying stairs tutorial above.
- *Step 3*: **CLICK** the stair run or landing you want to modify.
- *Step 4*: **CLICK** the **CONVERT** button in the **TOOLS** panel.
- *Step 5*: **CLICK** the **EDIT SKETCH** button in the **TOOLS** panel.
- *Steps 6-7*: Delete the current stair run edge. Add a new edge with the **DRAW TOOLS**.
- *Step 8*: **CLICK** the **FINISH SKETCH** button to finish the stair run sketch.
- *Step 9*: **CLICK** the **FINISH EDIT MODE** button to finish the stair modification.

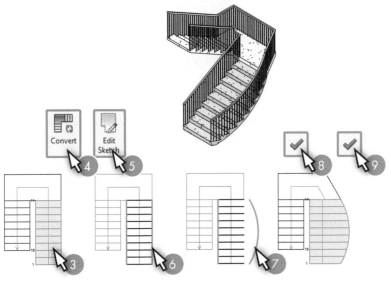

STAIRS (continued)

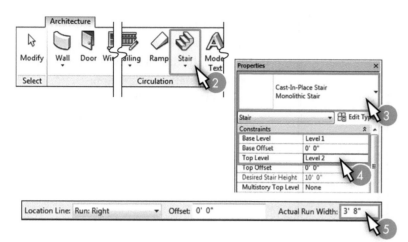

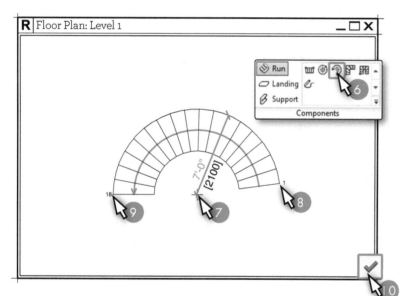

Adding Curved Stairs

- *Step 1 (not shown):* **OPEN** the **LEVEL 1** view in the **PROJECT BROWSER**.
- *Step 2:* **CLICK** the **STAIR** button in the **ARCHITECTURE** tab.
- *Step 3:* **CHANGE** the **STAIR TYPE** to **CAST-IN-PLACE STAIR** in the stair **PROPERTIES** box.
- *Step 4:* For this example, verify the **BASE LEVEL** is set to **LEVEL 1** and that the **TOP LEVEL** is set to **LEVEL 2**. When drawing stairs, set the **BASE LEVEL** and **TOP LEVEL** to match the start and end levels in your project.
- *Step 5:* In the **MODIFY | CREATE STAIR** tab, **SET** the **ACTUAL RUN WIDTH** to match the desired stair width. In this example, the width is set to **3'-8"**.

  The SI measurement for this step is **1100**.

- *Step 6:* **CLICK** the **CENTER-ENDS-SPIRAL** button in the stair **COMPONENTS** panel.

In the Level 1 plan view, sketch the stair following these steps:

- *Step 7:* **CLICK ONCE** to locate the center of the curved stair.
- *Step 8:* **MOVE** the **CURSOR** away from the center of the stair. **CLICK ONCE** to determine the radius of the stair.
- *Step 9:* **MOVE** the **CURSOR** along the path of the stair to reveal the stair treads. **CLICK ONCE** at the end of the stair run.
- *Step 10:* **CLICK** the **FINISH SKETCH** button to end the Stair sketch. Revit will complete the stair and add handrails.

- These two drawings show a plan and elevation view of the resulting curved stair.

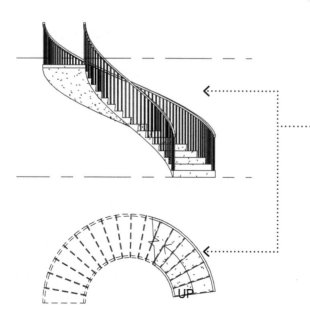

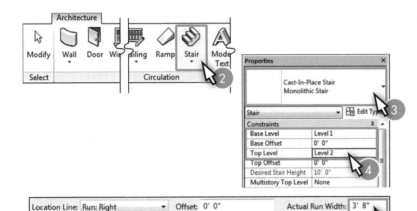

Adding Spiral Stairs

- *Step 1 (not shown)*: **OPEN** the **LEVEL 1** view in the **PROJECT BROWSER**.
- *Step 2*: **CLICK** the **STAIR** button in the **ARCHITECTURE** tab.
- *Step 3*: **CHANGE** the **STAIR TYPE** to **CAST-IN-PLACE STAIR** in the stair **PROPERTIES** box.
- *Step 4*: For this example, verify the **BASE LEVEL** is set to **LEVEL 1** and that the **TOP LEVEL** is set to **LEVEL 2**. When drawing stairs, set the **BASE LEVEL** and **TOP LEVEL** to match the start and end levels in your project.
- *Step 5*: In the **MODIFY | CREATE STAIR** tab, **SET** the **ACTUAL RUN WIDTH** to match the desired stair width. In this example, the width is set to **3'-8"**.

> The SI measurement for this step is **1100**.

- *Step 6*: **CLICK** the **FULL-STEP-SPIRAL** button in the stair **COMPONENTS** panel.

In the Level 1 plan view, sketch the stair following these steps:

- *Step 7*: **CLICK ONCE** to locate the center of the spiral stair.
- *Step 8*: **MOVE** the **CURSOR** away from the center of the stair. **CLICK ONCE** to determine the radius of the stair. The second click also determines the start position of the bottom tread.
- *Step 9*: **CLICK** the **FINISH SKETCH** button to end the stair sketch. Revit will complete the stair and add handrails.

- These two drawings show a plan and elevation view of the resulting spiral stair.

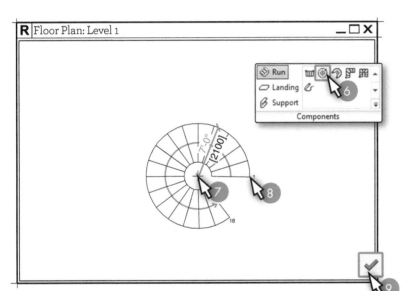

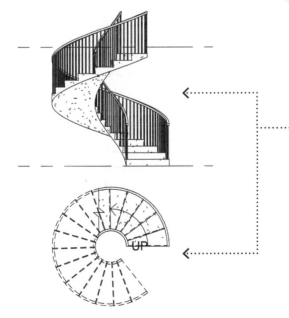

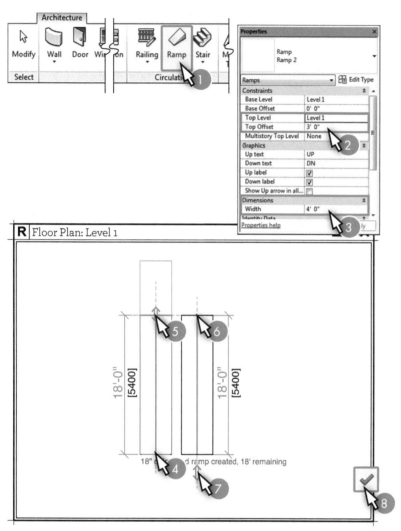

Adding Ramps

- *Step 1*: **CLICK** the **RAMP** button in the **ARCHITECTURE** tab.
- *Step 2*: **SET** the **TOP LEVEL** to **LEVEL 1** and **SET** the **TOP OFFSET** to **3'-0"** in the ramp **PROPERTIES** box.

> The SI measurement for this step is **900**.

- *Step 3*: **SET** the **WIDTH** to **4'-0"**.

> The SI measurement for this step is **1200**.

In the floor plan view, sketch the ramp following these steps:

- *Step 4*: **CLICK** to locate the start of the ramp.
- *Step 5*: **MOVE** the **CURSOR UP. CLICK ONCE** when the temporary dimension is **18'-0"**. These first two clicks define the first run of the ramp.

> The SI measurement for this step is **5400**.

- *Step 6*: **MOVE** the **CURSOR** to the **RIGHT. CLICK ONCE** to match the example.
- *Step 7*: **MOVE** the **CURSOR DOWN. CLICK ONCE** when the temporary dimension is **18'-0"**.

> The SI measurement for this step is **5400**.

Step 8: **CLICK** the **FINISH SKETCH** button in the **MODIFY | CREATE RAMP SKETCH** tab to finish the ramp sketch. Revit completes the ramp and adds handrails.

Modifying Ramps

Change the shape of a ramp with the edit boundary button.

- *Step 1*: In the floor plan view, **CLICK** on the **EDGE OF THE RAMP.**
- *Step 2*: **CLICK** the **EDIT BOUNDARY** button in the **MODIFY | RAMP BOUNDARY** tab.
- *Steps 3–4*: Delete the ramp run edge. Add a new edge with the **DRAW TOOLS**.
- *Step 5*: Use the **DRAW TOOLS** to align the ramp landing with the new ramp run edge.
- *Step 6*: **CLICK** the **FINISH SKETCH** button to finish the ramp sketch changing the right edge of the ramp to a curved edge.

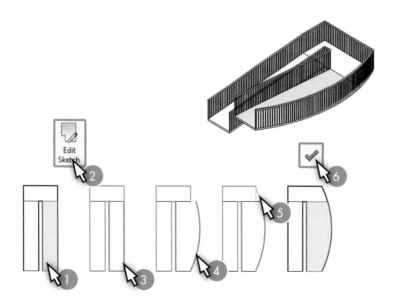

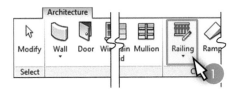

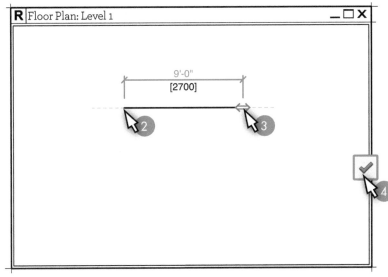

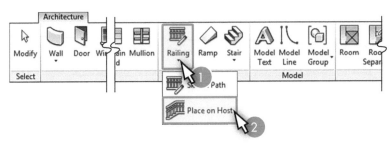

Adding Railings (Sketch Path)

Use the Railing Sketch Path method to add a railing to a slab edge, balcony, or interior condition.

- *Step 1*: **CLICK** the **RAILING** button in the **ARCHITECTURE** tab.

- *Step 2*: In the floor plan view, **CLICK** to locate the first edge of the railing.
- *Step 3*: **MOVE** the **CURSOR** and **CLICK** to locate the second edge of the railing. In this example, the railing is **9'-0"** long.

  The SI measurement for this step is **2700**.

- *Step 4*: **CLICK** the **FINISH SKETCH** button to finish the railing sketch.

Adding Railings (Place on Host)

Use the Railing Place on Host method to add a railing to an existing stair or ramp.
- *Step 1*: **CLICK** the **RAILING DOWN ARROW** in the **ARCHITECTURE** tab.
- *Step 2*: In the Drop-down menu, **CLICK** the **PLACE ON HOST** button.
- *Step 3 (not shown)*: In a floor plan view, **CLICK** on an **EXISTING STAIR**. Revit adds the railing to the selected object.

Railing Family Types

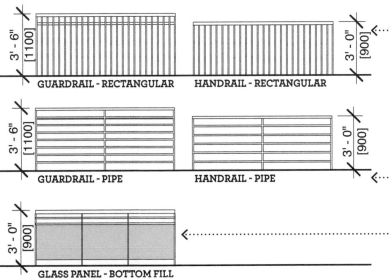

- The **GUARDRAIL - RECTANGULAR** and **HANDRAIL - RECTANGULAR** family types are made of 2"x 2" vertical posts spaced 4" apart.

  The default SI guardrail's vertical posts are **25mm x 25mm** spaced **275mm** apart.

- The **GUARDRAIL - PIPE** and **HANDRAIL - PIPE** family types are made of 1-1/2" horizontal pipes spaced 4" apart.
- The **GLASS PANEL** family type is made of 2'-8" wide glass panels supported by steel bars.

Guided Discovery Exercise

Guided Discovery 3.1 Multi-Level Building

- To begin this exercise download the AutoCAD building shell drawing at **WWW.RAFDBOOK.COM/DOWNLOADS**.
- Follow the step-by-step exercises in Chapter 2 on page 49 to link the AutoCAD building shell to a new Revit project.
- Add the following items to the project:
  - Levels
  - Column grid lines
  - Columns
  - Exterior walls
  - Floor slabs (with slab openings)
  - Stairs

Application Exercises

Using an assignment from your instructor or a previously completed studio project, convert a building shell to a Revit project. Add the following items to the new project:

- Levels
- Column grid lines
- Columns
- Exterior walls
- Floor slabs (with slab openings)
- Stairs

PRESENTATION DRAWINGS

PRESENTATION PLANS

The previous chapters introduced basic tools to create and modify a floor plan in Revit. Now that you have mastered the basics, it is time to explore the advanced skills you need to start a new multi-level Revit project. Chapter 4 also introduces specialized glass walls. Curtain wall and storefront systems are glazed panel systems. While these systems are traditionally used as exterior building surfaces, they can be easily adapted to interior glass wall systems.

IN THIS CHAPTER

PRESENTATION PLANS

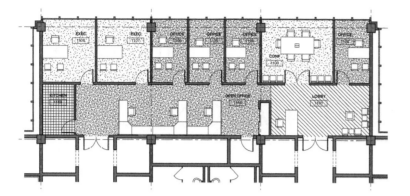

The presentation plan is an important drawing that communicates the design intent of a project. This type of plan often includes walls, doors, furniture, room names, and floor finishes. In AutoCAD you could create a presentation plan using specific layers and viewports. In Revit, you will duplicate a plan view with the categories of information you want to include in the floor plan.

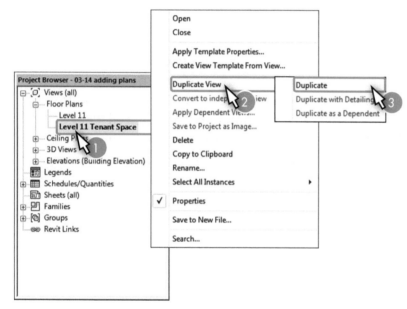

Creating a Presentation Plan View

Once you've added walls, doors, and furniture to the Revit project, it is time to create a unique view for the presentation drawing.

- *Step 1*: **RIGHT-CLICK** on the existing **LEVEL 11 TENANT SPACE** view in the **PROJECT BROWSER**.
- *Step 2*: **SELECT DUPLICATE VIEW** from the context menu.
- *Step 3*: **CLICK** on **DUPLICATE** in the secondary context menu.

This action duplicates the existing plan view as **LEVEL 11 TENANT SPACE COPY 1**.

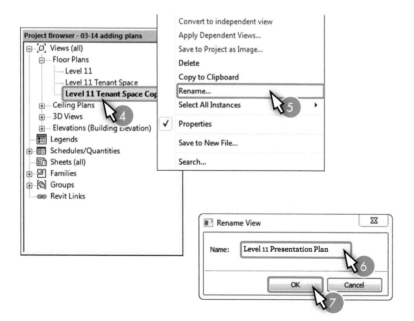

Renaming the Plan View

- *Step 4*: **RIGHT-CLICK** on the new **LEVEL 11 TENANT SPACE COPY 1** view in the **PROJECT BROWSER**.
- *Step 5*: **SELECT RENAME** from the context menu.

- *Step 6*: **RENAME** the plan view to **LEVEL 11 PRESENTATION PLAN**.
- *Step 7*: **CLICK** the **OK** button.

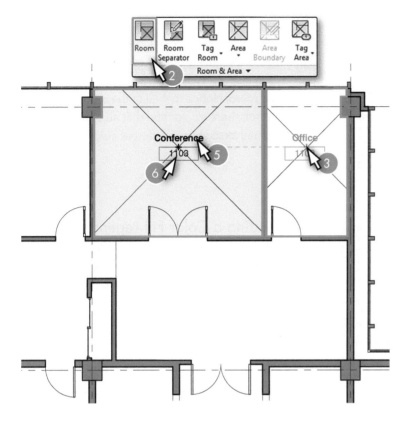

Adding Room Boundaries and Tags

The Room button creates a room bounded by walls in the project. The button also adds a room tag, which is a view-specific element.

- *Step 1 (not shown)*: **OPEN** the **PRESENTATION PLAN** view.
- *Step 2*: **CLICK** the **ROOM** button in the **ARCHITECTURE** tab.
- *Step 3*: **CLICK** inside any room to create both the room boundary and the room tag.
- Repeat *Step 3* to add room boundaries to each space in the plan view.
- *Step 4 (not shown)*: **PRESS** the **ESC** key on the keyboard to end the Room command.
- *Step 5*: **DOUBLE-CLICK** the **ROOM NAME** portion of the room tag to name the room. In this example, the room is renamed to **CONFERENCE**.
- *Step 6*: **DOUBLE-CLICK** the **ROOM NUMBER** portion of the room tag to number the room. In this example, the room is renumbered to **1103**.

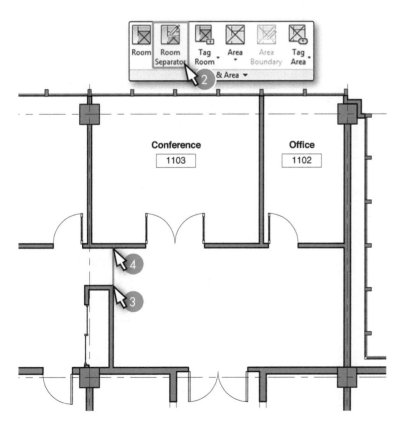

Adding Room Separators

Room separator lines define room boundaries between spaces that are not already separated by a wall.

- *Step 1 (not shown)*: **OPEN** the **CONSTRUCTION PLAN** view.
- *Step 2*: **CLICK** the **ROOM SEPARATOR** button in the **ARCHITECTURE** tab.
- *Steps 3–4*: **CLICK** in the plan view to create the room separator line.
- *Step 5 (not shown)*: **PRESS** the **ESC** key **TWICE** on the keyboard to end the Room Separator command.

Tip: Room numbers are usually sequenced in the floor plan so adjacent rooms have adjacent numbers. In multi-story commercial projects, the first two numbers of the room should match the floor level in the building.

COLOR FILL ROOM LEGEND

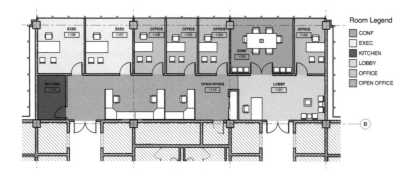

The Color Fill Legend tool is a quick way to add color or texture to rooms in your Revit project. In this example, each room is rendered with a specific color based on the name of the room. Notice that all of the rooms named **OFFICE** share a color and that all of the rooms named **EXEC** share a different color.

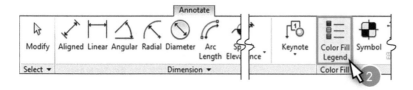

Adding a Color Fill Legend

Step 1 (not shown): In the **PROJECT BROWSER**, **OPEN** the **LEVEL 11 PRESENTATION PLAN** view.
Step 2: **CLICK** the **COLOR FILL LEGEND** button in the **ANNOTATE** tab.

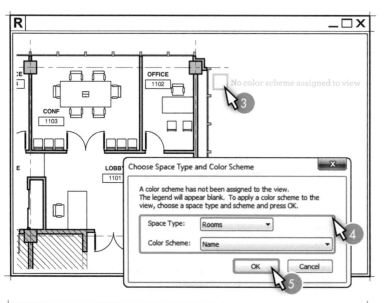

Step 3: **CLICK ONCE** in the plan view where you want to insert the Color Fill Legend. The Choose Space Type and Color Scheme dialog box opens if you have not assigned a color scheme to the active plan view.

Step 4: **SELECT ROOMS** as the Space Type and **NAME** as the Color Scheme. This tells Revit to automatically assign colors based on the name of the room.
Step 5: **CLICK** the **OK** button.

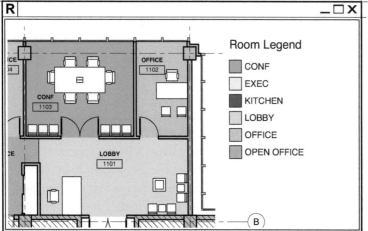

- The Room Legend contains a list of all the rooms in the project and their corresponding fill color.
- Each room in the plan view is filled with the color indicated in the Room Legend.

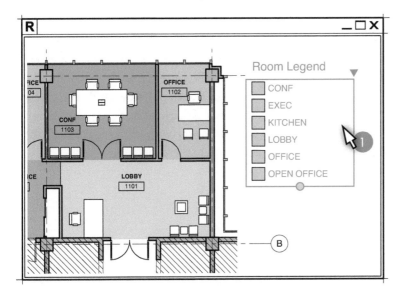

Editing the Color Scheme

You can modify the default color scheme in Color Fill Legends to include colors and patterns that support your design presentation.

Step 1: **SELECT** the **COLOR FILL LEGEND** in the active view.

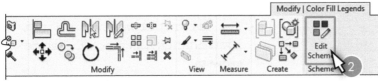

Step 2: **CLICK** the **EDIT SCHEME** button in the **MODIFY | COLOR FILL LEGENDS** tab.

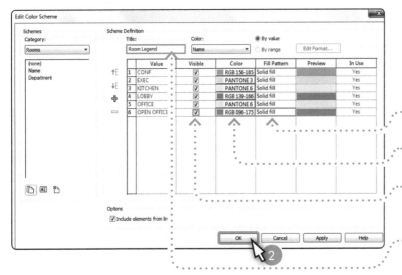

The Edit Color Scheme dialog box allows you to change the color scheme used in the Color Fill Legend. Because color schemes are shared across views in a Revit project, there may be room names defined in the Scheme Definition that are not located on the current level.

- **CLICK** the **FILL PATTERN** to change the room's fill pattern in the plan.
- **CLICK** the **COLOR** swatch to change the color for a room name.
- **UNCHECK** the **VISIBLE** parameter to hide a room fill pattern from the plan and hide the room name in the legend.
- **EDIT** the **TITLE** to rename the legend in the plan view.

Step 3: **CLICK** the **OK** button to close the **EDIT COLOR SCHEME** dialog box and apply the changes to the Color Fill Legend.

Tip: Change the **COLOR** definition in the **EDIT COLOR SCHEME** dialog box to set room fills based on a different room parameter. For example, the Department parameter would allow you to render similar zones/departments in your presentation plan with the same color.

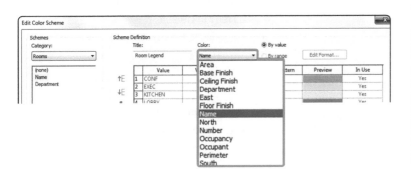

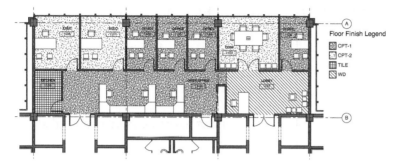

The Color Fill Legend tool is also a quick way to add floor finish patterns to rooms in Revit. In this example, each room is rendered with a specific pattern based on floor finish parameter. The steps below guide you through the process of duplicating your presentation plan view so you can assign a separate Color Fill Legend to the floor plan.

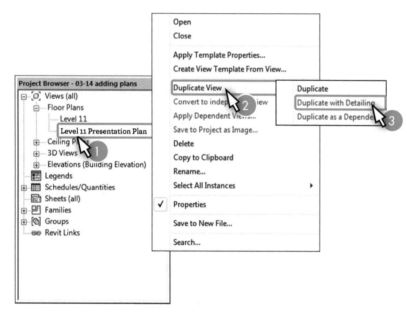

Creating a Presentation Finish Plan

This instruction will build on the Color Fill Legend added to the presentation plan view on page 80.

- *Step 1*: **RIGHT-CLICK** on the existing **LEVEL 11 PRESENTATION PLAN** view in the **PROJECT BROWSER**.
- *Step 2*: **SELECT DUPLICATE VIEW** from the context menu.
- *Step 3*: **CLICK** on **DUPLICATE WITH DETAILING** in the secondary context menu.

> **Tip:** The **DUPLICATE VIEW > DUPLICATE** option creates a duplicate view that only contains model elements from the duplicated view.
>
> The **DUPLICATE VIEW > DUPLICATE WITH DETAILING** option creates a duplicate view with all model and all annotative elements from the duplicated view.

Renaming the Plan View

- *Step 4*: **RIGHT-CLICK** on the new **LEVEL 11 PRESENTATION PLAN COPY 1** view in the **PROJECT BROWSER**.
- *Step 5*: **SELECT RENAME** from the context menu.

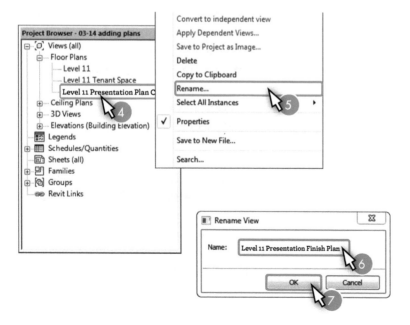

- *Step 6*: **RENAME** the plan view to **LEVEL 11 PRESENTATION FINISH PLAN**.
- *Step 7*: **CLICK** the **OK** button.

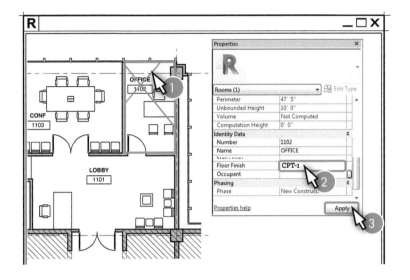

Defining Room Floor Finishes

You must define each room's floor finish before modifying a Color Fill Legends to display fill patterns based on floor finish.

- *Step 1:* **MOVE** the **CURSOR** over a room until you see the **BLUE X** and the **BLUE ROOM BOUNDARY. CLICK ONCE** on the **BLUE X.**
- *Step 2:* **CHANGE** the **FLOOR FINISH** parameter in the **PROPERTIES** box to appropriate floor finish abbreviation. In this example **CPT-1** indicates carpet style 1.
- *Step 3:* **CLICK** the **APPLY** button.

Repeat *Steps 1* and *2* above for each room in the presentation plan.

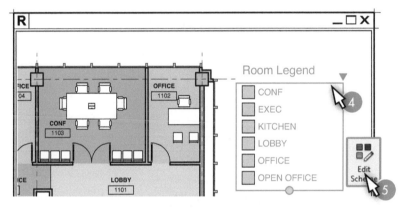

Editing the Color Scheme

After adding floor finish parameters for each room in the plan view, modify the color scheme in Color Fill Legends to include patterns based on a room's floor finish.

- *Step 4:* **SELECT** the **COLOR FILL LEGEND** in the active view.
- *Step 5:* *Click* the **EDIT SCHEME** button in the **MODIFY | COLOR FILL LEGENDS** tab.

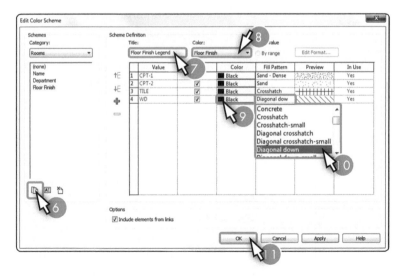

Step 6: **DUPLICATE** the **NAME** color scheme and name the duplicated scheme **FLOOR FINISH.**

Step 7: **CHANGE** the legend **TITLE** to **FLOOR FINISH LEGEND.**

Step 8: **CHANGE** the scheme **COLOR** to render based on **FLOOR FINISH.**

Step 9: **CHANGE** each finish **COLOR** to **BLACK.**

Step 10: **CHANGE** each finish **FILL PATTERN** to match the example.

Step 11: **CLICK** the **OK** button to close the **EDIT COLOR SCHEME** dialog box and apply the changes to the Color Fill Legend.

ROOM AREA SCHEDULES

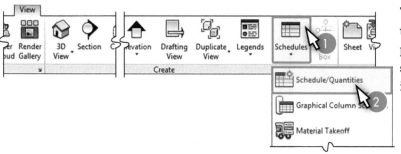

The Room Area Schedule is useful to compare the current design square footage to the programming document. This schedule should be customized to include fields important to the current project.

- *Step 1*: **CLICK** the **SCHEDULES DROP-DOWN ARROW** in the **VIEW** tab.
- *Step 2*: **CLICK** the **SCHEDULES/QUANTITIES** option in the Drop-down menu.

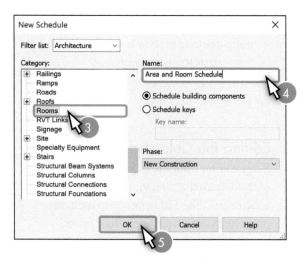

- *Step 3*: **SELECT** the **ROOMS** category in the **NEW SCHEDULE** dialog box.
- *Step 4*: **CHANGE** the schedule name to **ROOM AREA SCHEDULE**.
- *Step 5*: **CLICK** the **OK** button.

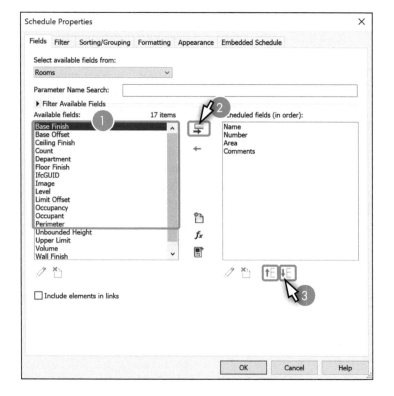

Adding Fields

- *Step 1*: **CLICK ONCE** on the **NAME** field in the available fields column.
- *Step 2*: **CLICK** the **ADD** button.

Repeat *Steps 1* and *2* to add the following fields to the schedule (in this order):

- **NAME**
- **NUMBER**
- **DEPARTMENT** (optional)
- **OCCUPANT** (optional)
- **OCCUPANCY** (optional)
- **AREA**
- **COMMENTS**

- *Step 3*: Use the **MOVE UP** and **MOVE DOWN** buttons to change the order of the fields in the schedule to match the order listed above.

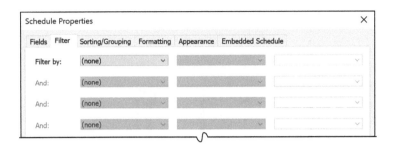

Filtering the Schedule

The Filter tab provides the ability to limit the rooms that appear in the schedule. For example, filtering rooms with numbers between 1100 and 1199 would show rooms on the 11th floor in the schedule. Do not make any changes to this tab at this time.

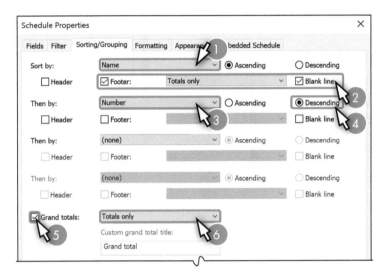

Sorting the Schedule

The Sorting/Grouping tab contains multiple sort criteria for the schedule. Room schedules are sorted by room number.

- *Step 1*: **CHANGE** the primary **SORT BY** parameter to **NAME**.
- *Step 2*: Add the following parameters for the primary sort: **FOOTER, TOTALS ONLY**, and **BLANK LINE**.
- *Step 3*: **CHANGE** the secondary **SORT BY** parameter to **NUMBER**.
- *Step 4*: **CHANGE** the secondary **SORT ORDER** to **DESCENDING**.
- *Step 5*: **CHECK** the **GRAND TOTALS** box.
- *Step 6*: **SELECT** the **TOTALS ONLY** option in the Drop-down menu.

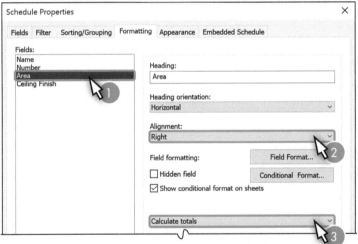

Formatting the Schedule

The Formatting tab contains individual format settings for each column in the schedule.

- *Step 1*: **CLICK ONCE** on the **AREA** field to change its format properties.
- *Step 2*: **CHANGE** the **ALIGNMENT** field to **RIGHT**.
- *Step 3*: **CHANGE** the **CALCULATE** field to **CALCULATE TOTALS**.
- *Step 4 (not shown)*: **CLICK** the **OK** button to close the **SCHEDULE PROPERTIES** dialog box.

Viewing the Schedule

The Room Area Schedule view is used to update room finish properties in a project.

- *Step 1 (not shown)*: **DOUBLE-CLICK** on the **SCHEDULE NAME** in the **PROJECT BROWSER**.

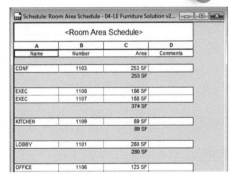

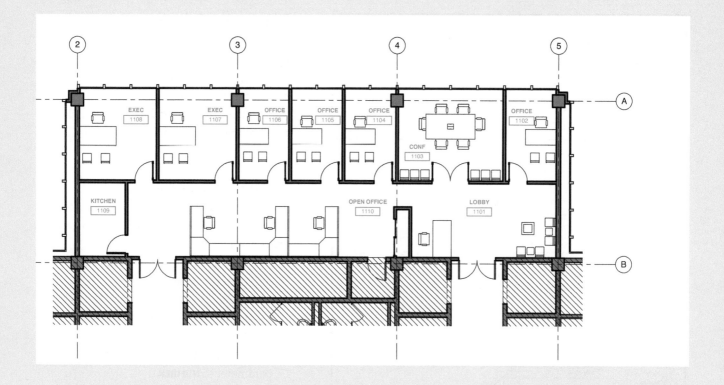

Learning Exercises

These exercises are intended to help you improve your
understanding of Presentation Plans in Revit. To begin this
exercise, open the Revit project created in Learning Exercises 2.1 at
the end of Chapter 2.

Learning Exercise 4.1: Adding Room Tags

- Duplicate the **LEVEL 11 TENANT SPACE** plan view in the
  PROJECT BROWSER.
- Rename the new view to **LEVEL 11 PRESENTATION PLAN.**
- Add Room Boundaries and Tags for each room in the project.
- Rename and renumber each room to match the example above.
- **SAVE** the project to your computer or a portable drive.

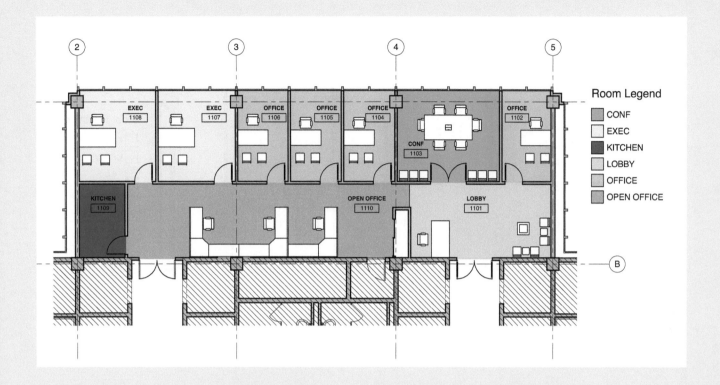

Learning Exercises (continued)

Learning Exercise 4.2: Adding Room Legend
- Duplicate with detailing the **LEVEL 11 PRESENTATION PLAN** view from Learning Exercise 4.1.
- Rename the duplicated view to **LEVEL 11 PRESENTATION PLAN ROOM LEGEND.**
- Add a Color Fill Legend to the plan view.
- Adjust the legend's Color Scheme to match the example above. (Reference page 80 for more information.)
- **SAVE** the project to your computer or a portable drive.

Revit Tips
- Floor plans are commonly drawn at 1/8″ = 1′-0″.

> The equivalent SI scale is **1:100**.

- Use a Color Fill Legend to graphically emphasize the room adjacencies in a project.

Annotation Tips
- Set an appropriate architectural scale before annotating plans.
- Make the furniture category visible in this plan view.
- Add room tags to every room in the project.

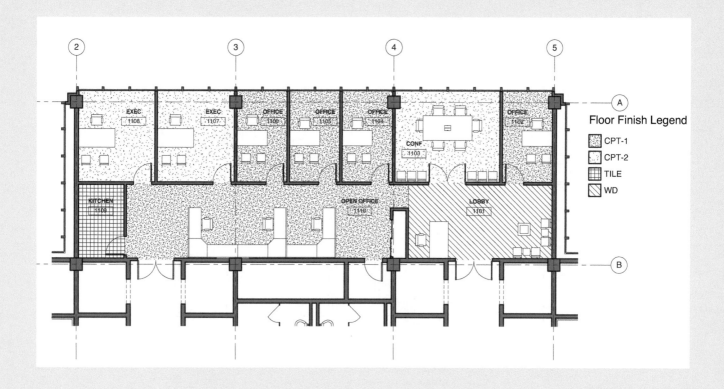

Learning Exercises (continued)

Learning Exercise 4.3: Adding Floor Finish Legend

- Duplicate with detailing the **LEVEL 11 PRESENTATION PLAN ROOM LEGEND** view from Learning Exercise 4.2.
- Rename the duplicated view to **LEVEL 11 PRESENTATION PLAN FLOOR FINISH LEGEND.**
- Adjust the Color Fill Legend's Color Scheme to display the Floor Finish parameter.
- Adjust each room's floor finish parameter and the legend's Color Scheme to match the example above. (Reference page 82 for more information.)
- **SAVE** the project to your computer or a portable drive.

Revit Tips

- Floor plans are commonly drawn at 1/8″ = 1′-0″.

  The equivalent SI scale is **1:100.**

- Use a Color Fill Legend to add room finish patterns to the plan.

Annotation Tips

- Set an appropriate architectural scale before annotating plans.
- Make the furniture category visible in this plan view.
- Add room tags to every room in the project.

chapter 5

PRESENTATION RCPS

Ceiling plans are useful drawings to communicate the location of ceiling-mounted building systems including lighting, HVAC, fire sprinklers, and egress signage. Ceilings and lighting are also visible in interior perspective discussed in Chapter 6. In Revit, ceilings and light fixtures provide the artificial light for photorealistic renderings.

IN THIS CHAPTER

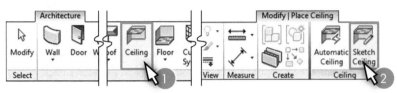

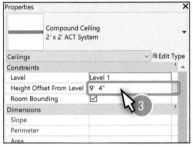

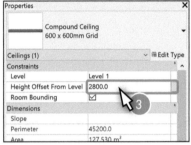

The Sketch Ceiling method is the most common method used to add a ceiling in Revit.

- *Step 1*: From the ceiling plan view, **CLICK** the **CEILING** button in the **ARCHITECTURE** tab. This changes the ribbon to the **MODIFY | PLACE CEILING** tab.
- *Step 2*: **CLICK** the **SKETCH CEILING** button to draw a ceiling. This opens the **MODIFY | CREATE CEILING BOUNDARY** ribbon.
- *Step 3*: **SET** the **HEIGHT** of the ceiling in the **PROPERTIES** box. In this example, the height is set to **9′ 4″**.

> The SI measurement for this step is **2800**.

Sketching a Ceiling Boundary

- *Step 4*: In the **MODIFY | CREATE CEILING BOUNDARY** tab, **CLICK** the **DRAW LINE** button.

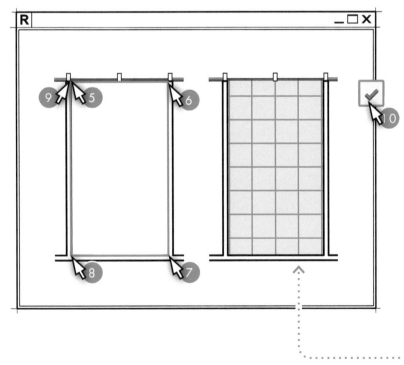

- *Step 5*: In the ceiling plan, **CLICK** on the upper-left corner of the room.
- *Steps 6–9*: Following the example, **CLICK** on each corner of the room.
- *Step 10*: **CLICK** the **FINISH SKETCH** button in the **MODIFY | CREATE CEILING BOUNDARY** tab to finish the ceiling sketch.

> **Tip**: When sketching ceilings, it is important that you close the ceiling's shape. In this example, the boundary line between *Steps 8* and *9* complete the rectangle shape.

> **Guided Discovery 5.1**: Using the Sketch Ceiling command, add a second 2′ x 2′ ceiling to the ceiling plan to match this example. The SI equivalent ceiling is 600mm x 600mm.
>
> Support files for this exercise are at **WWW.RAFDBOOK.COM/DOWNLOADS**.

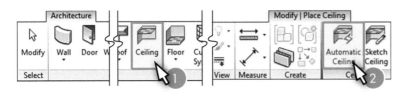

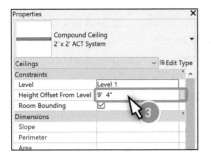

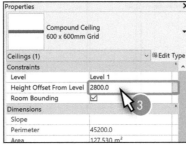

The Automatic Ceiling method fills rooms (fully enclosed by walls) with the selected ceiling surface. While this method appears to save time, it often results in multiple/overlapping ceilings in the Revit project.

- *Step 1*: From the ceiling plan view, **CLICK** the **CEILING** button in the **ARCHITECTURE** tab. This changes the ribbon to the **MODIFY | PLACE CEILING** tab.
- *Step 2*: By default, the Place Ceiling method is set to **AUTOMATIC CEILING**.
- *Step 3*: **SET** the **HEIGHT** of the ceiling in the **PROPERTIES** box. In this example, the height is set to **9′ 4″**.

The SI measurement for this step is **2800**.

Tip: The ceiling's height must be below the next level's height or the added ceiling will not be visible in the RCP view.

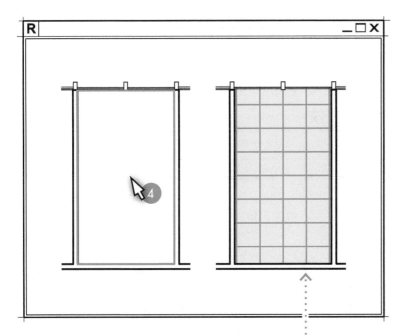

As you move the mouse over rooms in the ceiling plan, Revit indicates the room boundary with a blue border.

- *Step 4*: **CLICK** on any room to add a ceiling.

Guided Discovery 5.1 (continued):
Following the example to the left, add a 2′ x 2′ ACT Ceiling to the ceiling plan with the Automatic Ceiling method. The SI equivalent ceiling is 600mm x 600mm.

CEILINGS (continued)

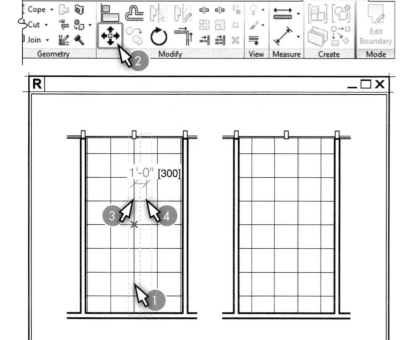

Moving Ceiling Grids

Moving ceiling grids is similar to moving walls, doors, and furniture in Revit.

- *Step 1*: **CLICK** on the **CEILING GRID LINE** that you want to move.
- *Step 2*: In the **MODIFY | CEILINGS** tab, **CLICK** the **MOVE** button.
- *Step 3*: **CLICK** on the **CEILING GRID LINE** again to set the initial point of the move.
- *Step 4*: **MOVE** the mouse to the right or left.
- *Step 5 (not shown)*: **TYPE** the **MOVE DISTANCE** (e.g., 1'), and **PRESS ENTER**. In this example, the grid is moved a distance of **1'** to the **RIGHT**.

> The SI measurement for this step is **300**.

Rotating Ceiling Grids

Rotating ceiling grids is similar to rotating furniture in Revit.

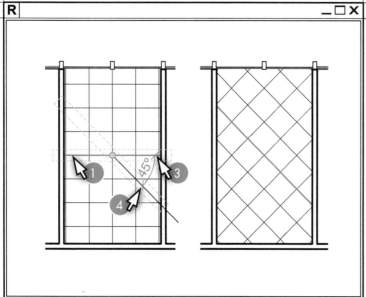

- *Step 1*: **CLICK** on the **CEILING GRID LINE** that you want to rotate.
- *Step 2*: In the **MODIFY | CEILINGS** tab, **CLICK** the **ROTATE** button.
- *Step 3*: **CLICK** on the **CEILING GRID LINE** again to set the initial angle of the rotate.
- *Step 4*: **MOVE** the mouse clockwise or counterclockwise.
- *Step 5 (not shown)*: **TYPE** the **ROTATION ANGLE** (e.g., **45°**), and **PRESS ENTER**. In this example, the grid is rotated **45°** in the **CLOCKWISE** direction.

> **Guided Discovery 5.1 (continued)**: Follow the steps on this page to adjust the position of a ceiling grid.
> Follow the instructions on the next page to change the ceiling type.

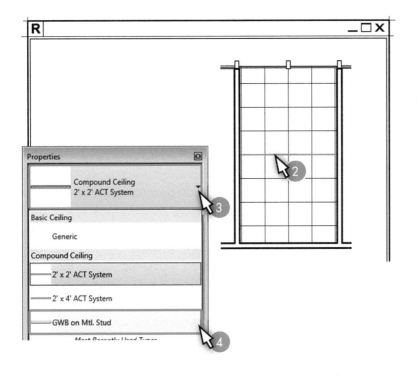

Changing ceiling materials (or types) is similar to changing door families and types. The default ceiling family in Revit is Compound Ceiling.

Changing Ceiling Types

- *Step 1 (not shown)*: **OPEN** a **CEILING PLAN** view.
- *Step 2*: **CLICK** on any line in the ceiling grid to select the ceiling. The **PROPERTIES** palette updates to show the current ceiling family (**COMPOUND CEILING**) and **TYPE** (**2' X 2' ACT SYSTEM**).

  The SI equivalent ceiling type is 600 x 600.

- *Step 3*: **CLICK** on the down arrow in the **PROPERTIES** palette to show the available ceiling families and types.
- *Step 4*: **CLICK** on the **GWB ON MTL. STUD** family type to change the ceiling material. The selected ceiling updates to reflect the graphic properties of the new ceiling type. In this instance, the grid lines disappear.

Changing GWB Ceiling Types

GWB ceilings are more difficult to select in the ceiling plan view because there are no lines to click.

- *Steps 1–2*: **DRAG** a window over one corner of the ceiling surface.
- *Step 3*: **CLICK** the **FILTER** button in the **MODIFY | MULTI-SELECT** tab.
- *Step 4*: **DESELECT** all items except **CEILINGS**.
- *Step 5*: **CLICK** the **OK** button to close the **FILTER SELECTION** box. The **PROPERTIES** palette updates to show the current ceiling family (**COMPOUND CEILING**) and type (**GWB ON MTL STUD**)
- *Step 6 (not shown)*: **CLICK** on the down arrow in the **PROPERTIES** palette to show the available ceiling families and types.
- *Step 7 (not shown)*: **CLICK** on the **2' X 4' ACT SYSTEM** family type to change the ceiling material. The selected ceiling updates to reflect the graphic properties of the **2' X 4' ACT** ceiling type.

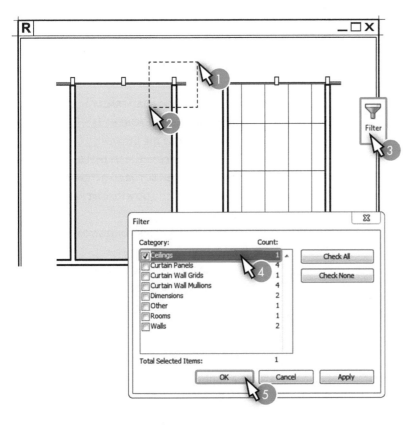

LIGHT FIXTURES

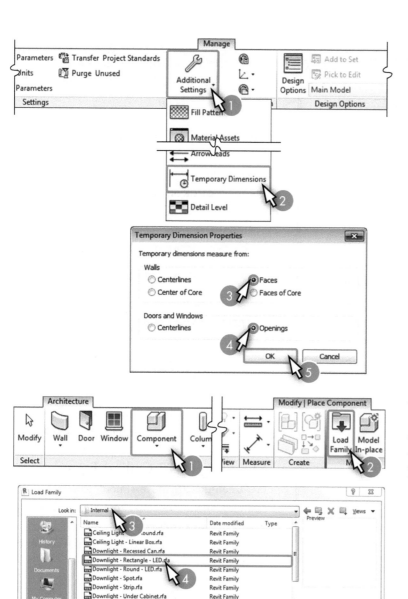

Temporary Dimensions

By default, Revit's temporary dimensions provide dimensional information to the center lines of walls, doors, and windows. It is easier to locate light fixtures from the edge of the fixture to the closest wall face.

- *Step 1*: **CLICK** the **ADDITIONAL SETTINGS** button in the **MANAGE** tab.
- *Step 2*: **CLICK** the **TEMPORARY DIMENSIONS** button in the Drop-down menu. This opens the **TEMPORARY DIMENSION PROPERTIES** dialog box.
- *Step 3*: **CLICK** the **FACES** option for temporary dimensions from walls.
- *Step 4*: **CLICK** the **OPENINGS** option for temporary dimensions from doors and windows.
- *Step 5*: **CLICK** the **OK** button.

Adding Ceiling Components

Ceiling components must be hosted by a ceiling. This means you must add ceilings to the ceiling plan before you can add light fixtures.

- *Step 1*: From the ceiling plan view, **CLICK** the **COMPONENT** button in the **ARCHITECTURE** tab.
- *Step 2*: **CLICK** the **LOAD FAMILY** button in the **MODIFY | PLACE COMPONENT** tab. This opens the **LOAD FAMILY** file browser.
- *Step 3*: **NAVIGATE** to the **US IMPERIAL> LIGHTING>ARCHITECTURAL>INTERNAL** folder.
- *Step 4*: **SELECT** the **DOWNLIGHT - RECTANGLE - LED** light family.
- *Step 5*: **CLICK** the **OPEN** button to load the family into the Revit project.
- *Step 6*: **CLICK** the **PLACE ON FACE** button in the **MODIFY | PLACE COMPONENT** tab.

As you move the cursor in the drawing area, Revit shows the light fixture and temporary dimensions to the closest wall.

- *Step 7*: **CLICK ONCE** to insert the fixture in the ceiling plan.
- *Step 8 (not shown)*: **PRESS** the **ESC** key **TWICE** to end the Component command.

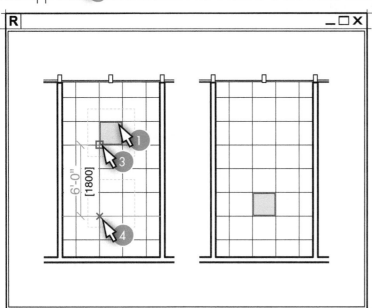

The **MODIFY | LIGHTING FIGURES** tab provides tools that allow you to precisely locate light fixtures in a ceiling plan.

Moving Light Fixtures

- *Step 1*: **CLICK** on the **LIGHT FIXTURE** as shown in the example.
- *Step 2*: **CLICK** the **MOVE** button in the **MODIFY | LIGHTING FIXTURES** tab.
- *Step 3*: Use the **ENDPOINT OBJECT SNAP** (indicated by a magenta square) to start the Move command at the bottom-left corner of the light fixture.
- *Step 4*: Use the **INTERSECT OBJECT SNAP** (indicated by a magenta x) to snap the light fixture to a ceiling grid intersection.
- *Step 5 (not shown)*: **PRESS** the **ESC** key on the keyboard to end the Move command.

> **Tip**: You can also use the **ALIGN** command to locate a light fixture inside a ceiling grid or in relation to another fixture in the RCP.

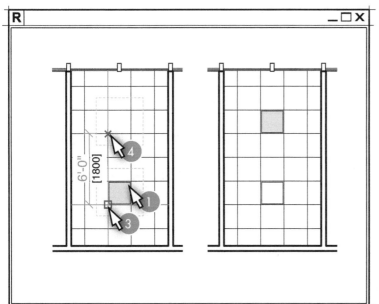

Copying Light Fixtures

- *Step 1*: **CLICK** on the light fixture as shown in the example.
- *Step 2*: **CLICK** the **COPY** button in the **MODIFY | LIGHTING FIXTURES** tab.
- *Step 3*: Use the **ENDPOINT OBJECT SNAP** to start the Copy command at the bottom-left corner of the light fixture.
- *Step 4*: Use the **INTERSECT OBJECT SNAP** to snap the copied light fixture to a ceiling grid intersection.
- *Step 5 (not shown)*: **PRESS** the **ESC** key on the keyboard to end the Move command.

> **Guided Discovery 5.2**: Follow the steps on this page to add light fixtures to the ceiling plan.

LIGHT FIXTURES (continued)

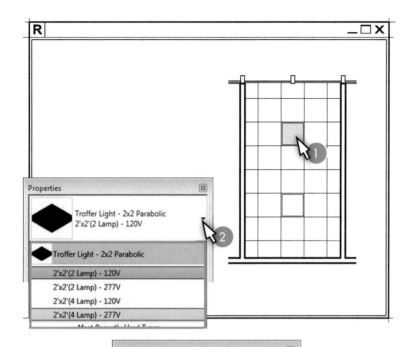

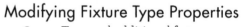

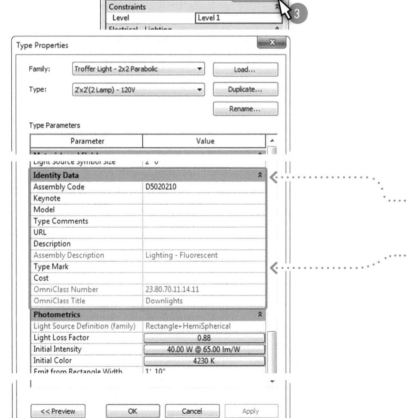

Similar to doors and windows, light fixtures belong to families. In addition to the default light families, several lighting manufacturers have developed Revit families.

Selecting Family Types

- *Step 1*: **CLICK** on the light fixture as shown in the example. The **PROPERTIES** dialog box contains information about the selected light fixture.

- *Step 2*: **CLICK** the fixture type down arrow in the **PROPERTIES** box to reveal additional family types. Most light fixture families contain lamp and voltage options.

Modifying Fixture Type Properties

- *Step 3*: To reveal additional fixture properties, **CLICK** the **EDIT TYPE** button in the **PROPERTIES** box. The **TYPE PROPERTIES** dialog box contains material, electric, and photometric data for the selected fixture.

- The **IDENTITY DATA** section contains information that can be referenced in a light schedule.
- The **TYPE MARK** variable will appear in both an RCP light fixture tag and the lighting schedule. Changing this variable will update all instances of the fixture type in the project.

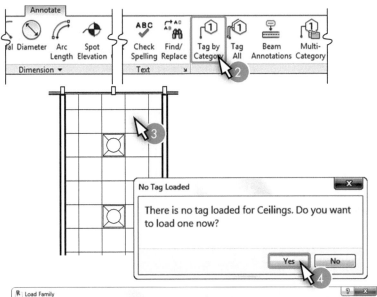

Loading the Ceiling Tag

Ceiling tag annotations display the ceiling material and ceiling height in the ceiling view. The first time you annotate ceiling tags in a Revit project, Revit will prompt you to load the ceiling tag.

- *Step 1 (not shown)*: **OPEN** a **CEILING VIEW** in Revit.
- *Step 2*: **CLICK** the **TAG BY CATEGORY** button in the **ANNOTATE** tab.
- *Step 3*: **CLICK** on any **CEILING** in the view. Revit will prompt with the **NO TAG LOADED** alert box.
- *Step 4*: **CLICK** the **YES** button in the **NO TAG LOADED** alert box. This opens the **LOAD FAMILY** file browser.

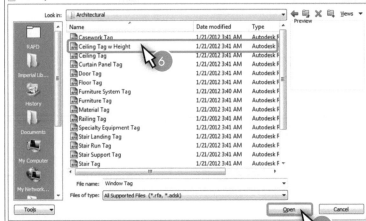

- *Step 5 (not shown)*: **NAVIGATE** to the **US IMPERIAL>ANNOTATIONS>ARCHITECTURAL** folder.
- *Step 6*: **CLICK** the **CEILING TAG W HEIGHT** annotation family.

> The SI equivalent tag is located at:
> **ENGLISH>US>ANNOTATIONS> ARCHITECTURAL>M_CEILING TAG W HEIGHT.RFA**

- *Step 7*: **CLICK** the **OPEN** button to load the family into the Revit project.

As you move the cursor over the ceilings in the ceiling plan, Revit shows the Ceiling Tag with Height annotation attached to each ceiling.

- *Step 8*: **CLICK** on any ceiling to add the annotation to your drawing.

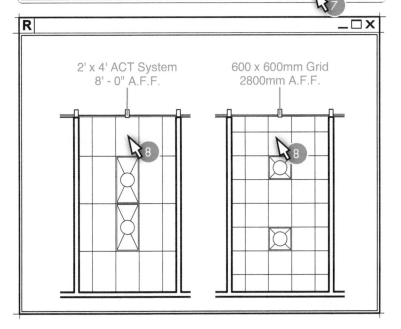

> **Guided Discovery 5.4**:
> Insert **CEILINGS** and **CEILING TAGS** to match both ceiling plans in this example. The support file for this exercise is at **WWW.RAFDBOOK.COM/DOWNLOADS.**

VIEW RANGE

Design firms often show the location of door openings in reflected ceiling plans. By default, doors and door openings are not visible in Revit ceiling plans.

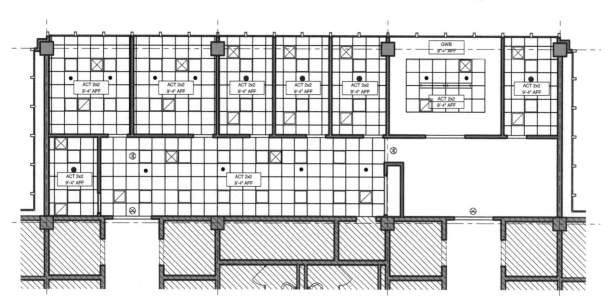

Changing the View Range

Plan and ceiling plan views in Revit are dynamic slices through a three-dimensional model. The view range settings tells Revit how high to slice through the model. Distance is measured from the floor.

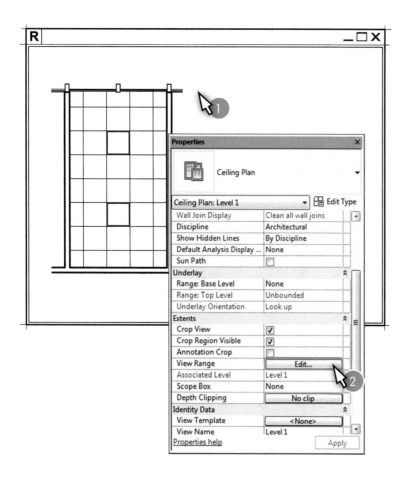

- *Step 1*: **OPEN** a **CEILING PLAN** view and **CLICK ONCE** in an empty portion of the drawing area. This deselects all elements.

- *Step 2*: In the **CEILING PLAN PROPERTIES** palette, **CLICK** the **VIEW RANGE EDIT** button.

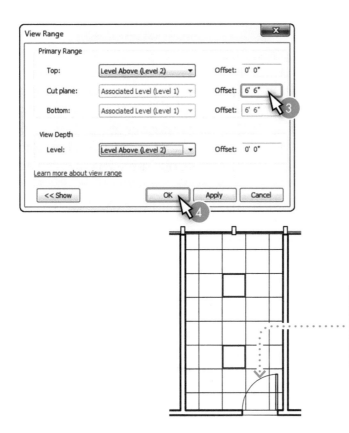

- *Step 3*: **CHANGE** the **CUT PLANE OFFSET** to **6′ 6″**. The offset is the distance between the floor of the associated level and the cut plane for the reflected ceiling plan. It is important that this offset is lower than the height of the doors in the project.

  The SI measurement for this step is **2000**.

- *Step 4*: **CLICK** the **OK** button to close the dialog box and apply the view range changes.

> **Tip:** The door swing, door, and door opening are all visible in the ceiling plan. Follow the steps below to hide the door in a RCP view.

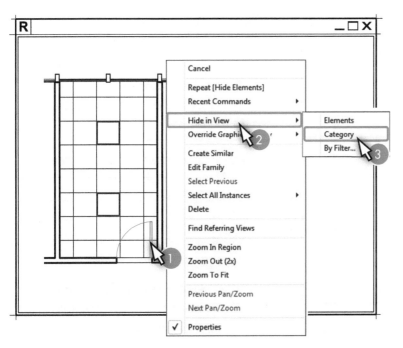

Hiding Doors in the Ceiling Plan

Lowering the cut plane in the ceiling plane exposed both the door openings and the doors. Hide the door category to remove the doors from the view.

- *Step 1*: **RIGHT-CLICK** any **DOOR ELEMENT** in the ceiling plan view.
- *Step 2*: **SELECT HIDE IN VIEW** from the context menu.
- *Step 3*: **CLICK** on **CATEGORY** in the secondary context menu. This action hides the door category in the current ceiling plan view.

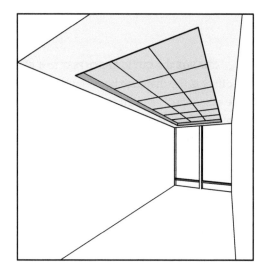

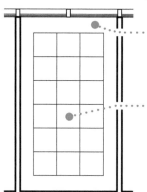

The ceiling in this example is designed with two separate materials at two different heights.

- The **OUTER CEILING** material is **GYPSUM WALLBOARD (GWB)** and has a 6′ x 12′ opening. The GWB ceiling is 9′-0″ **ABOVE FINISH FLOOR (AFF)**.
- The **INNER CEILING** material is **ACOUSTIC CEILING TILE (ACT)** and is slightly higher than the GWB ceiling. The ACT ceiling is 9′-4″ AFF.

Sketching the Outer Ceiling

- *Step 1 (not shown):* **CLICK** the **CEILING** button in the **ARCHITECTURE** tab and **CLICK** the **SKETCH CEILING** button.

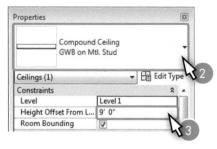

- *Step 2:* **SET** the **CEILING MATERIAL** to **GWB ON MTL. STUD**.
- *Step 3:* **SET** the **CEILING HEIGHT** to **9′ 0″**.

  The SI measurement for this step is **2700**.

- *Step 4:* **CLICK** the **RECTANGLE** button in the **MODIFY | CREATE CEILING BOUNDARY** tab.

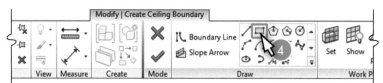

> **Tip:** Do not complete/finish the ceiling sketch in this exercise until *Step 9*.

- *Steps 5-6:* In the ceiling plan, **CLICK** on the **LOWER-LEFT CORNER** of the room and then **CLICK** on the **UPPER-RIGHT CORNER** of the room.
- *Steps 7-8:* To create the opening in the outer ceiling, **DRAW** a **SECOND RECTANGLE** inside the outer rectangle. Adjust the size of the rectangle to match the dimensions in the example.

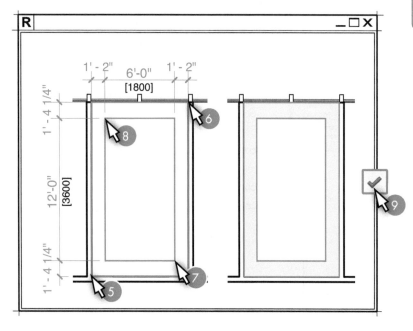

  The SI measurement for the interior rectangle is **1800mm x 3600mm**.

- *Step 9:* **CLICK** the **FINISH SKETCH** button in the **MODIFY | CREATE CEILING BOUNDARY** tab to finish the ceiling sketch.

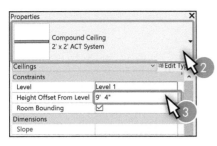

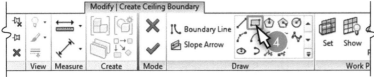

Sketching the Inner Ceiling

- *Step 1 (not shown)*: **CLICK** the **CEILING** button in the **ARCHITECTURE** tab and **CLICK** the **SKETCH CEILING** button.

- *Step 2*: **SET** the **CEILING MATERIAL** to **2′ X 2′ ACT SYSTEM**.

  The SI ceiling family is **600 X 600MM GRID**.

- *Step 3*: **SET** the **CEILING HEIGHT** to **9′ 4″**.

  The SI measurement for this step is **2850**.

- *Step 4*: **CLICK** the **RECTANGLE** button in the **MODIFY | CREATE CEILING BOUNDARY** tab.

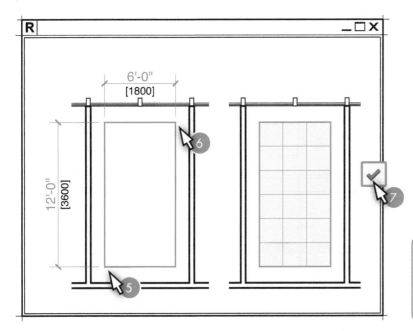

- *Step 5*: In the ceiling plan, **CLICK** on the **LOWER-LEFT CORNER** of the opening created in the outer ceiling.
- *Step 6*: **CLICK** on the **UPPER-RIGHT CORNER** of the opening created in the outer ceiling.
- *Step 7*: **CLICK** the **FINISH SKETCH** button in the **MODIFY | CREATE CEILING BOUNDARY** tab to finish the ceiling sketch.

> **Guided Discovery 5.3**:
> Create a two-material ceiling to match this example. The support file for this exercise is at **WWW.RAFDBOOK.COM/DOWNLOADS.**

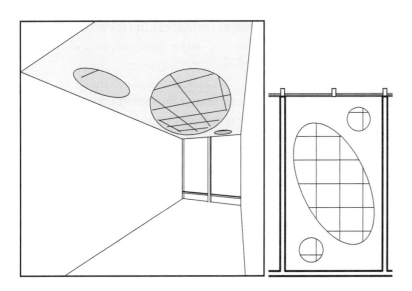

Curved Ceiling Openings

Openings in ceilings are not limited to rectangles. The **DRAW** panel in the **MODIFY | CREATE CEILING BOUNDARY** tab (*Step 4* above) contains curve and line tools to sketch different ceiling openings.

In this example, the **CIRCLE** and **ELLIPSE** drawing tools were used to sketch openings in the GWB ceiling (9′-0″ AFF or 2700mm AFF).

The ACT ceiling (9′-4″ AFF or 2850mm AFF) extends to the perimeter of the room.

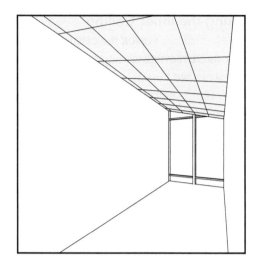

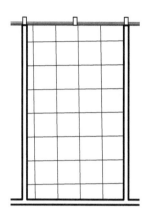

The **ACT** ceiling in this example is designed with a slope. This basic example can be combined with other ceilings and ceiling openings described earlier in this chapter.

Sketching a Sloped Ceiling

- *Step 1 (not shown)*: **CLICK** the **CEILING** button in the **ARCHITECTURE** tab and then **CLICK** the **SKETCH CEILING** button.
- *Step 2 (not shown)*: In the **PROPERTIES** box, set the **CEILING MATERIAL** to **2′ X 2′ ACT** and the **CEILING HEIGHT** to **9′ 0″**.

> The SI equivalent ceiling is **600 X 600MM GRID**. The SI equivalent height is **2700**.

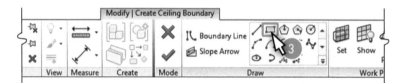

- *Step 3*: In the **MODIFY | CREATE CEILING BOUNDARY** tab, **CLICK** the **RECTANGLE** button.
- *Steps 4–5*: In the ceiling plan, **CLICK** on the **UPPER-LEFT CORNER** of the room and then **CLICK** on the **LOWER-RIGHT CORNER** of the room.

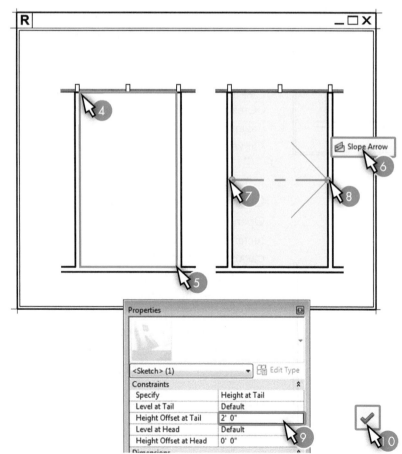

You can add a slope to any ceiling while in ceiling sketch mode.

- *Step 6*: **CLICK** the **SLOPE ARROW** button in the **MODIFY | CREATE CEILING BOUNDARY** tab.
- *Steps 7–8*: **DRAW** the slope arrow as indicated in the example.
- *Step 9*: Once you've drawn the slope arrow, change the **HEIGHT OFFSET AT TAIL** dimension to **2′ 0″**.

> The SI equivalent offset is **600**.

In this example, because the ceiling height is **9′ 0″** [2700mm], the height at the Tail is **11′ 0″** [3300mm].

- *Step 10*: **CLICK** the **FINISH SKETCH** button in the **MODIFY | CREATE CEILING BOUNDARY** tab to finish the ceiling sketch.

In addition to interior light fixtures, the RCP indicates the location of the HVAC supply diffuser and return registers, fire sprinklers, and life safety signage.

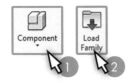

Loading Symbols

- *Step 1*: From any ceiling plan view, **CLICK** the **COMPONENT** button in the **ARCHITECTURE** tab.
- *Step 2*: **CLICK** the **LOAD FAMILY** button in the **MODIFY | PLACE COMPONENT** tab. This opens the **LOAD FAMILY** file browser.

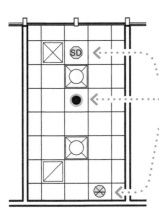

Life Safety Symbols

Imperial Life safety families are located in the **US IMPERIAL>SPECIALTY EQUIPMENT> FIRE PROTECTION** folder.

- The **SMOKE DETECTOR** symbol is **SMOKE DETECTOR.RFA**
- The **FIRE SPRINKLER** symbol is **SPRINKLER.RFA**
- The **EXIT SIGN** symbol is **EXIT SIGN.RFA**

> SI Life safety families are located in the **ENGLISH>US>SPECIALTY EQUIPMENT> FIRE PROTECTION** folder.

Fire sprinklers should be located by a licensed plumbing engineer. Smoke detectors and egress signage should be located as required by local building codes.

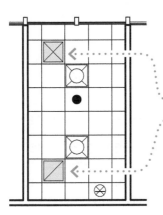

HVAC Symbols

Imperial HVAC families are located in **US IMPERIAL>MECHANICAL>ARCHITECTURAL> AIR-SIDE COMPONENTS>AIR TERMINALS** folder.

- The **HVAC SUPPLY DIFFUSER** symbol is **SQUARE SUPPLY DIFFUSER.RFA**
- The **HVAC RETURN REGISTER** symbol is **SQUARE RETURN REGISTER.RFA**

> SI HVAC families are located in the **ENGLISH>US>MECHANICAL>ARCHITECTURAL> AIR-SIDE COMPONENTS>AIR TERMINALS** folder.

HVAC supply diffusers and return registers should be located by a licensed mechanical engineer.

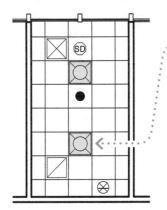

Light Fixture Families

- The **LIGHT FIXTURE** families are located in the **US IMPERIAL>LIGHTING> ARCHITECTURAL>INTERNAL** folder.

> SI light fixture families are located in the **ENGLISH>US>LIGHTING> ARCHITECTURAL>INTERNAL** folder.

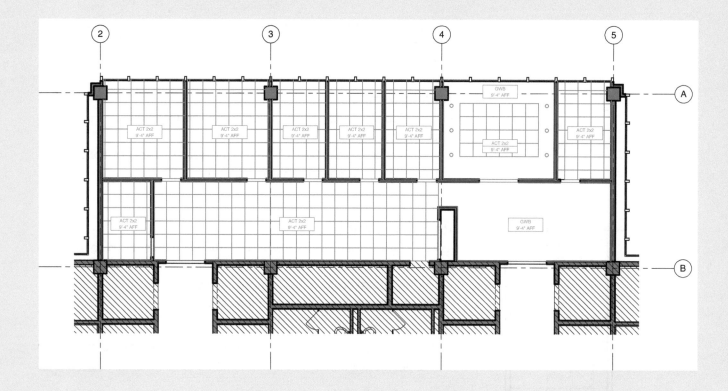

Learning Exercises

These exercises are intended to help you improve your understanding of Presentation Reflected Ceiling Plans in Revit.

Learning Exercise 5.1: Adding Ceilings

To begin this exercise, open the Revit project completed in Learning Exercises 4.3 at the end of Chapter 4. You can also download a support file for these exercises at **WWW.RAFDBOOK.COM/DOWNLOADS.**

- Open the **LEVEL 11** ceiling plan view in the **PROJECT BROWSER.**
- Change the view range cut plane offset to 6'-6".

> The SI equivalent cut plan offset is **2000.**

- Hide the door category in the RCP view.
- Add ceilings to RCP view. Use the example above as a guide.
- **SAVE** the project to your computer or a portable drive.

Revit Tips

- RCPs are commonly drawn at the same scale as the floor plan or 1/8" = 1'-0".

> The equivalent SI scale is **1:100.**

- Set an appropriate architectural scale before annotating plans.
- Add room tags to every room in the project.
- In Revit, the default cut plane for RCPs is 7'-0" or 2300mm above the finish floor. To change this default height, adjust the cut plane in the plan's view range.

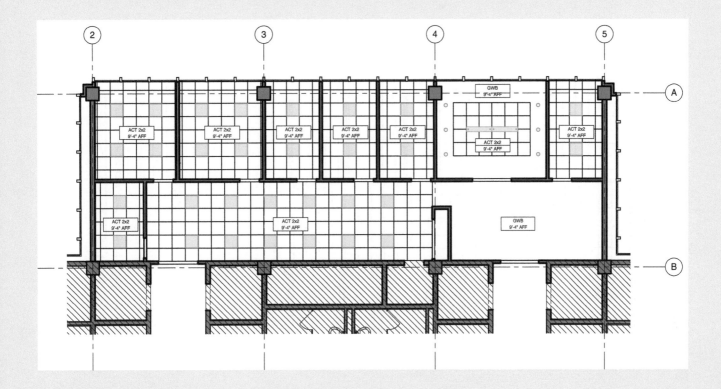

Learning Exercise 5.2: Adding Light Fixtures

- Open the Revit project completed in Learning Exercise 5.1.
- Open the **LEVEL 11** ceiling plan view in the **PROJECT BROWSER**.
- Add light fixtures to the RCP using the **US IMPERIAL LIBRARY** or the **US METRIC LIBRARY**. Use the fixtures below as a guide.
- **SAVE** the project to your computer or a portable drive.

- ○ ⟨····· • **DOWNLIGHT - RECESSED CAN.RFA**
- ☐ ⟨····· • **DOWNLIGHT - RECESSED - LED.RFA**
- ▭ ⟨····· • **1X4 PENDENT FIXTURE**
  (downloaded from **BIMOBJECT.COM**)

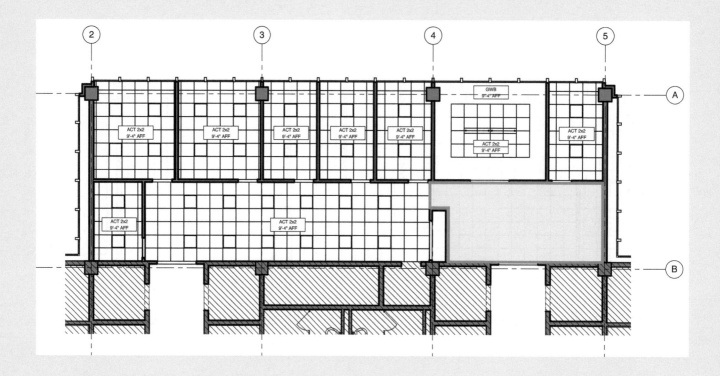

Learning Exercise 5.3: Ceiling Design

In this exercise, you will design a ceiling for the lobby in the space above. To begin this exercise, open the Revit project completed in Learning Exercise 5.2.

Add the following items to the ceiling design:
- Ceiling(s)
- Lighting
- Egress signage
- Ceiling tags with height

Application Exercises

Using an assignment from your instructor or a previously completed studio project, create a **PRESENTATION CEILING PLAN** view.

Add the following items to the ceiling plan as appropriate:
- Ceilings
- Lighting
- Ceiling tags with height
- Dimensions and annotations

chapter 6

PERSPECTIVE AND ISOMETRIC DRAWINGS

Perspective and isometric views leverage the most powerful aspect of BIM for young designers: with Revit you can simultaneously work on a project in two dimensions and three dimensions. The chapter explains how to create interior perspectives from an existing floor plan. You will also learn how to create cutaway isometric drawings of the Revit model.

IN THIS CHAPTER

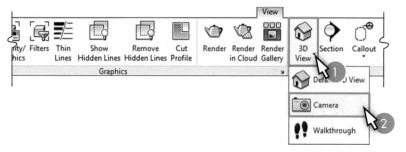

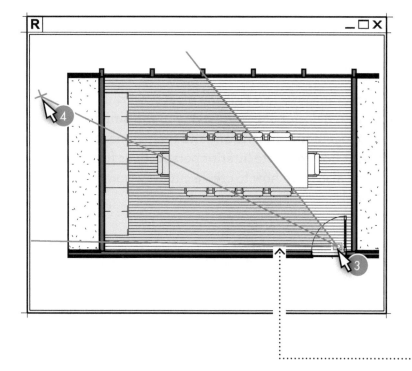

Creating Perspectives

The Camera button creates a perspective view of the Revit project from the plan view. Building components updated in a plan view will automatically update in perspective views.

- *Step 1*: Open a plan view and **CLICK** the **3D VIEW DOWN ARROW** in the **VIEW** tab.
- *Step 2*: In the Drop-down menu, **CLICK** the **CAMERA** button. The mouse cursor icon will change to a camera.

- *Step 3*: **CLICK ONCE** on the floor plan to locate the camera position. In this example, the camera is located near the door into the conference room.
- *Step 4*: **MOVE** the mouse in the direction you want to point the camera. **CLICK ONCE** to set the camera's target.

Tip: Note that in this example, the camera target is outside the room. This is important because the target determines both the **ORIENTATION** and **DEPTH** of the perspective. Anything beyond the target will not be visible in the perspective.

- The outside blue lines indicate the **FIELD OF VIEW** for the perspective. Only the shaded elements in this example will be visible in the perspective.

Viewing the Perspective

The second click in *Step 4* above opens the perspective as a new 3D view in Revit.

The perspective view is also available in the 3D Views category of the Project Browser.

Guided Discovery 6.1: Create a conference room perspective to match this example. The support file for this exercise is at **WWW.RAFDBOOK.COM/DOWNLOADS**.

Reposition the Camera

Once you have created a perspective, you may want to recompose the view by changing the camera location or target location.

- *Step 1 (not shown)*: **OPEN** both the **PLAN VIEW** and the **PERSPECTIVE VIEW**. Close all other views except these two views.
- *Step 2 (not shown)*: On the keyboard, **PRESS** the **W** and **T** keys in sequence to tile the two views in Revit.
- *Step 3*: In the perspective view, **CLICK ONCE** on the **PERSPECTIVE FRAME**. This activates the camera icon and field of view graphic in the floor plan view.
- *Step 4*: In the plan view, **CLICK AND DRAG** the **CAMERA** icon or **TARGET** icon to recompose the perspective.

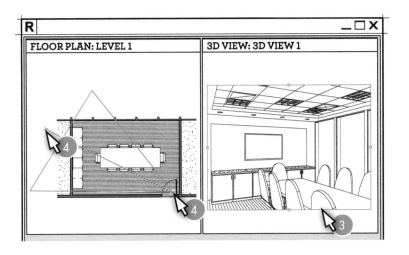

Resize/Crop Perspectives

Resize or crop perspective views to match other 3D views in the project.

- *Step 1*: In the perspective view, **CLICK ONCE** on the **PERSPECTIVE FRAME**.
- *Step 2*: **DRAG** the **CROP MODEL HANDLES** to adjust the width and height of the perspective.

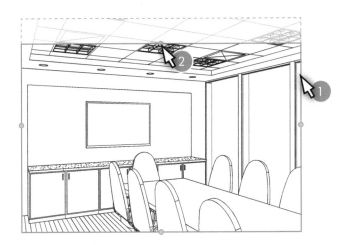

Scale Perspectives

- *Step 1 (not shown)*: **OPEN** the **PERSPECTIVE VIEW** and **CLICK** the **PERSPECTIVE FRAME**.
- *Step 2*: **CLICK** the **SIZE CROP** button in the **MODIFY | CAMERAS** tab. This opens the **CROP REGION SIZE** dialog box.
- *Step 3*: **SELECT** the **SCALE** button to change the **SIZE** of the perspective.
- *Step 4*: Change the width or height dimensions. In this example, the perspective **WIDTH** is **SET** to **17″** [425mm] and the **HEIGHT** automatically adjusted to **9 9/16″** [240mm].
- *Step 5*: **CLICK** the **OK** button.

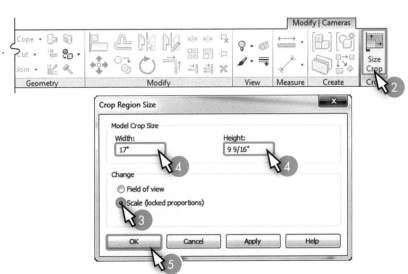

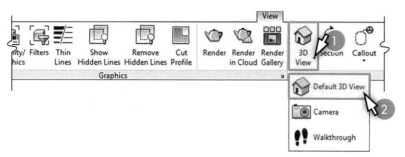

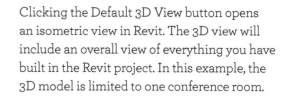

The Default 3D View button creates an isometric view of the Revit project. Building components updated in a plan view will automatically update in the isometric view.

- *Step 1*: **CLICK** the **3D VIEW DOWN ARROW** in the **VIEW** tab.
- *Step 2*: In the Drop-down menu, **CLICK** the **DEFAULT 3D VIEW** button.

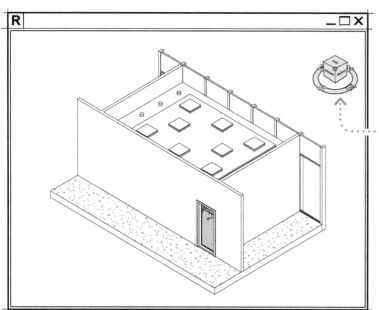

Clicking the Default 3D View button opens an isometric view in Revit. The 3D view will include an overall view of everything you have built in the Revit project. In this example, the 3D model is limited to one conference room.

- The **VIEW CUBE** is located in the top-right corner of the window.

3D views often contain building elements you would not see inside a building. In this example, we see the space above the ceiling in the conference room, including the tops of the fluorescent and recessed light fixtures.

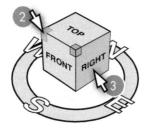

Adjusting 3D Views with the View Cube

Use the view cube to change the angle of the 3D view.

- *Step 1 (not shown)*: **OPEN** or create a **3D** view as shown in the instructions above.
- *Step 2*: **CLICK** on any **CORNER** to see an isometric view from that angle.
- *Step 3*: **CLICK** on any of the **FACES** to see an elevation view of the model.

> **Guided Discovery 6.2**: Create a conference room section-isometric to match this example. The support file for this exercise is at **WWW.RAFDBOOK.COM/DOWNLOADS**.

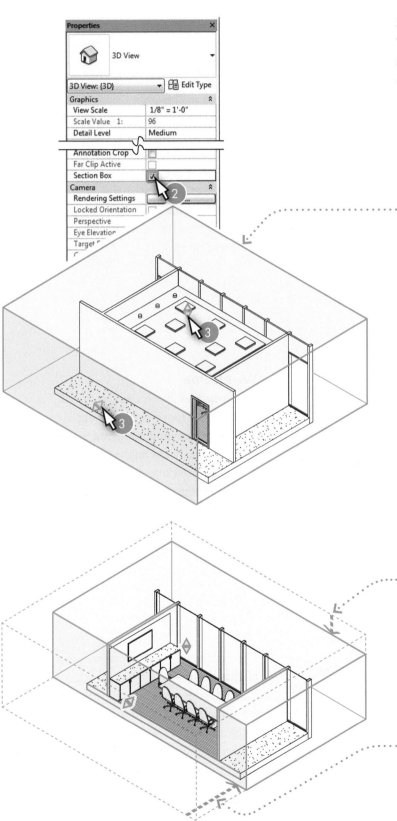

Section Box

The section box allows you to dynamically slice a 3D view. In this example, we will create a cutaway view of the conference room.

- *Step 1 (not shown)*: **OPEN** a **3D VIEW** in the **PROJECT BROWSER.**
- *Step 2*: **CLICK** the **SECTION BOX** option in the **PROPERTIES** box. You may need to scroll down to locate the section box parameter.

- 3D views with an activated section box display a blue wireframe section box at the boundaries of the model. Each face of the blue section box contains a double arrow that allows you to change the location of that face relative to the building model.

- *Step 3*: **DRAG** the **RESIZE ARROWS** toward the model to create a dynamic slice of the model.

- In this example, the top face of the section box is moved down about two feet.

- The front face of the section box is moved toward the conference room.

VISUAL STYLES

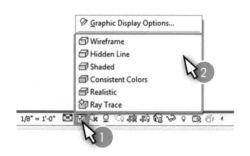

The Visual Style button allows you to change the graphic display in the current view. Styles can be changed for both two-dimensional drawings (e.g., plans and elevations) and three-dimensional drawings. Changes made to the visual style of a view are saved with that view.

- *Step 1*: To change the visual style of a view, **CLICK ONCE** on the **VISUAL STYLE** button in the status bar.
- *Step 2*: **CLICK ONCE** on the new graphic **DISPLAY STYLE**. Each of Revit's visual styles is described in detail below and on the facing page.

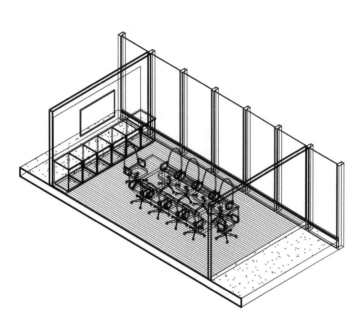

Wireframe

While the wireframe visual style will significantly speed up your computer, most designers find it difficult to work with because of the intensity of lines in the drawing. Wireframe drawings are black and white and contain line weight and material surface patterns. Images with this style can be exported as vector artwork.

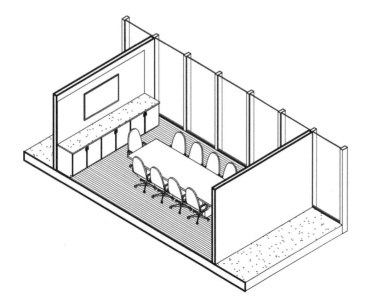

Hidden Line

The hidden line visual style is the default style for new 3D views. Hidden line drawings are black and white and contain line weight and material surface patterns. Images with this style can be exported as vector artwork.

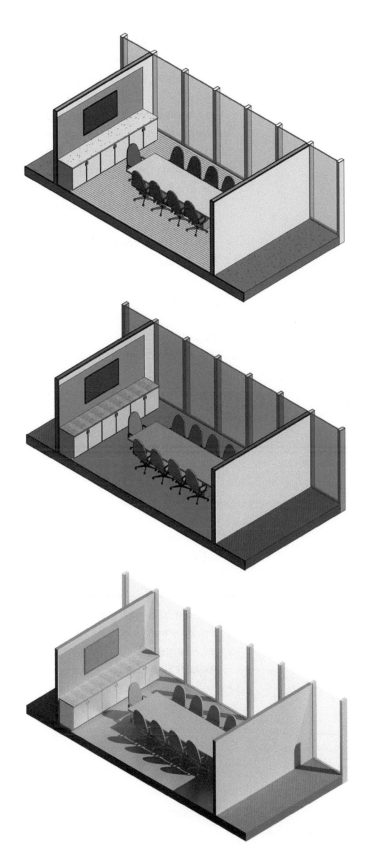

Companion Download 6.1: View color images of these visual style examples online at **WWW.RAFDBOOK.COM/DOWNLOADS**.

Shaded/Consistent Colors

The shaded visual style produces a color image that contains both the material's color and the material's surface pattern. Surfaces in these images are shaded to simulate the way light changes the value of a surface.

The consistent color visual style (not pictured) is identical to the shaded visual style with one exception. The consistent color style does not contain any surface shading.

Realistic

The realistic visual style produces a color image that combines the surface edges with some texture mapping as defined for each material.

Ray Trace

The Ray Trace visual style produces a realistic color image that contains shadows as produced by the sun and/or artificial light. In Ray Traced images, you will also see variation in value across a material or surface. Depending on the speed of your computer, these images can take several minutes to update with each change you make to your model.

Renaming Views

Every time you create a new perspective view, Revit names it 3D View 1. Additional views are named 3D View 2, 3D View 3, and 3D View 4. It does not take very long before the Project Browser is filled with 3D views, making it difficult to find a specific view. As you create views, rename the views you want to keep with a descriptive title.

- *Step 1*: **RIGHT-CLICK** on the **VIEW** in the **PROJECT BROWSER**.
- *Step 2*: **SELECT RENAME** from the context menu.
- *Step 3*: **TYPE** a **DESCRIPTIVE NAME** in the dialog box.

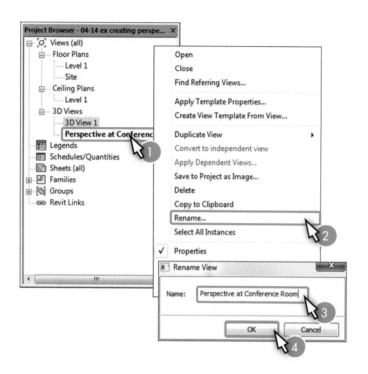

Descriptive names include both the type of 3D drawing and the name of the room shown in the drawing. Perspective at Lobby and Isometric of Reception Desk are two examples of descriptive view names.

- *Step 4*: **CLICK** the **OK** button.

Deleting Views

When you determine you no longer need a view in your project, delete it from the project to minimize the number of views in the Project Browser.

- *Step 1*: **RIGHT-CLICK** on the **VIEW NAME** in the **PROJECT BROWSER**.
- *Step 2*: **SELECT DELETE** from the context menu.

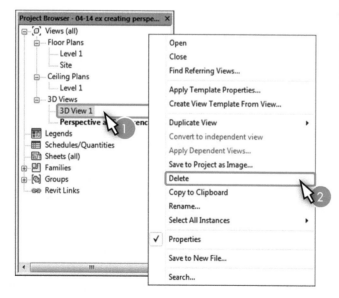

Checklist for 3D Drawings

General

- As you create each 3D view, make sure it communicates the three-dimensional properties of your project.
- Two-point perspectives from the corner of a room create a good sense of depth in the image.
- One-point perspectives tend to shorten the depth of the perspective and should be avoided.
- Use the section box with isometric views to create a cutaway view of the project.
- Stay organized: rename 3D views with descriptive titles.
- Delete unwanted 3D views from the **PROJECT BROWSER**.
- Resize, scale, or crop each of the 3D drawings to create a consistent set of presentation drawings.

Learning Exercises

Learning Exercise 6.1: Interior Perspectives

To begin this exercise, open the Revit project completed in Learning Exercises 5.1 at the end of Chapter 5. You can also download a support file for these exercises at **WWW.RAFDBOOK.COM/DOWNLOADS**.

Follow Guided Discovery 6.1 in the chapter to create the following **3D VIEWS** in the companion Revit project:

- Perspective at conference room
- Perspective at lobby

Learning Exercise 6.2: Section-Isometrics

To begin this exercise, open the Revit project completed in Learning Exercises 6.1. You can also download a support file for these exercises at **WWW.RAFDBOOK.COM/DOWNLOADS**.

Follow Guided Discovery 6.2 in the chapter to create the following **3D VIEWS** in the companion Revit project:

- Isometric at conference room (section box)
- Isometric of Level 11 plan (section box)

Application Exercises

Using an assignment from your instructor or a previously completed studio project, create the following **3D VIEWS**:

- Perspective at entry
- Perspective of a significant interior space
  - Overall model isometric
  - Isometric with section box of a significant interior space

chapter 7

PHOTOREALISTIC RENDERING

Photorealistic renderings are powerful design communication tools. This chapter explores creating renderings of three-dimensional drawings in Revit including light sources, materials, and rendering settings. Rendering interior perspectives with Revit is a multi-stage process that is time consuming. Before you begin the rendering process, make sure you've completed the following in your Revit model:

- Include all walls, doors, windows, and floors.
- Include ceilings and interior lights in the ceiling plan for interior perspectives.
- While entourage (i.e., furniture and people) is not required, adding it to the model will provide a sense of scale to the rendered image.

IN THIS CHAPTER

Material Properties and Assets

In Revit, material properties are organized into assets that control the behavior of a material. Designers most commonly use the Graphics and Appearance Assets to control the way a material looks in the project.

GRAPHICS ASSETS are unique to each material in a project. This asset controls how a material displays in most Visual Styles including Hidden Line, Shaded, and Consistent Colors.

In the three examples below, the Graphics Asset parameters for each material are slightly different, resulting in the materials displaying differently in Shaded views.

- The **GYPSUM WALL BOARD CEILING** material is similar to the **GYPSUM WALL BOARD** material with one exception: the **SURFACE PATTERN** parameter is set to **GYPSUM PLASTER**. This allows a stipple pattern on GWB in RCPs.
- The **SHADING** parameter for the **GYPSUM WALL BOARD SW 6517 REGATTA** material is set to **USE RENDER APPEARANCE**. This tells Revit to display the paint's color on surfaces.

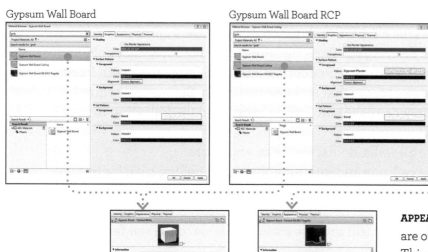

Gypsum Wall Board   Gypsum Wall Board RCP   Gypsum Wall Board SW 6517 Regatta

Gypsum Board - Painted White   Gypsum Board - Painted SW 6517 Regatta

APPEARANCE ASSETS are unique to a project and are often shared between multiple materials. This asset controls how a material displays in the Realistic Visual Style and in photorealistic renderings.

- The **GYPSUM BOARD - PAINTED WHITE** asset is shared by two materials. Changes to this asset will impact both materials.
- The **GYPSUM BOARD - PAINTED SW 6517 REGATTA** asset was created for the **GYPSUM WALL BOARD SW 6517 REGATTA** material. This allows us to change the paint color in the **SW 6517 REGATTA** without affecting the other two materials.

The **ASSET BROWSER** contains the Appearance Library. Assets from this library can be imported into an existing or new material in the Revit project.

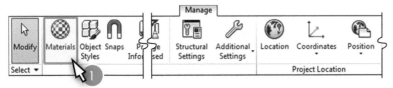

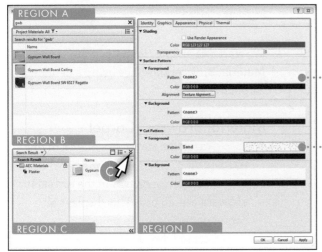

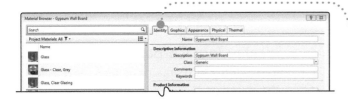

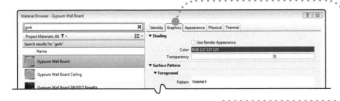

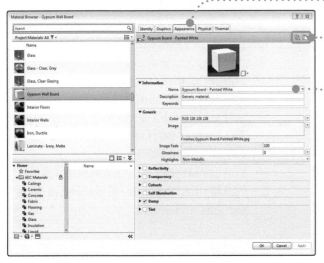

Material Browser Overview

- *Step 1*: **CLICK** the **MATERIALS** button in the **MANAGE** tab to open the **MATERIAL BROWSER**.

- *Region A*: The **SEARCH BOX** is the quickest method to locate materials in the active project.
- *Region B*: **PROJECT MATERIALS** are displayed in this portion of the **MATERIAL BROWSER**. In this example, we see search results for "gwb".
- *Region C*: The **LIBRARY PANEL** contains additional materials which can be added to the active project. **CLICK** the **SHOW/HIDE** button to display the library panel.
- *Region D*: The **MATERIAL EDITOR PANEL** contains multiple tabs that control how the material displays on elements in Revit.

- In the Graphics Tab, the **SURFACE PATTERN** controls the pattern on an object's surface (e.g., a carpet's pattern in plan view).
- The **CUT PATTERN** controls the graphic pattern when an object is cut (e.g., a concrete floor slab in a building section).

- The **MATERIAL EDITOR > IDENTITY** tab allows you to adjust the name, description, and class (category) for materials in the active project.
- The **MATERIAL EDITOR > GRAPHICS** tab controls how a material displays in most Visual Styles.

- The **MATERIAL EDITOR > APPEARANCE** tab controls how a material displays in most Photorealistic Renderings.
- The **REPLACE ASSET** and **DUPLICATE ASSET** buttons allow you to modify the material's appearance properties.
- Adjust the name of the Appearance Asset in the **INFORMATION** section.

Understanding material definitions in Revit is the first step in generating photorealistic renderings of your Revit model. Revit's Material Browser is the central location for default materials, imported materials, and custom materials.

We start this chapter looking at the Material Browser interface using a default carpet material.

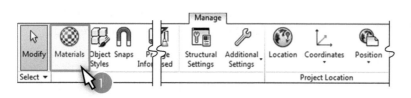

Material Browser: Carpet

- *Step 1*: **CLICK** the **MATERIALS** button in the **MANAGE** tab.
- *Step 2*: **SEARCH** for **CARPET** in the **MATERIAL BROWSER** search box. This displays all carpet materials in the project.
- *Step 3*: **SELECT** the **CARPET(1)** material.

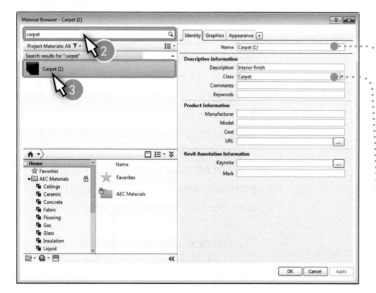

Identity Tab: Carpet

The Identity tab contains general settings for the material.
- The **NAME** field contains the material's name.
- The **CLASS** field contains the material's category.

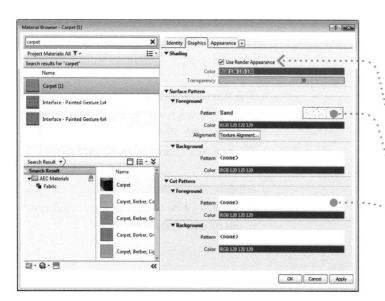

Graphics Assets: Carpet

The Graphics tab defines the material's visual properties in views with visual styles set to hidden line, consistent colors, and shaded.

- The **USE RENDER APPEARANCE** option assigns a color to the material based on the **APPEARANCE** tab's settings.
- The **SURFACE PATTERN** is the material hatch visible in plan and elevation.
- The **CUT PATTERN** is the material hatch visible when the material is sliced in plan, sections, and details.

Appearance Tab: Carpet

The Appearance Assets tab defines the material's visual properties in views with visual styles set to Realistic and Ray Trace. The settings for this tab can be loaded from Appearance Assets.

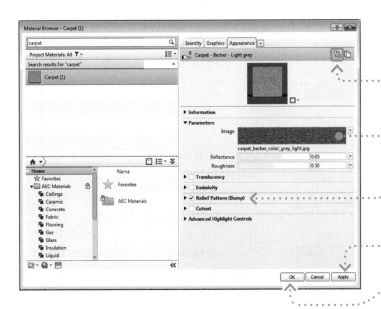

- The **REPLACE ASSET** button opens the Asset Browser where you can select a pre-defined Appearance Asset.
- The attached **IMAGE** is mapped to surfaces in renderings.
- **RELIEF PATTERN (BUMP)** maps are gray scale images that apply texture to a surface in renderings. Click on the image to change the bump map.
- The **APPLY** button saves changes made to the material.
- The **OK** button saves changes and closes the Material Browser.

Asset Browser: Carpet

The Asset Browser contains a large selection of pre-defined Appearance Assets. In this example, the Asset Browser is opened to the Appearance Library>Flooring>Carpet folder. The Carpet sub-category contains a variety of carpet selections.

- The **REPLACE ASSET** button loads the selected asset into the current material's **APPEARANCE** tab.

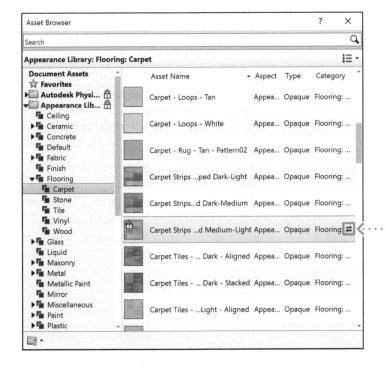

Adding Materials: Custom Carpet

In this example, a custom carpet material is created to match an Interface carpet tile.

- *Step 1*: **SEARCH** for a carpet tile at **WWW.INTERFACE.COM**.
- *Steps 2–3*: **DOWNLOAD** high-res images of the carpet tile (in top view).

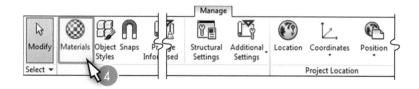

- *Step 4*: **CLICK** the **MATERIALS** button in the **MANAGE** tab.

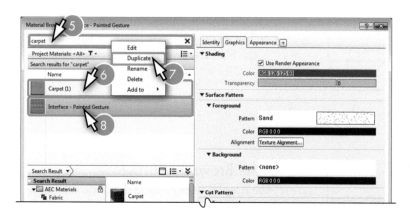

- *Step 5*: **SEARCH** for **CARPET** in the **MATERIAL BROWSER**.
- *Steps 7–8*: **RIGHT-CLICK** the **CARPET (1)** in the **MATERIAL BROWSER** and **SELECT DUPLICATE**.
- *Steps 9*: **RIGHT-CLICK** the duplicated **MATERIAL** and **RENAME** it to **INTERFACE - PAINTED GESTURE**.

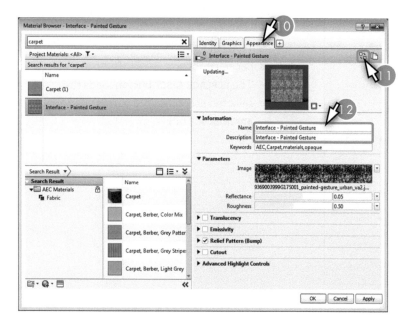

- *Step 10*: **CLICK** the **APPEARANCE** tab in the Interface - Painted Gesture material.
- *Step 11*: **CLICK** the **DUPLICATE ASSET** button. By duplicating the Appearance Asset, we can change the materials for the Interface - Painted Gesture material without changing the color of the original Carpet (1) material.
- *Step 12*: **CHANGE** the duplicated **MATERIAL ASSET** name to match the material's name.

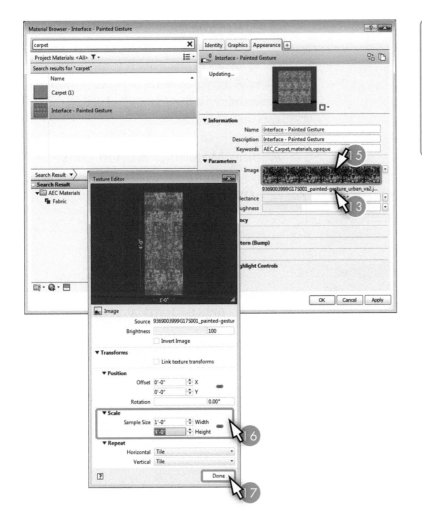

- *Step 13*: **CLICK** the **IMAGE NAME** to load a new texture. In this example, we loaded the carpet tile image downloaded from Interface's website.
- *Step 14 (not shown)*: Locate the downloaded image file in the **SELECT FILE** dialog box and **CLICK** the **OK** button.

- *Step 15*: **CLICK** the **IMAGE PREVIEW** to open the texture editor.
- *Step 16*: In the texture editor, **SET** the **WIDTH** and **HEIGHT** of the sample texture. This tells Revit how large to make the image in renderings. In this example, the carpet tile's scale is set to 1'-0" wide and 4'-0" tall.
- *Step 17*: **CLICK** the **DONE** button to close the texture editor.

- *Step 18*: In the **GRAPHICS** tab, **CHECK** the **USE RENDER APPEARANCE** option.

- *Step 19*: **CLICK** the **OK** button to save changes to this material.

In addition to image maps and textures, Revit can also render reflections and transparency in materials. A frosted glass material is created on these pages to illustrate transparency, reflection, and refraction appearance properties.

Adding Materials: Frosted Glass

- *Step 1*: **CLICK** the **MATERIALS** button in the **MANAGE** tab.

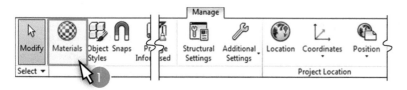

- *Step 2*: **SEARCH** for **FROSTED GLASS** in the **MATERIAL BROWSER**.
- *Step 3*: **OPEN** the **MATERIAL LIBRARY** if it is not visible.
- *Step 4*: **SELECT** the **IMPORT** button for **GLASS, FROSTED** in the **MATERIAL LIBRARY**.

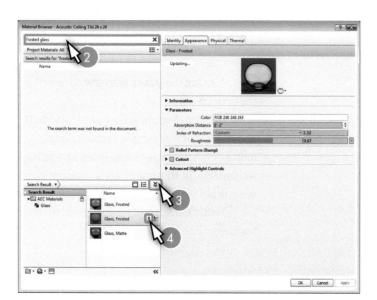

The Graphics tab defines the material's visual properties in views with visual styles set to hidden line, consistent colors, and shaded.

- *Step 5*: **SELECT FROSTED GLASS** in the **MATERIAL BROWSER**.
- *Step 6*: **CHECK** the **USE RENDER APPEARANCE** option in the **GRAPHICS** tab.
- *Step 7*: **CLICK** the **OK** button to save changes to this material.

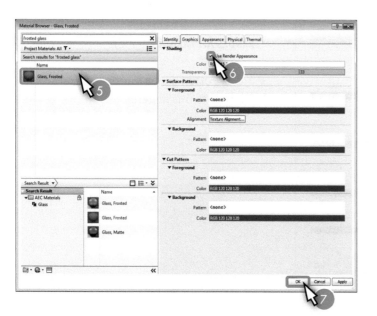

Adding Materials: Custom Paint

In this example, a custom paint material is created to match a Sherwin-Williams paint color.

- *Step 1*: **SEARCH** for a paint color at **WWW.SHERWIN-WILLIAMS.COM**.
- *Steps 2–3*: **CLICK** the **DETAILS** tab and write down the RGB value for the selected color.

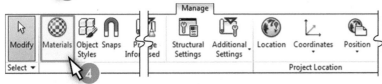

- *Step 4*: **CLICK** the **MATERIALS** button in the **MANAGE** tab.

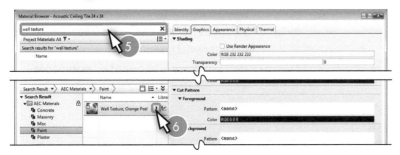

- *Step 5*: **SEARCH** for **WALL TEXTURE** in the **MATERIAL BROWSER**.

- *Step 6*: **SELECT** the **IMPORT** button for **WALL TEXTURE, ORANGE PEEL** in the Material Library.
- *Steps 7–8*: **RIGHT-CLICK** the imported **MATERIAL** in the **MATERIAL BROWSER** and **SELECT DUPLICATE**.

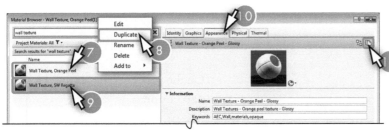

- *Steps 9*: **RIGHT-CLICK** the duplicated **MATERIAL** and **RENAME** it to **WALL TEXTURE, SW REGATTA**.
- *Steps 10–11*: **CLICK** the **APPEARANCE** tab in the SW Regatta material and then click the **DUPLICATE ASSET** button. By duplicating the Appearance Asset, we can change the color for the SW Regatta material without changing the color of the original material.
- *Step 12*: **CHANGE** the duplicated **MATERIAL ASSET** name to match the material's name.
- *Step 13*: **CLICK** the **COLOR** parameter.
- *Step 14*: In the **COLOR** dialog box, **SET** the **RGB** values to **RED: 33**, **GREEN: 87**, and **BLUE: 114**.
- *Step 15*: **CLICK** the **OK** button.

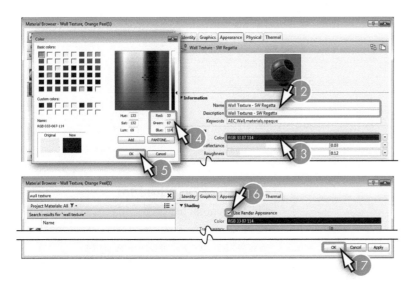

- *Step 16*: **CHECK** the **USE RENDER APPEARANCE** option in the **GRAPHICS** tab.
- *Step 17*: **CLICK** the **OK** button to save changes to this material.

Downloading Material Library (AD-SKLIB) Files

In this example, a three-color scheme was created at Sherwin-Williams's website. Sherwin-Williams paint was selected for this example because of the large paint catalog available for Revit models.

- *Step 1*: **NOTE** the **SW PAINT COLORS** that you want to use in your project.

- *Step 2*: **OPEN** a **WEB BROWSER** and navigate to **WWW.BIMSMITH.COM**. BIMsmith is a website that aggregates manufacturer objects created for Revit.
- *Step 3*: In the **SEARCH** box, **SEARCH** for **SHERWIN-WILLIAMS**.
- *Step 4*: **CLICK** the **PROMAR 200 SEMI-GLOSS** search result.

- *Step 5*: On the product page, **CLICK** the **DOWNLOAD** button.

Companion Download 7.1:
Find the latest list of manufacturers and Revit downloads at **WWW.RAFDBOOK.COM/DOWNLOADS**.

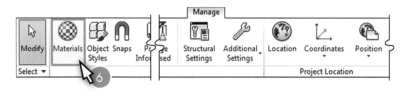

Loading Materials

Once you have downloaded the Sherwin-Williams material library you will need to open the library and load each paint material into the Revit project.

- *Step 6*: **CLICK** the **MATERIALS** button in the **MANAGE** tab.

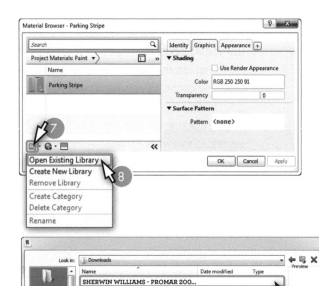

- *Steps 7–8*: **CLICK** the **OPEN EXISTING LIBRARY** in the **MATERIAL BROWSER**.

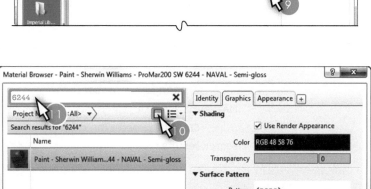

- *Step 9*: **NAVIGATE** to the **DOWNLOADS** folder and **SELECT** the **SHERWIN-WILLIAMS PROMAR 200 ADSKLIB** file.

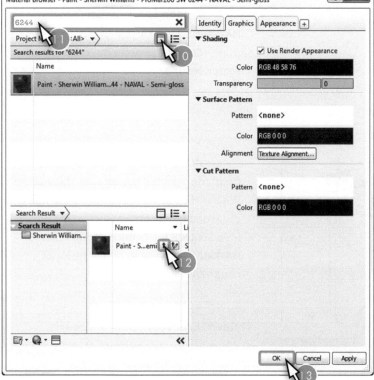

The final steps load the desired paint materials from the Material Library. In this example, we will load SW 6244 into the Revit project.

- *Step 10*: **CLICK** the **SHOW/HIDE LIBRARY PANEL** button to review the loaded material libraries.
- *Step 11*: **SEARCH** for **6244** in the **SEARCH** box.

- *Step 12*: **CLICK** the **ADD MATERIAL TO DOCUMENT** button.

Repeat *Steps 11-12* to add the **SW7667** and **SW7076** materials.

- *Step 13*: **CLICK** the **OK** button.

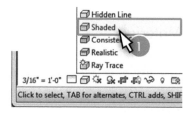

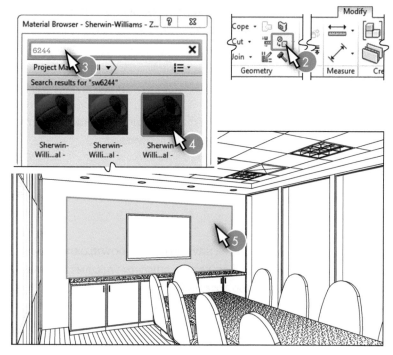

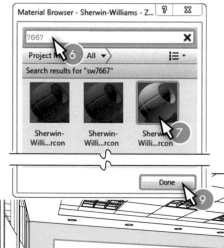

Painting Walls

The Paint button applies materials to wall, floor, and ceiling surfaces in the model. The Paint button does not work with families including furniture, doors, and windows.

- *Step 1*: **OPEN** a **PERSPECTIVE VIEW** and **CHANGE** the **VISUAL STYLE** to **SHADED**.
- *Step 2*: **CLICK** the **PAINT** button in the **MODIFY** tab. This **OPENS** the **MATERIAL BROWSER**.

- *Step 3*: **SEARCH** for paint **6244** in the **MATERIAL BROWSER**.
- *Step 4*: **SELECT** the paint material in the search results. If the material names are truncated, hover the cursor over the samples to see their full name.

- *Step 5*: **CLICK ONCE** on a **WALL SURFACE** to paint the selected material. In this example, the SW6244 paint is applied to the wall surface behind the LCD TV.

- *Step 6*: **SEARCH** for paint **7667** in the **MATERIAL BROWSER**.
- *Step 7*: **SELECT** the paint material in the search results.

- *Step 8*: **CLICK ONCE** on a **WALL SURFACE** to paint the selected material. In this example, the SW7667 paint is applied to the wall area indicated in light blue.
- *Step 9*: **CLICK** the **DONE** button in the **MATERIAL BROWSER** to finish the Paint command.

> **Guided Discovery 7.1**: Download the support file for this exercise at **WWW.RAFDBOOK.COM/DOWNLOADS**.

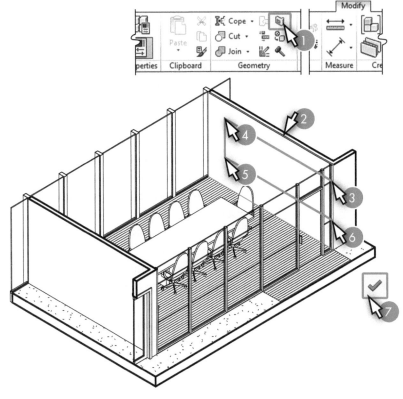

Splitting Wall Faces

- *Step 1*: **OPEN** an **ELEVATION** or **ISOMETRIC** view and **CLICK** the **SPLIT FACE** button in the **MODIFY** tab.

- *Step 2*: **CLICK ONCE** on the perimeter of the **WALL** in the view.
- *Steps 3-6*: **USE** the **LINE** draw tool to **OUTLINE** the split surface.

> **Tip**: Because the split area in this example is at the edge of the wall, the split face sketch does not include a line between *Step 3* and *Step 6*.

- *Step 7*: **CLICK** the **FINISH EDIT** button in the **MODIFY | SPLIT FACE > CREATE BOUNDARY** tab.

Painting Split Walls

- *Step 8*: **CLICK** the **PAINT** button in the **MODIFY** tab.

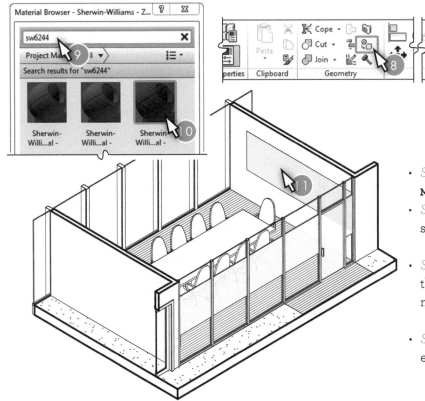

- *Step 9*: **SEARCH** for paint **6244** in the **MATERIAL BROWSER**.
- *Step 10*: **SELECT** the paint material in the search results.

- *Step 11*: **CLICK** the **SPLIT WALL SURFACE** in the conference room to apply the selected material.

- *Step 12 (not shown)*: **PRESS** the **ESC** key to end the Paint command.

PAINTING MATERIALS (continued)

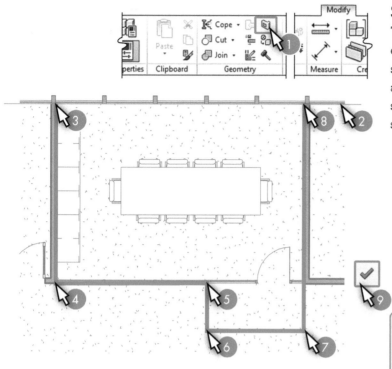

Splitting Floor Faces

The Paint button will apply a material to an entire floor because floors are defined as a single surface. The Split Face button divides a floor into multiple areas. After a floor is split, you can apply unique materials on each split surface.

- *Step 1*: **OPEN** a **PLAN** view and **CLICK** the **SPLIT FACE** button in the **MODIFY** tab.
- *Step 2*: **CLICK ONCE** on the perimeter of the **SLAB** in plan view.
- *Steps 3–8*: **USE** the **LINE** draw tool to **OUTLINE** the split surface.
- *Step 9*: **CLICK** the **FINISH EDIT** button in the **MODIFY | SPLIT FACE > CREATE BOUNDARY** tab.

Tip: Because the room in this example is at the edge of the building slab, the split face sketch does not include a line between *Step 3* and *Step 8*.

Painting Split Floors

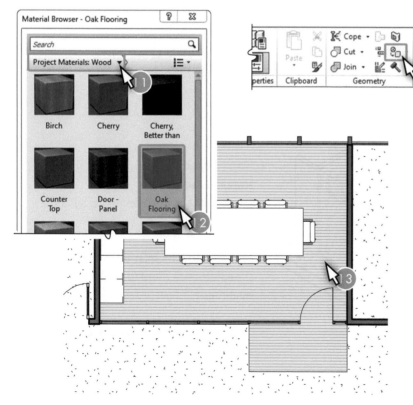

- *Step 10*: **CLICK** the **PAINT** button in the **MODIFY** tab.

- *Step 11*: **SELECT** the **WOOD** category in the **MATERIAL BROWSER**.
- *Step 12*: **SELECT** the **OAK FLOORING** material in the **MATERIAL BROWSER**.

- *Step 13*: **CLICK** the **SPLIT FLOOR SURFACE** in the conference room to apply the selected material.

- *Step 14 (not shown)*: **PRESS** the **ESC** key to end the Paint command.

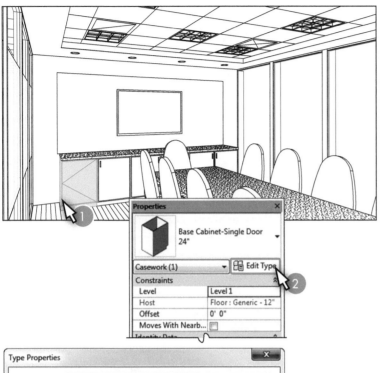

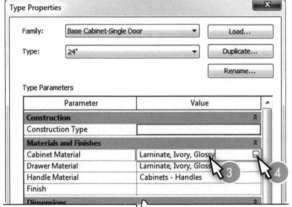

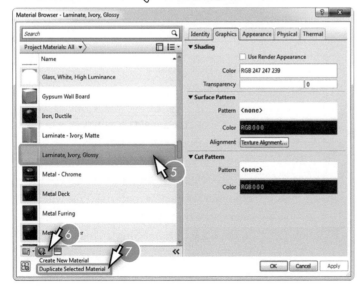

Changing a Family's Material

Most families allow unique changes to materials for each family type or family member. For example, a base cabinet family may have several family types with varying widths.

In the Base Cabinet-Single Door 24″ family type, the cabinet, drawer, and handle materials can be assigned one set of materials. In the Base Cabinet-Single Door 30″ family type, the cabinet, drawer, and handle materials can be assigned a different set of materials.

- *Step 1*: **CLICK ONCE** on the **BASE CABINET** in the perspective view.
- *Step 2*: **CLICK** the **EDIT TYPE** button in the **PROPERTIES** dialog box.

Assigning a New Material to a Family Type

Note that there are three material properties for the Base Cabinet family: Cabinet Material, Drawer Material, and Handle Material.

- *Step 3*: **CLICK ONCE** on the **CABINET MATERIAL NAME** in the **TYPE PROPERTIES** box.
- *Step 4*: **CLICK** the **MATERIAL SELECTION** button. This opens the **MATERIAL BROWSER**.

The easiest way to create a new material is to duplicate an existing material that is similar to the material you want to create.

- *Step 5*: The current material assigned to the family is automatically selected in the **MATERIAL BROWSER**.
- *Step 6*: **CLICK** the **NEW MATERIAL** button.
- *Step 7*: **CLICK** the **DUPLICATE SELECTED MATERIAL** option from the Drop-down menu.

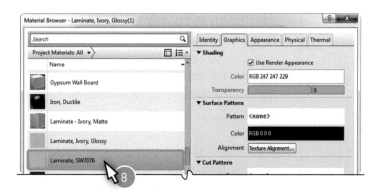

Assigning a New Material to a Family Type (continued)

- *Step 8*: **RENAME** the duplicated material (**LAMINATE, IVORY, GLOSSY COPY**) to **LAMINATE, SW7076**.

Appearance Assets tell Revit about a material's photorealistic properties. When we duplicated the ivory laminate material, it maintained its physical properties (even though we renamed it to Laminate, SW7076). To change the physical appearance of a duplicated material, you need to replace its Appearance Asset.

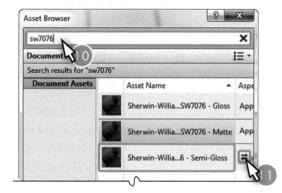

- *Step 9*: **CLICK** the **REPLACE ASSET** button in the new material's **APPEARANCE** tab. This opens the Asset Browser.

- *Step 10*: **SEARCH** for **7076** in the **ASSET BROWSER**.

- *Step 11*: **CLICK** the **REPLACE ASSET** button next to the **SW7076 SEMI-GLOSS** material. This replaces the **SMOOTH-IVORY** Appearance Asset with the **SHERWIN-WILLIAMS SW7076** Appearance Asset loaded earlier in this chapter.

- *Step 12*: **CHECK** the **REFLECTIVITY** box in the new material's **APPEARANCE** tab.
- *Step 13*: **SET** the **DIRECT** reflectivity to **5**.
- *Step 14*: **CLICK** the **OK** button to accept the changes to the new material. This will also assign the material to the cabinet material in the Base Cabinet-Single Door 24" family type.

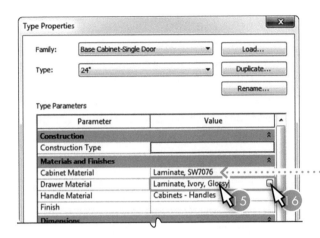

Assigning an Existing Material to a Family Type

In *Steps 1-14* we created a new material and assigned it to the Base Cabinet-Single Door 24″ family type's cabinet material. Because the material is now defined in the Revit project, assigning it to a new portion of the Base Cabinet family is an easier process.

- Note the new material (**LAMINATE, SW7076**) is identified in the **CABINET MATERIAL** field.

- *Step 15*: **CLICK ONCE** on the **DRAWER MATERIAL NAME** in the **TYPE PROPERTIES** box.

- *Step 16*: **CLICK** the **MATERIAL SELECTION** button. This opens the **MATERIAL BROWSER**.

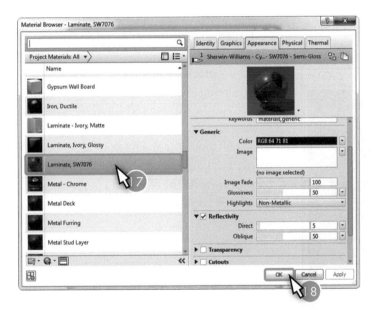

- *Step 17*: **SELECT** the **LAMINATE, SW7076** material in the **MATERIAL BROWSER**.

- *Step 18*: **CLICK** the **OK** button to assign the laminate to the drawer material in the Base Cabinet-Single Door 24″ family type.

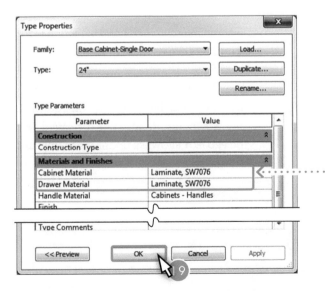

- The **TYPE PROPERTIES** box now displays the **LAMINATE, SW7076** material assigned to both the **CABINET MATERIAL** and **DRAWER MATERIAL** for the Base Cabinet-Single Door 24″ family type.

- *Step 19*: **CLICK** the **OK** button to close the **TYPE PROPERTIES** palette and apply the family type's material changes to the Revit project.

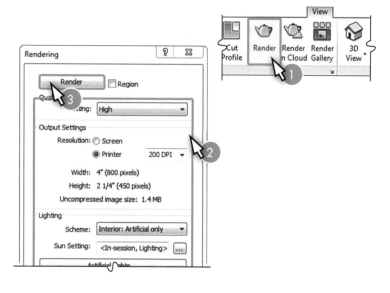

Render Method

The time required to photorealistically render a Revit view is directly related to the size of the rendering (pixels), the quality of the rendering, the quantity of light sources, and the processing power of your computer. Depending on the speed of your computer, these images can take several hours to fully render.

- *Step 1*: **OPEN** any **3D** view and **CLICK** the **RENDER** button in the **VIEW** tab.
- *Step 2*: **ADJUST** the **QUALITY**, **OUTPUT**, and **LIGHTING** settings. Each of these is discussed in greater detail on the following pages.
- *Step 3*: **CLICK** the **RENDER** button to start the rendering process.

The first 15 percent of the rendering process consists of a square jumping around a black screen. As the rendering progresses, the square begins to reveal portions on the rendering.

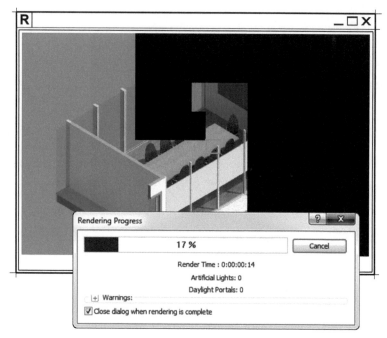

- *Step 4*: Once the rendering is complete, **CLICK** the **SAVE TO PROJECT** button.

- *Steps 5–6*: **PROVIDE** a **DESCRIPTIVE NAME** for the rendering, then **CLICK** the **OK** button to save the image. Renderings are saved in the **PROJECT BROWSER** under the **RENDERING** category.

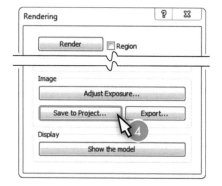

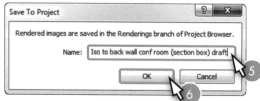

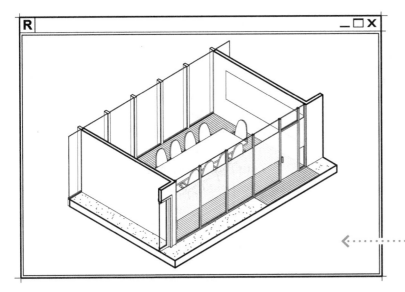

Interactive Ray Trace Mode

The Ray Trace visual style produces interactive photorealistic images in any 3D view. The image contains shadows as produced by the sun and/or artificial light. In Ray Traced images you will also see variation in value across a material or surface. Depending on the speed of your computer, these images can take several minutes to update every time you make a change to your model.

- *Step 1*: **OPEN** a **3D** view in the Revit project.

- *Step 2*: **CLICK ONCE** on the **VISUAL STYLE** button.
- *Step 3*: **SELECT** the **RAY TRACE** graphic display style.

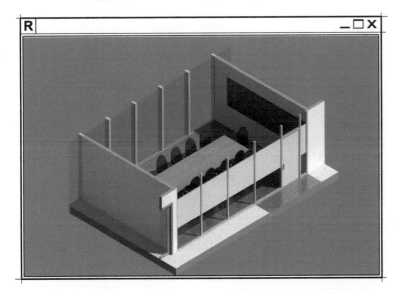

Revit will immediately begin to render the 3D view using the Ray Trace method. Adjusting the view or changing an element within the view will restart the Ray Trace rendering process.

- *Step 4*: Once the rendering is complete, **CLICK** the **SAVE** button in the **INTERACTIVE RAY TRACE** panel of the ribbon.
- *Steps 5-6*: **PROVIDE** a **DESCRIPTIVE NAME** for the rendering, then **CLICK** the **OK** button to save the image to the Revit project.

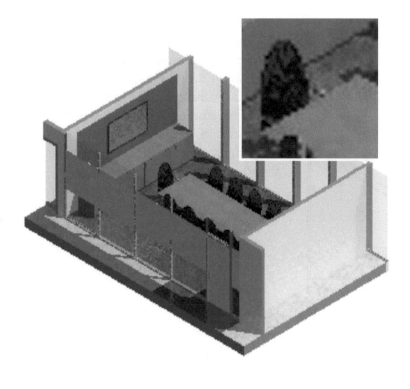

Draft-Quality Renderings

Because rendering high-quality images is very time consuming, it is important to select the appropriate render quality setting every time you start a new rendering.

- **USE** the **DRAFT** rendering quality to quickly check the material mappings, quantity, and quality of light.
- **USE** the **HIGH** or **BEST** rendering quality for presentation images.

- The render quality setting for this image is **DRAFT**. It is rendered with a **SUN ONLY** lighting scheme.
- Evaluate the image quality in the enlarged portion of this draft-quality rendering.

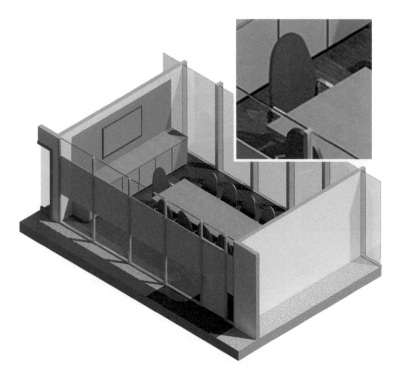

High-Quality Cloud Renderings

This image was rendered in Autodesk's Rendering in the Cloud service.

- The render quality setting for this image is **FINAL** quality. It is also rendered with a **SUN ONLY** lighting scheme.
- Evaluate the image quality in the enlarged portion of this high-quality rendering.

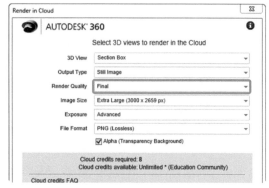

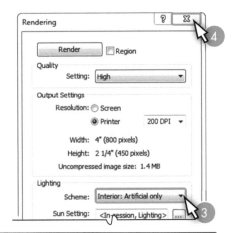

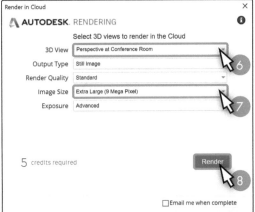

Lighting/Interior: Artificial Light

The examples on this page and the following pages show the same interior perspective rendered with different lighting scheme settings.

- *Step 1 (not shown)*: **OPEN** the **INTERIOR PERSPECTIVE** view.
- *Step 2*: **CLICK** the **RENDER** button in the **VIEW** tab.
- *Step 3*: **SET** the **LIGHTING SCHEME** to **INTERIOR: ARTIFICIAL ONLY**. This lighting scheme turns off the sun as a light source in the rendering.
- *Step 4*: **CLICK** the **CLOSE WINDOW** button.

- *Step 5*: **CLICK** the **RENDER IN CLOUD** button in the **VIEW** tab.
- *Step 6*: **SET** the **3D VIEW** to the proper interior perspective view.
- *Step 7*: **SET** the **IMAGE SIZE** to **EXTRA LARGE**.
- *Step 8*: **CLICK** the **RENDER** button.
- *Step 9*: **CLICK** the **RENDER GALLERY** button in the **VIEW** tab to monitor the rendering progress.

RENDER LIGHTING SCHEMES (continued)

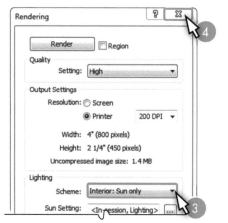

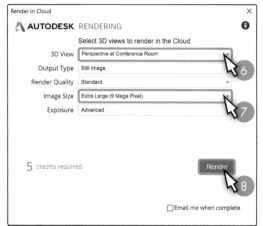

Lighting/Interior: Sunlight

- *Step 1 (not shown):* **OPEN** the **INTERIOR PERSPECTIVE** view.
- *Step 2:* **CLICK** the **RENDER** button in the **VIEW** tab.
- *Step 3:* **SET** the **LIGHTING SCHEME** to **INTERIOR: SUN ONLY.** You will notice in the rendered results that the interior lights are still "turned on" in the scene. This scheme adjusts the exposure for sunlight. Compare the image results with the renderings and settings on the next page.
- *Step 4:* **CLICK** the **CLOSE WINDOW** button.

- *Step 5:* **CLICK** the **RENDER IN CLOUD** button in the **VIEW** tab.
- *Step 6:* **SET** the **3D VIEW** to the proper interior perspective view.
- *Step 7:* **SET** the **IMAGE SIZE** to **EXTRA LARGE.**
- *Step 8:* **CLICK** the **RENDER** button.

- *Step 9:* **CLICK** the **RENDER GALLERY** button in the **VIEW** tab to monitor the rendering progress.

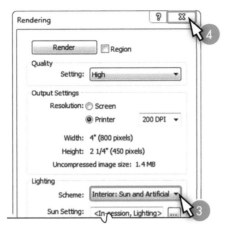

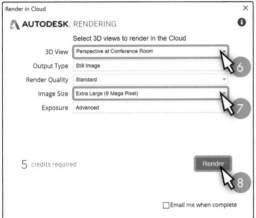

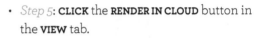

Lighting/Interior: Sunlight and Artificial Light

- *Step 1 (not shown)*: **OPEN** the **INTERIOR PERSPECTIVE** view.
- *Step 2*: **CLICK** the **RENDER** button in the **VIEW** tab.
- *Step 3*: **SET** the **LIGHTING SCHEME** to **INTERIOR: SUN AND ARTIFICIAL**. This scheme adjusts the exposure for a combination of both sunlight and artificial light.
- *Step 4*: **CLICK** the **CLOSE WINDOW** button.

- *Step 5*: **CLICK** the **RENDER IN CLOUD** button in the **VIEW** tab.
- *Step 6*: **SET** the **3D VIEW** to the proper interior perspective view.
- *Step 7*: **SET** the **IMAGE SIZE** to **EXTRA LARGE**.
- *Step 8*: **CLICK** the **RENDER** button.

- *Step 9*: **CLICK** the **RENDER GALLERY** button in the **VIEW** tab to monitor the rendering progress.

Real Time Rendering

Enscape is a real-time 3D rendering tool that works directly with Revit. This means that you can see a photorealistic rendering of your Revit project update in real time as you modify and change your Revit project file.

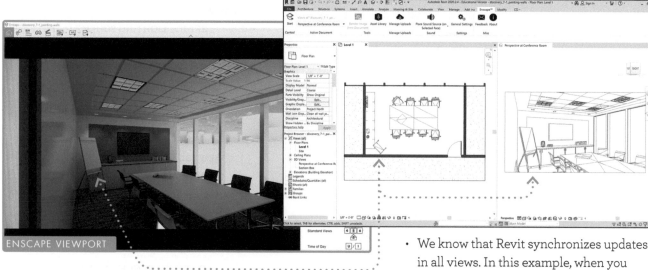

ENSCAPE VIEWPORT

- We know that Revit synchronizes updates in all views. In this example, when you move the easel in the plan view, Revit updates its location in perspective.
- The **Enscape viewport** also automatically updates the location of the easel in the rendered perspective. In addition to objects, the rendering also live-renders changes to materials and lighting.

Free Educational Licenses

Enscape has been very generous in providing free software to students. At the time of publication, students and educators can download a 24-month educational license of Enscape.

While the educational software incorporates all the functionality of the professional software, it may not be used for commercial or for-profit purposes.

- Apply for an educational license at **WWW.ENSCAPE3D.COM/EDUCATIONAL-LICENSE/**
- Professionals can learn more about purchasing a license at **WWW.ENSCAPE3D.COM/PRICING/**

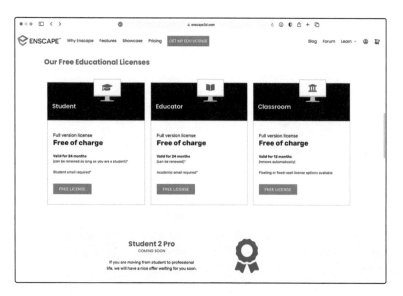

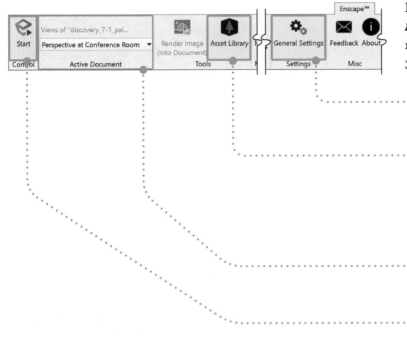

Enscape Revit Plugin

After installing Enscape on your computer, the Enscape ribbon should appear between the **ADD-INS** ribbon and **MODIFY** ribbon. You will need to open a Revit project with at least one 3D view.

- The **General Settings button** contains performance settings and license information.
- The **Asset Library** contains thousands of Enscape specific families including furniture and entourage. These assets only render in Enscape and typically do not look very good in plan view or when rendered with other software.
- The **Active Document panel** includes a drop-down selection with all 3D views in the current project.
- The **Start button** launches the Enscape Viewer (see below) and live rendering for the selected 3D view in the Active Document panel.

Enscape Viewer

The Enscape Viewer opens as a separate window when you click the start button in the Enscape ribbon.

- The **Visual Settings window** allows you to customize the rendering style including the horizon image, cloud cover, and atmosphere.
- The **View Management panel** shows the 3D views in your Revit project. Click on any view name to change the rendered view in Enscape.
- The **Help panel** includes the keyboard shortcuts needed to walk through your Enscape rendering.

Tip: Learn more about how to render Revit models using Enscape with video tutorials and more at **WWW.ENSCAPE3D.COM**.

Checklist for Rendering

General
- Strong renderings start with a strong perspective. Make sure you have carefully composed the perspective view and that you have added entourage to the scene.
- Render using a draft-quality setting until the light seems appropriate in the scene.
- Save the high-quality rendering settings for the one or two scenes you know will look great. These renderings can take several hours to complete.

Materials
- Materials can be assigned to multiple objects in a project. Duplicate materials before changing them so you don't inadvertently change another object in the project.
- Appearance Assets can be assigned to multiple materials. Duplicate Appearance Assets before changing them so you don't inadvertently change another material in the project.

Interior Rendered Perspective
Middlebury College Squash Center
ARC/Architectural Resources Cambridge

Companion Download 7.2
You can also download full-color images on these professional
renderings at **WWW.RAFDBOOK.COM/DOWNLOADS.**

Exterior Rendered Perspective
Middlebury College Squash Center
ARC/Architectural Resources Cambridge

Interior Rendered Perspective
Graduate Studio, Marymount University
Lisa Corrado, Kirsten Ederer, and Kurt Seip

Learning Exercises

Learning Exercise 7.1: Rendered Perspectives
To begin this exercise, open the Revit project completed in
Learning Exercises 6.2 at the end of Chapter 6. You can also
download a support file for these exercises at
WWW.RAFDBOOK.COM/DOWNLOADS.

Follow the step-by-step exercises in the chapter to add materials
and render the following **3D VIEWS** in the companion download:
- Perspective at conference room
- Perspective at lobby
- Isometric at conference room (section box)
- Isometric of level 11 plan (section box)

Application Exercises

Using an assignment from your instructor or a previously
completed studio project, create renderings for the following types
of drawings:
- Interior Perspectives
- Exterior Perspectives
- Isometric
- Isometric (section box)

Interior Rendered Perspective

Graduate Thesis, Marymount University

Lisa Corrado

chapter 8

ELEVATIONS AND SECTIONS

Elevations and sections are important drawings that communicate vertical surface conditions in a project. In Revit, you can simultaneously work on a project in plan view and elevation or section view. This is a powerful tool that allows designers to consider all aspects of a space in the design process. This chapter explains how to create interior elevations, building elevations, and sections from an existing floor plan.

IN THIS CHAPTER

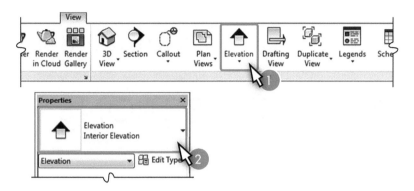

The Elevation button creates an elevation view of the Revit project from the plan view. Building components updated in a plan view will automatically update in elevation views.

Adding Interior Elevations

- *Step 1*: From any plan view, **CLICK** the **ELEVATION** button in the **VIEW** tab.
- *Step 2*: **CHANGE** the **ELEVATION TYPE** to **INTERIOR ELEVATION** in the **PROPERTIES** palette.

As you move the cursor around the room, the interior elevation arrow will automatically point to the closest wall in the floor plan.

- *Step 3*: **CLICK ONCE** in the floor plan to locate the interior elevation.
- *Step 4 (not shown)*: **PRESS** the **ESC** key to end the Elevation command.

> **Tip**: **PRESS** the **TAB** key when placing the Interior Elevation tag to cycle through alternate elevation positions.

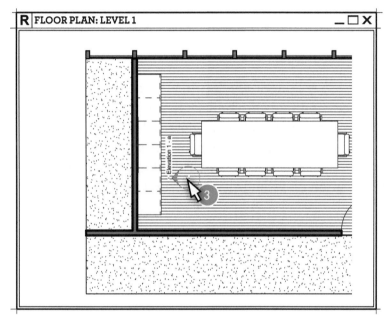

Adjusting the Elevation's Scope

- *Step 5*: **CLICK ONCE** on the **ELEVATION ARROW** in the plan view.
- *Step 6*: **DRAG** the **ELEVATION LINE** to change the cut location of the interior elevation.
- *Step 7*: **DRAG** the **SEGMENT HANDLE** to adjust the width of the interior elevation.
- *Step 8*: **DRAG** the **ARROWS** to adjust the depth of the interior elevation.

> **Guided Discovery 8.1**: Following the exercise on this and the following pages, create an interior elevation. The support file is at **WWW.RAFDBOOK.COM/DOWNLOADS**.

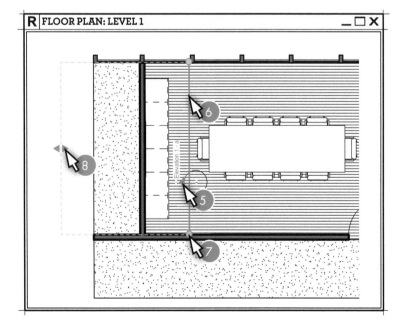

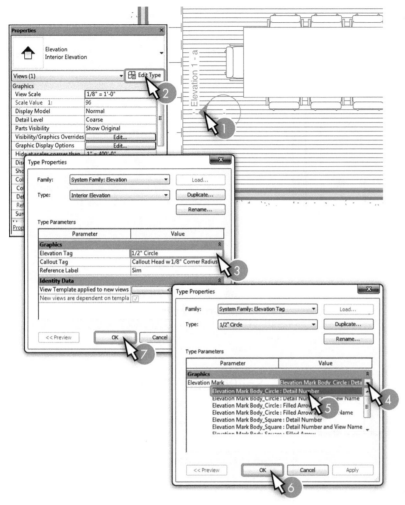

Adjusting the Interior Elevation Tag

The default Interior Elevation tag shows both the interior elevation view name and the drawing number. In a construction document set, the elevation's view name should be removed from the Interior Elevation tag.

- *Step 1*: **CLICK ONCE** on the **ARROW** portion of the interior elevation tag.
- *Step 2*: **CLICK** the **EDIT TYPE** button in the **PROPERTIES** dialog box.

- *Step 3*: **CLICK** the **ELEVATION TAG** graphics value. The default value is **1/2" CIRCLE**.

> The default SI elevation tag is **10mm CIRCLE**.

- *Steps 4-5*: **CHANGE** the **ELEVATION MARK** value to **ELEVATION MARK BODY_CIRCLE: DETAIL NUMBER**.
- *Step 6*: **CLICK** the **OK** button to close the **ELEVATION TAG PROPERTIES** dialog box.

- *Step 7*: **CLICK** the **OK** button to close the **ELEVATION PROPERTIES** dialog box.

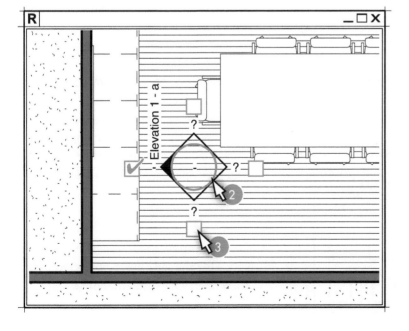

Adding Additional Elevations

When you need to draw multiple interior elevations for a single room or space, draw the first elevation using the Elevation button in the Revit ribbon.

- *Step 1 (not shown)*: **OPEN** a **PLAN VIEW** with an interior elevation symbol.
- *Step 2*: **CLICK ONCE** on the **CIRCLE** portion of the interior elevation symbol.
- *Step 3*: **CHECK** the **SHOW ARROW** box in the direction where you want to add an interior elevation.

> **Tip**: Removing a check from a **SHOW ARROW** box will delete the interior elevation from the Revit project.

INTERIOR ELEVATIONS (continued)

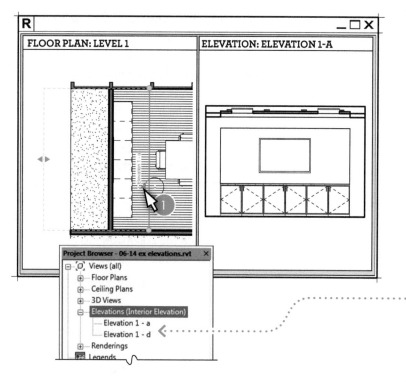

Viewing the Elevation

- *Step 1:* **RIGHT-CLICK** on the **ELEVATION ARROW** and **SELECT GO TO ELEVATION VIEW** from the context menu.

- The **ELEVATION VIEW** can also be opened in the **PROJECT BROWSER.**

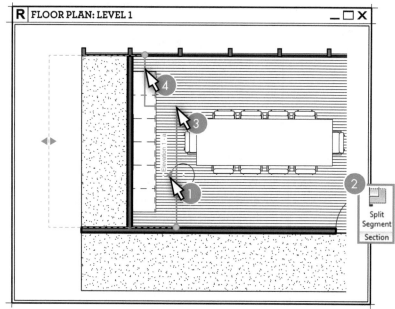

Splitting the Elevation View

A split elevation combines multiple elevation segments drawn or cut at different distances to the elevated surface. Split elevations are useful when attempting to draw an elevation through a slab opening or when creating an elevation/section combination drawing.

- *Step 1:* **CLICK ONCE** on the **ELEVATION ARROW** in the plan view.
- *Step 2:* **CLICK** the **SPLIT SEGMENT** button in the **MODIFY | VIEWS** tab.
- *Step 3:* **CLICK ONCE** on the **ELEVATION LINE** to set the split location.
- *Step 4:* **MOVE** the **CURSOR** toward the wall and **CLICK** as shown in this example.
- *Step 5 (not shown):* **PRESS** the **ESC** key **TWICE** to end the Split Segment command.

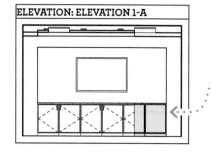

- The resulting split elevation is shown here. Notice the shaded blue region is redrawn as a section view through the casework.

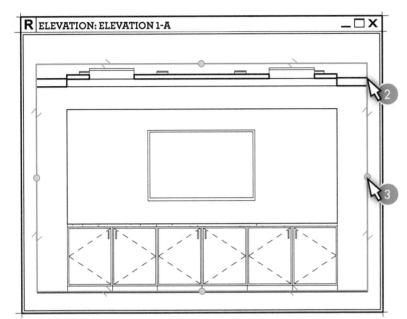

Adjusting the Crop Region

The scope of the elevation can be adjusted or cropped in the elevation view.

- *Step 1 (not shown):* **OPEN** the **ELEVATION VIEW**.
- *Step 2:* **CLICK ONCE** on the **CROP REGION FRAME** around the elevation.
- *Step 3:* **DRAG** the **SEGMENT HANDLE** to adjust the width or height of the interior elevation. By default, the crop window will not print, so it is important to make the crop region slightly larger than the elevation.

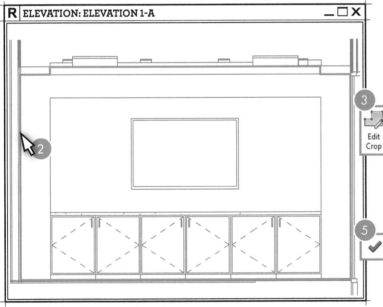

Sketching the Crop Region

The scope of the elevation can be adjusted or cropped in the elevation view.

- *Step 1 (not shown):* **OPEN** the **ELEVATION VIEW**.
- *Step 2:* **CLICK ONCE** on the **CROP REGION FRAME**.
- *Step 3:* **CLICK** the **EDIT CROP** button in the **MODIFY | VIEWS** tab.
- *Step 4 (not shown):* Use the **DRAW TOOLS** to adjust the crop line to match this example.
- *Step 5:* **CLICK** the **FINISH EDIT MODE** button in the **MODIFY | EDIT PROFILE** tab.

Adjusting Lineweight (Linework)

The Linework command adjusts line weight in the active view. In this example, we add a wide line to the elevation perimeter.

- *Step 1:* **CLICK ONCE** on the **LINEWORK** button in the **MODIFY** tab.
- *Steps 2–3:* **SELECT** the **WIDE LINES** in the **LINE STYLE** Drop-down menu.
- *Steps 4–5:* **CLICK ONCE** on each perimeter line in the elevation view to change it to a wide line.
- *Step 6 (not shown):* **PRESS** the **ESC** key **TWICE** to end the Linework command.

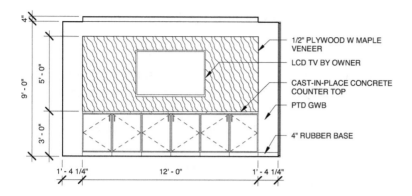

- 1/2" PLYWOOD W MAPLE VENEER
- LCD TV BY OWNER
- CAST-IN-PLACE CONCRETE COUNTER TOP
- PTD GWB
- 4" RUBBER BASE

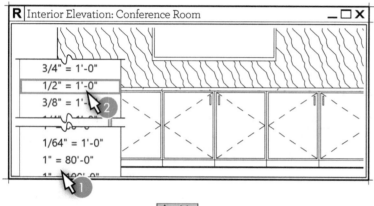

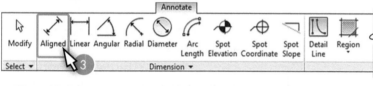

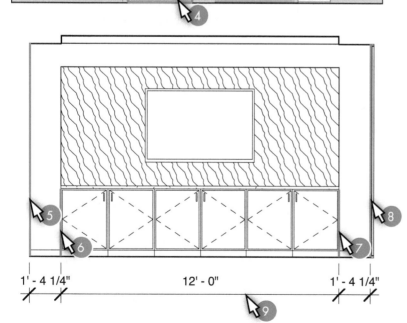

In Revit, you will need to add the following annotations to each interior elevation view: dimensions, material descriptions, and material hatches.

Architectural Drawing Scale

Before annotating a drawing, it is important to set the architectural scale.

- Interior elevations are typically drawn at 1/4" = 1'-0" or SI scale 1:50.
- Kitchen and bath elevations are often drawn at 1/2" = 1'-0" or SI scale 1:25.
- *Step 1:* **CLICK** on the **ARCHITECTURAL SCALE** in the status bar.
- *Step 2:* **SELECT** the **PREFERRED SCALE** from the list of possible architectural scales.

Adding Dimension Strings

In elevations, dimensions are usually limited to elements unique to the elevation like vertical distances on walls, built-in cabinets, and changes in wall material.

- *Step 3:* **CLICK** the **ALIGNED DIMENSION** button in the **ANNOTATE** tab.
- *Step 4:* In the green **MODIFY | PLACE DIMENSIONS** tab, **SELECT WALL FACES** as shown in this example. This allows you to start dimension strings from the faces of walls in the elevation view.
- *Step 5:* Following the example to the left, **CLICK** on the **LEFT INTERIOR WALL** in the elevation.
- *Steps 6–7:* **CLICK** on the **LEFT AND RIGHT EDGES** of the built-in cabinets.
- *Step 8:* **CLICK** on the **RIGHT INTERIOR WALL** in the elevation.
- *Step 9:* As you move the mouse, you will see the dimension string following the cursor position. Position the dimension string below the elevation and **CLICK ONCE** to **LOCATE** the dimension string.
- *Step 10 (not shown):* **PRESS** the **ESC** key **TWICE** to end the Dimension command.

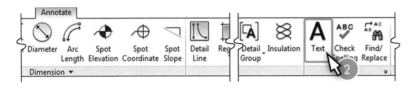

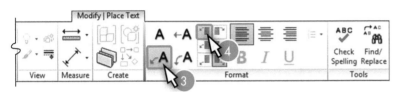

Adding Text Leaders

In elevation views, text annotations identify materials in the view.

- *Step 1 (not shown):* **OPEN** the **ELEVATION VIEW**.
- *Step 2:* **CLICK** the **TEXT** button in the **ANNOTATE** tab.
- *Step 3:* **CLICK** the **TWO-SEGMENT LEADER** button in the **MODIFY | PLACE TEXT** tab.
- *Step 4:* **CLICK** the **LEADER AT TOP-LEFT** button in the **MODIFY | PLACE TEXT** tab.

- *Step 5:* **CLICK ONCE** in the elevation view to locate the leader's arrow.
- *Step 6:* **CLICK ONCE** in the elevation view to locate the leader's elbow.
- *Step 7:* **CLICK ONCE** in the elevation view to locate the end of the leader line.
- *Step 8:* **TYPE** the **TEXT** that describes the element identified with the leader. In this example, we typed: **1/2" PLYWOOD W MAPLE VENEER**.

> The equivalent SI material is **12.5MM PLYWOOD W MAPLE VENEER**.

- *Step 9:* **CLICK ANYWHERE** in the **VIEW** to finish editing the text.
- *Step 10 (not shown):* **PRESS** the **ESC** key **TWICE** to end the Text command.

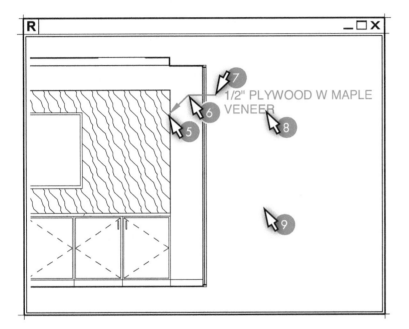

Adjusting the Leader's Appearance

Click once on the leader text you want to adjust.

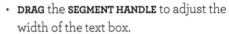

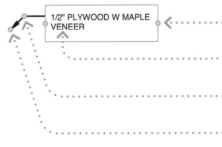

- **DRAG** the **SEGMENT HANDLE** to adjust the width of the text box.
- **DOUBLE-CLICK** the **TEXT** to edit. **CLICK ANYWHERE** in the **VIEW** to finish editing.
- **DRAG** the **ELBOW HANDLE** to adjust the position of the leader elbow.
- **DRAG** the **ARROW HANDLE** to adjust the position of the leader arrow.

ANNOTATING INTERIOR ELEVATIONS (continued)

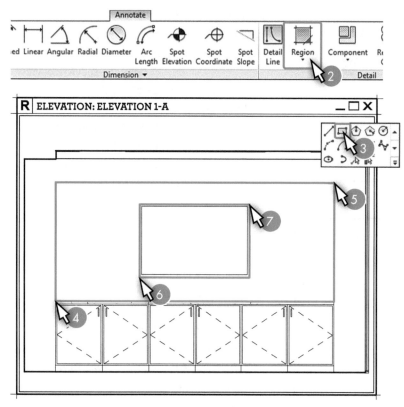

Adding Material Hatches

The Region Hatch button allows you to add material hatches to interior elevations.

- *Step 1 (not shown)*: **OPEN** the **ELEVATION VIEW**.
- *Step 2*: **CLICK ONCE** on the **REGION** button in the **ANNOTATE** tab.
- *Step 3*: **CLICK ONCE** on the **RECTANGLE** button in the **DRAW** panel of the **MODIFY | CREATE FILLED REGION BOUNDARY** tab.

- *Steps 4–5*: **CLICK ONCE** on the opposite corners of the rectangle in the elevation to define the hatch region.
- *Steps 6–7*: **CLICK ONCE** on the opposite corners of the LCD television in the elevation to define a hole in the hatch region.

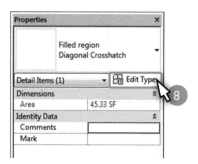

Defining a New Material

It's time to define a new material hatch in the project. In the following steps, we will define a wood hatch and apply it to the region in this elevation.

- *Step 8*: **CLICK** the **EDIT TYPE** button in the **PROPERTIES** palette. This opens the **TYPE PROPERTIES** dialog box.

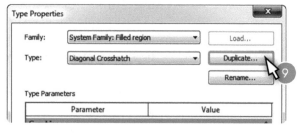

- *Step 9*: **CLICK** the **DUPLICATE** button in the **TYPE PROPERTIES** dialog box.

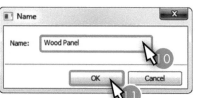

- *Step 10*: **TYPE** a **NAME** for the new material hatch. In this example, we typed **WOOD PANEL**.
- *Step 11*: **CLICK** the **OK** button to close the **NAME** dialog box and return to the **TYPE PROPERTIES** dialog box.

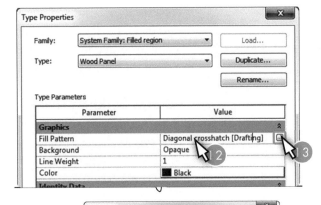

Defining a New Material (continued)

- *Step 12*: **CLICK** to edit the **FILL PATTERN NAME**.
- *Step 13*: **CLICK** the **FILL PATTERN SELECT** button to open the **FILL PATTERNS** dialog box.

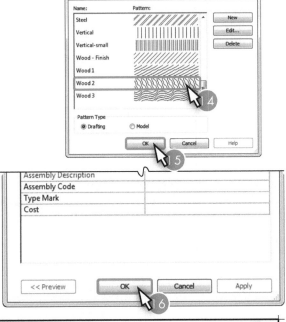

- *Step 14*: **SELECT** the **WOOD 2** fill pattern.
- *Step 15*: **CLICK** the **OK** button to close the **FILL PATTERNS** dialog box and return to the **TYPE PROPERTIES** dialog box.

- *Step 16*: **CLICK** the **OK** button to close the **TYPE PROPERTIES** dialog box.

Finishing the Hatch

- *Step 17*: **CLICK** the **FINISH EDIT MODE** button in the **MODIFY | CREATE FILLED REGION BOUNDARY** tab.
- *Step 18 (not shown)*: **PRESS** the **ESC** key to end the Hatch command.

The hatched elevation is shown here. Note that the wood material hatch does not cover the LCD television.

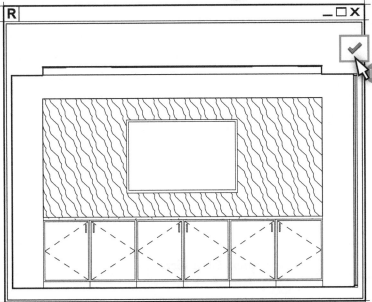

Tip: Annotation elements (including Region Hatches) are visible only in the view where they are created. For example, this wood grain will not be visible in 3D views or other interior elevations.

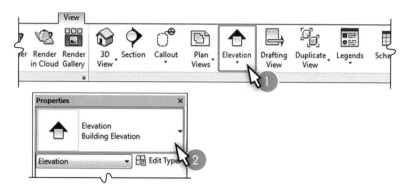

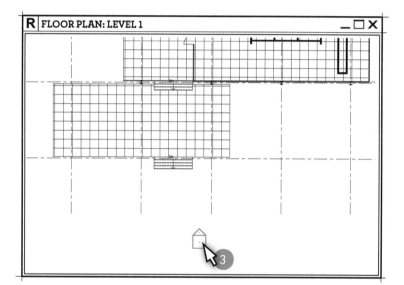

The Elevation button creates an elevation view of the Revit project from the plan view. Building components updated in a plan view will automatically update in elevation views.

Adding Building (Exterior) Elevations

- *Step 1*: From any plan view, **CLICK** the **ELEVATION** button in the **VIEW** tab.
- *Step 2*: **CHANGE** the **ELEVATION TYPE** to **BUILDING ELEVATION** in the **PROPERTIES** palette.

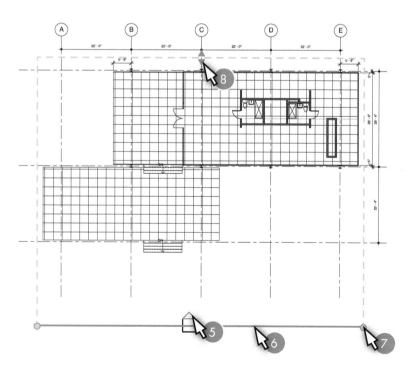

As you move the cursor around the exterior of the building, the elevation arrow will automatically point to the closest exterior wall in the floor plan. **PRESS** the **TAB** key on the keyboard to cycle through alternate elevation positions before you add the elevation.

- *Step 3*: **CLICK ONCE** in the floor plan to locate the exterior elevation.
- *Step 4 (not shown)*: **PRESS** the **ESC** key **TWICE** to end the Elevation command.

Adjusting the Elevation's Scope

- *Step 5*: **CLICK ONCE** on the **ELEVATION ARROW** in the plan view.
- *Step 6*: **DRAG** the **ELEVATION LINE** to change the cut location of the interior elevation.
- *Step 7*: **DRAG** the **SEGMENT HANDLE** to adjust the width of the interior elevation.
- *Step 8*: **DRAG** the **ARROWS** to adjust the depth of the building elevation.

Main Floor Plan

Farnsworth House (1951)
Mies van der Rohe

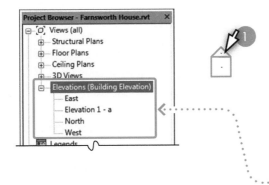

Viewing the Building Elevation

- *Step 1*: **RIGHT-CLICK** on the **ELEVATION ARROW** and **SELECT GO TO ELEVATION VIEW** from the context menu.

The elevation view can also be opened in the **PROJECT BROWSER**. New Revit projects include a **NORTH, EAST, SOUTH,** and **WEST** building elevation.

- In this example, the south elevation was deleted and replaced with **ELEVATION 1 - A**.

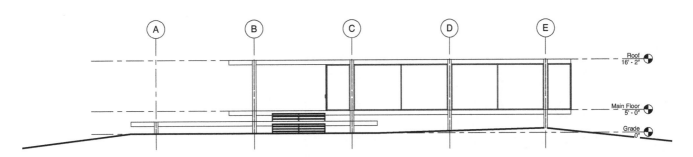

South Building Elevation

Farnsworth House (1951)

Mies van der Rohe

This drawing is the south building elevation created in *Steps 1–8* on the previous page. Exterior elevations are typically drawn at 1/8″ = 1′-0″.

The equivalent SI scale is **1:100.**

The following annotations should be located on the exterior elevation view:

- Add significant vertical dimensions.
- Add material hatches to identify special wall surfaces.
- Add text labels to identify wall finishes.
- Show the Levels annotation category to turn on the floor level symbols.
- Show the Grids annotation category to turn on the column grid symbols.

Guided Discovery 8.2: Following the exercise on this and the following pages, create a building elevation. The support file is at **WWW.RAFDBOOK.COM/DOWNLOADS.**

BUILDING SECTIONS

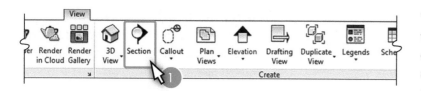

The Section button creates a section view of the Revit project from the plan view. Building components updated in a plan view will automatically update in the corresponding section view.

Adding Sections

- *Step 1*: From any plan view, **CLICK** the **SECTION** button in the **VIEW** tab.

- *Step 2*: **CLICK ONCE** in the floor plan to locate the first end of the section cut line.

- *Step 3*: **CLICK ONCE** in the floor plan to locate the second end of the section cut line.
- *Step 4 (not shown)*: **PRESS** the **ESC** key to end the Section command.

Adjusting the Section's Graphics

Click once on a section line to adjust its visual properties.

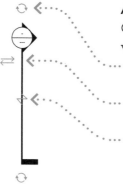

- **CLICK** the **CYCLE SECTION TAIL** symbol to change the graphics for each section tail.
- **CLICK** the **FLIP SECTION** symbol to flip to direction of the section view.
- **CLICK** the **GAPS IN SEGMENTS** symbol to remove the portion of the section line that overlaps the floor plan.

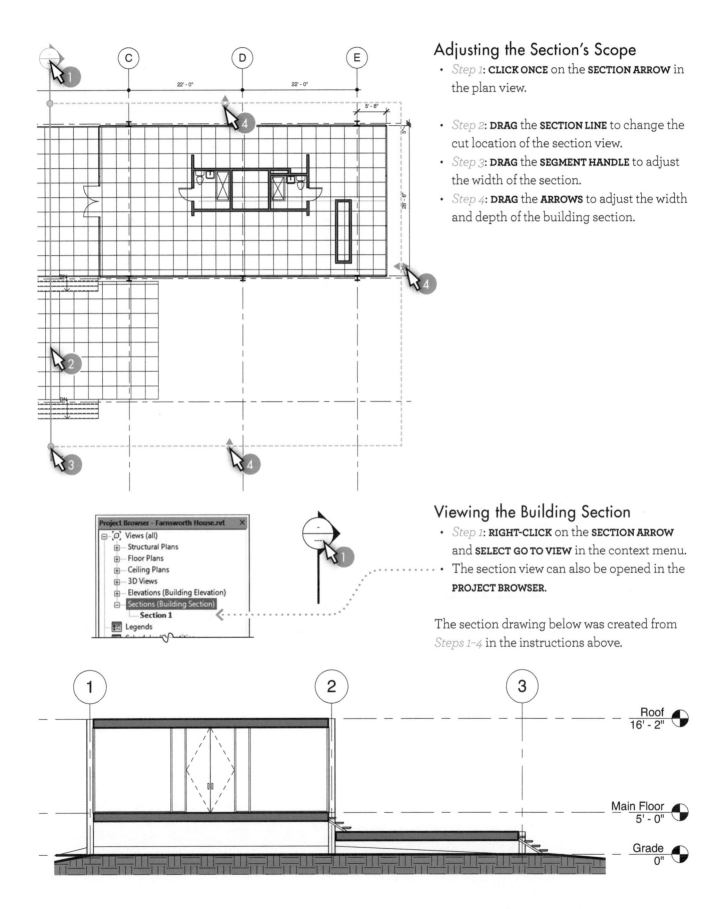

Adjusting the Section's Scope

- *Step 1:* **CLICK ONCE** on the **SECTION ARROW** in the plan view.

- *Step 2:* **DRAG** the **SECTION LINE** to change the cut location of the section view.
- *Step 3:* **DRAG** the **SEGMENT HANDLE** to adjust the width of the section.
- *Step 4:* **DRAG** the **ARROWS** to adjust the width and depth of the building section.

Viewing the Building Section

- *Step 1:* **RIGHT-CLICK** on the **SECTION ARROW** and **SELECT GO TO VIEW** in the context menu.
- The section view can also be opened in the **PROJECT BROWSER.**

The section drawing below was created from *Steps 1-4* in the instructions above.

BUILDING SECTIONS (continued)

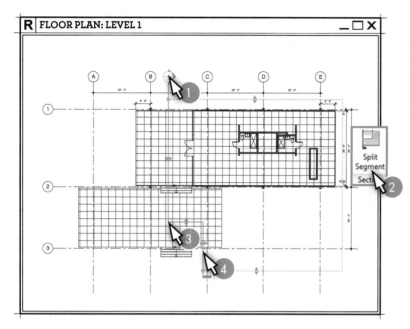

Splitting the Section View

A split section combines multiple parallel section segments drawn or cut at different locations. Split sections are useful when you need to jog the section line to communicate an idea about adjacent spaces.

- *Step 1*: **CLICK ONCE** on the **SECTION ARROW** in the plan view.
- *Step 2*: **CLICK** the **SPLIT SEGMENT** button in the **MODIFY | VIEWS** tab.
- *Step 3*: **CLICK ONCE** on the **SECTION LINE** to set the split location.
- *Step 4*: **MOVE** the **CURSOR** to shift the bottom portion of the section in front of the stairs and **CLICK** as shown in this example.
- *Step 5 (not shown)*: **PRESS** the **ESC** key **TWICE** to end the Split Segment command.

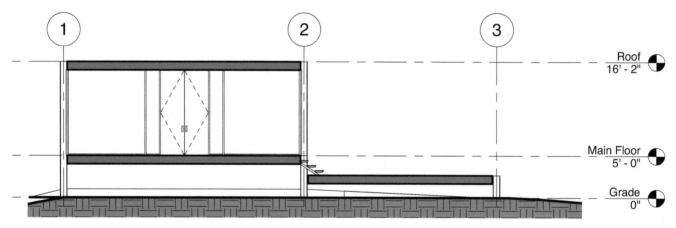

The resulting split section is shown here. Notice the bottom set of stairs is no longer visible in the view.

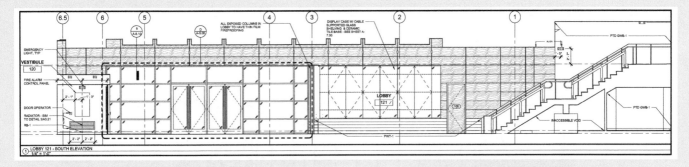

Interior Elevation at Lobby
Middlebury College Squash Center
ARC/Architectural Resources Cambridge

Guided Discovery Exercise

Guided Discovery 8.1: Interior Elevations

- To begin this exercise download the support file at **WWW.RAFDBOOK.COM/DOWNLOADS.**
- Follow the step-by-step exercises on page 148 to add the following **INTERIOR ELEVATIONS** to the companion Revit project:
  - East interior elevation at conference room
  - South interior elevation at conference room
  - West interior elevation at conference room

- For each elevation, add the following annotations:
  - Use region hatches to add material hatches.
  - Add text leaders to identify materials.
  - Dimension elements unique to the elevation view, such as vertical dimensions on walls and built-in cabinets.

Revit Interior Elevation Tips

- Interior elevations are usually drawn at 1/4" = 1'-0" scale.

  > The equivalent SI scale is **1:50**.

- Revit will automatically cross-reference the Interior Elevation tag in the floor plan when you place the elevation view on a sheet.

Annotation Tips

- In Revit, set an appropriate architectural scale before annotating each interior elevation.
- Draw the perimeter of the elevation with a dark annotation detail line.
- Add material hatches to identify special wall materials.
- Add text labels to identify wall surface finishes and wall base materials and finishes.
- Hide the Levels annotation category for single-level elevations.
- Hide the Grids annotation category for single-room interior elevations.

Dimension Tips

- In Revit, set an appropriate architectural scale before dimensioning an interior elevation.
- Limit dimensions to objects and elements that are not already dimensioned in the floor plan.
- Dimension the location for each change in wall material.
- Start dimension strings from the nearest wall.

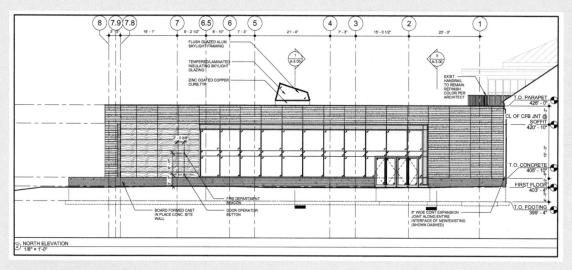

North Building Elevation

Middlebury College Squash Center

ARC/Architectural Resources Cambridge

Guided Discovery Exercise

Guided Discovery 8.2: Building Elevations

- To begin this exercise download the support file at **WWW.RAFDBOOK.COM/DOWNLOADS.**
- Follow the step-by-step exercises on page 156 to add the following **BUILDING ELEVATIONS** to the companion Revit project:
  - North building elevation
  - East building elevation
  - South building elevation
  - West building elevation

- For each elevation, add the following annotations:
  - Use region hatches to add material hatches.
  - Add text leaders to identify materials.
  - Dimension elements unique to the elevation view, such as vertical dimensions for windows and doors.

Revit Building Elevation Tips

- Building elevations are usually drawn at 1/8″ = 1′-0″ scale.
- Revit will automatically cross-reference the Building Elevation tag in the floor plan when you place the elevation view on a sheet.

Annotation Tips

- In Revit, set an appropriate architectural scale before annotating each elevation.
- Add material hatches to identify special wall surfaces.
- Add text labels to identify wall finishes.
- Show the Levels annotation category.
- Show the Grids annotation category.

Dimension Tips

- In Revit, set an appropriate architectural scale before dimensioning a building elevation.
- Limit dimensions to objects and elements that are not already dimensioned in the floor plan.
- Dimension the location for each change in wall material.
- Start dimension strings from the nearest column grid line or floor level grid line.

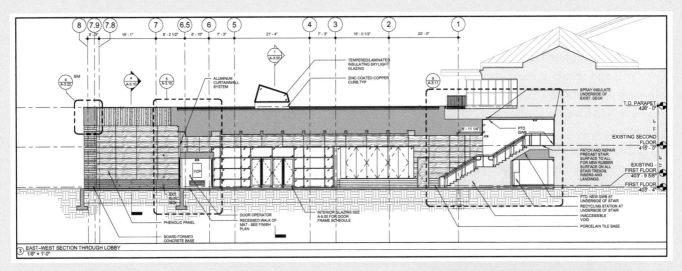

East–West Building Section Elevation
Middlebury College Squash Center
ARC/Architectural Resources Cambridge

Revit Building Section Tips

- Building sections are usually drawn at 1/8″ = 1'-0″ scale.

  > The equivalent SI scale is **1:100**.

- Revit will automatically cross-reference the building section symbol in the floor plan when you place the section view on a sheet.

Annotation Tips

- In Revit, set an appropriate architectural scale before annotating each section.
- In each section view, add material hatches to identify special surfaces.
- Poché walls and slabs by changing the cut pattern to solid.
- Poché plenum spaces with a region hatch.
- Show the Levels annotation category.
- Show the Grids annotation category.

Dimension Tips

- In Revit, set an appropriate architectural scale before dimensioning a section.

  > The equivalent SI scale is **1:100**.

- Limit dimensions to objects and elements that are not already dimensioned in the floor plan.
- Start dimension strings from the nearest column grid line or floor level grid line.

APPLICATION EXERCISE

Application Exercise

Using an assignment from your instructor or a previously completed studio project, create elevations and sections. For each view, add the following annotations:

- Use region hatches to add material hatches.
- Add text leaders to identify materials.
- Dimension elements unique to the elevation view, such as vertical dimensions on walls and built-in cabinets.

chapter 9

ROOFS AND SITE PLANS

Roofs and site context are important elements to include in design presentations. While this chapter, on the surface, seems appropriate for architecture students, interior design students can also take advantage of these exterior elements to populate the space immediately outside their project. Creating an exterior environment in Revit is important for rendering interior perspectives and for describing access to and from a building site.

IN THIS CHAPTER

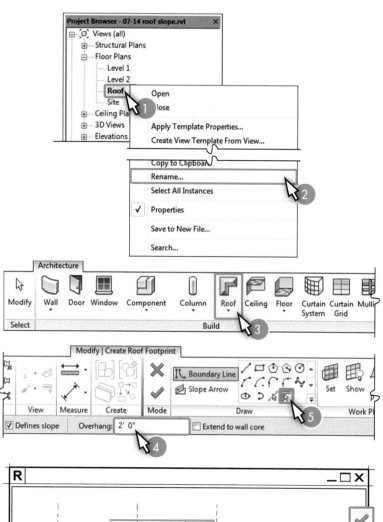

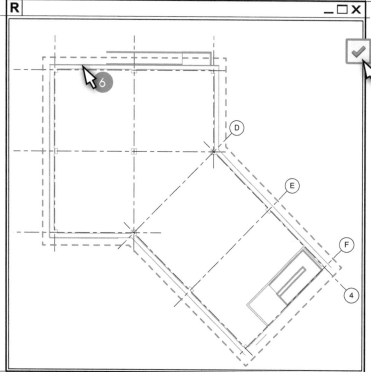

Adding Sloped Roofs

The Sloped Roof command creates a pitched roof from the perimeter of the building. Before you create a roof, verify that you've defined a level above the highest occupiable level in the project. For example, if you have Levels 1 and 2 as occupiable space, an additional Level 3 is required to build the roof.

- *Steps 1–2*: In the **PROJECT BROWSER**, **RENAME** the highest level in the project to **ROOF**. In this example, **LEVEL 3** was renamed to **ROOF**. Verify that the exterior walls have the **TOP CONSTRAINT** set to **UP TO LEVEL: ROOF**.

- *Step 3*: **OPEN** the **ROOF** plan view and **CLICK** the **ROOF** button in the **ARCHITECTURE** tab.

- *Step 4*: **SET** the **OVERHANG** to **2′-0″** in the **MODIFY | CREATE ROOF FOOTPRINT** tab.

  The SI measurement for this step is **600**.

- *Step 5*: **SELECT** the **PICK WALLS** button in the draw panel of the **MODIFY | CREATE ROOF FOOTPRINT** tab.

- *Step 6*: **HOVER** the **CURSOR** over the edge of an exterior wall.
- *Step 7 (not shown)*: **PRESS** the **TAB** key on the keyboard to select all of the exterior walls.
- *Step 8 (not shown)*: **CLICK ONCE** when you see a dashed line around the perimeter of the building.

- *Step 9*: **CLICK** the **FINISH EDIT MODE** button in the **MODIFY | CREATE ROOF FOOTPRINT** tab.

Guided Discovery 9.1: Following the exercise to the left, add a sloped roof to a Revit project. The support file is at **WWW.RAFDBOOK.COM/DOWNLOADS**.

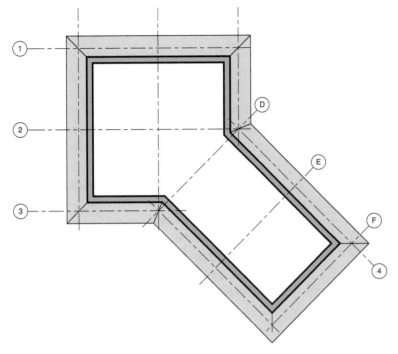

Viewing the Sloped Roof

The roof level will display a sliced view of the sloped roof, as seen in this example. This is because the default cut plane for all floor plan views is 4'-0" above the finish floor.

> The default SI cut plane for floor plan views is **1200**.

- *Step 1*: **CLICK** the **3D VIEW** button in the **VIEW** tab to see the sloped roof created in the previous steps.

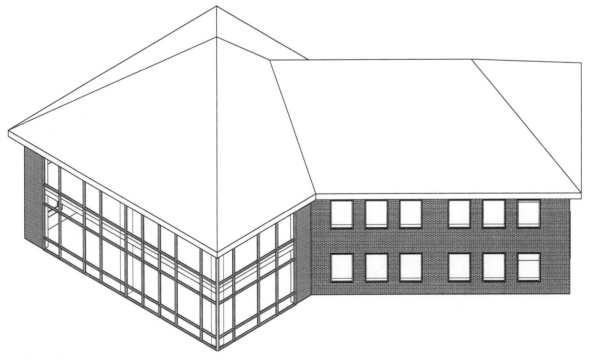

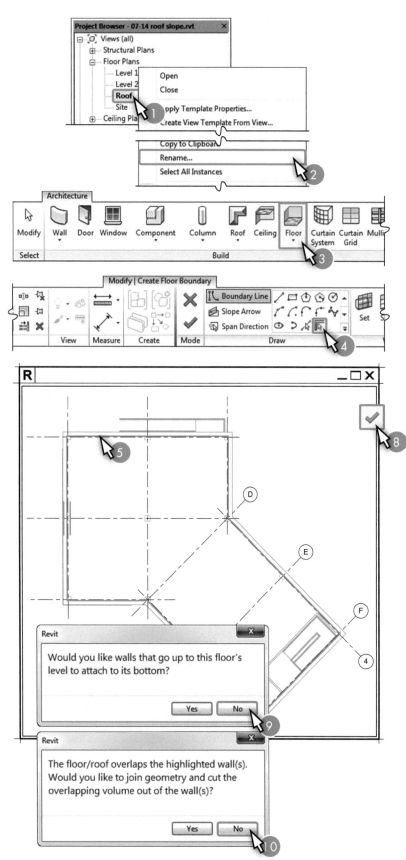

Adding Flat Roofs

Flat roofs can be created with a combination of floor slabs and heightened exterior walls. Before you create a roof, verify that you've defined a level above the highest occupiable level in the project. For example, if you have Levels 1 and 2 as occupiable space, an additional Level 3 is required to build the roof.

- *Steps 1-2*: In the **PROJECT BROWSER**, **RENAME** the highest level in the project to **ROOF**. In this example, **LEVEL 3** was renamed to **ROOF**. Verify that the exterior walls have the **TOP CONSTRAINT** set to **UP TO LEVEL: ROOF**.
- *Step 3*: **OPEN** the **ROOF** plan view and **CLICK** the **FLOOR** button in the **ARCHITECTURE** tab.
- *Step 4*: **SELECT** the **PICK WALLS** button in the draw panel of the **MODIFY | CREATE FLOOR BOUNDARY** tab.

- *Step 5*: **HOVER** the **CURSOR** over the interior edge of an exterior wall.
- *Step 6* (*not shown*): **PRESS** the **TAB** key on the keyboard to select all of the exterior walls.
- *Step 7* (*not shown*): **CLICK ONCE** when you see a blue line around the perimeter of the building.

- *Step 8*: **CLICK** the **FINISH EDIT MODE** button in the **MODIFY | CREATE FLOOR BOUNDARY** tab.

- *Step 9*: If you are prompted to attach walls to the bottom of the slab, **CLICK** the **NO** button. Answering **NO** will allow you to extend the exterior walls above the roof, creating a parapet.

- *Step 10*: If you are prompted to join geometry between the floor and walls, **CLICK** the **NO** button. Answering **NO** will keep the exterior wall geometry separate from the slab geometry.

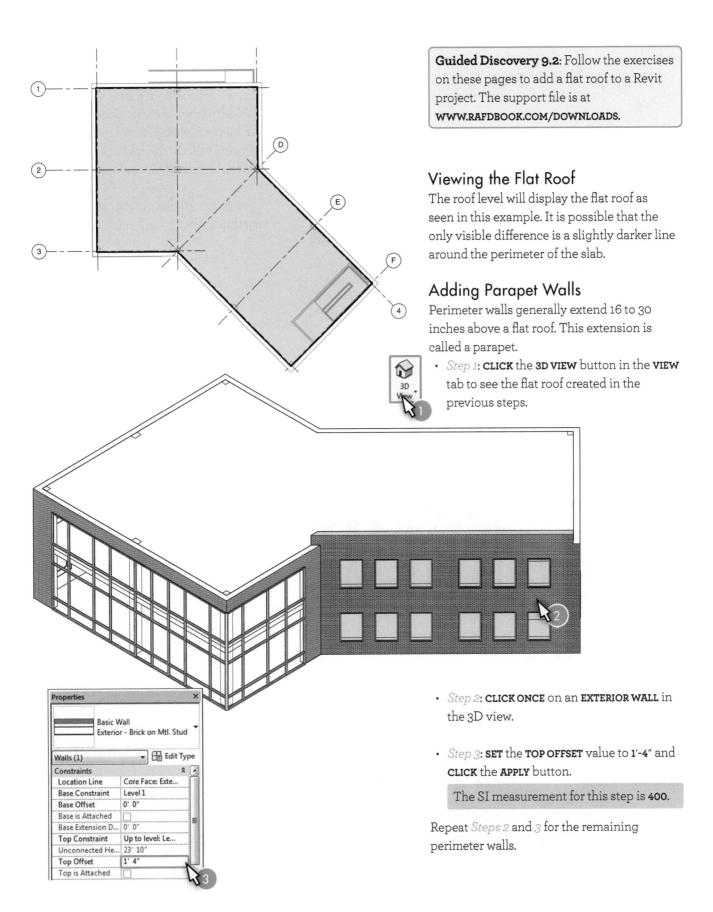

Guided Discovery 9.2: Follow the exercises on these pages to add a flat roof to a Revit project. The support file is at **WWW.RAFDBOOK.COM/DOWNLOADS.**

Viewing the Flat Roof

The roof level will display the flat roof as seen in this example. It is possible that the only visible difference is a slightly darker line around the perimeter of the slab.

Adding Parapet Walls

Perimeter walls generally extend 16 to 30 inches above a flat roof. This extension is called a parapet.

- *Step 1*: **CLICK** the **3D VIEW** button in the **VIEW** tab to see the flat roof created in the previous steps.

- *Step 2*: **CLICK ONCE** on an **EXTERIOR WALL** in the 3D view.

- *Step 3*: **SET** the **TOP OFFSET** value to **1'-4"** and **CLICK** the **APPLY** button.

  The SI measurement for this step is **400**.

Repeat *Steps 2* and *3* for the remaining perimeter walls.

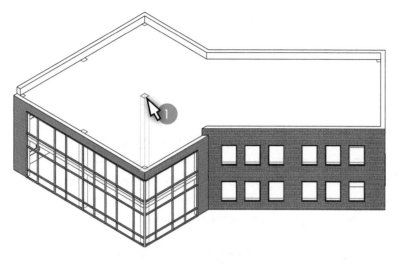

Attaching Walls and Columns to the Flat Roof

The first thing you might notice in the 3D view is that the tops of each column and interior walls are visible on the roof. Attaching columns and walls to the roof will connect them to the bottom of the roof.

- *Step 1*: In the 3D view, **CLICK ONCE** on a **VISIBLE COLUMN**.

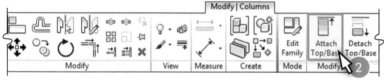

- *Step 2*: **CLICK** the **ATTACH TOP/BASE** button in the **MODIFY | COLUMNS** tab.

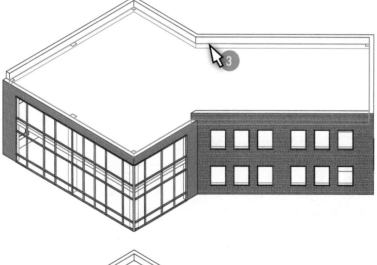

- *Step 3*: **CLICK ONCE** on the **ROOF EDGE** to identify it as the top constraint for the selected column. While the column will disappear from the view, it is still in the model.

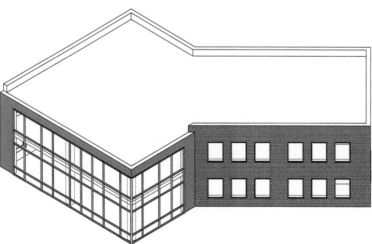

Repeat *Steps 1–3* for each column and wall visible on the roof.

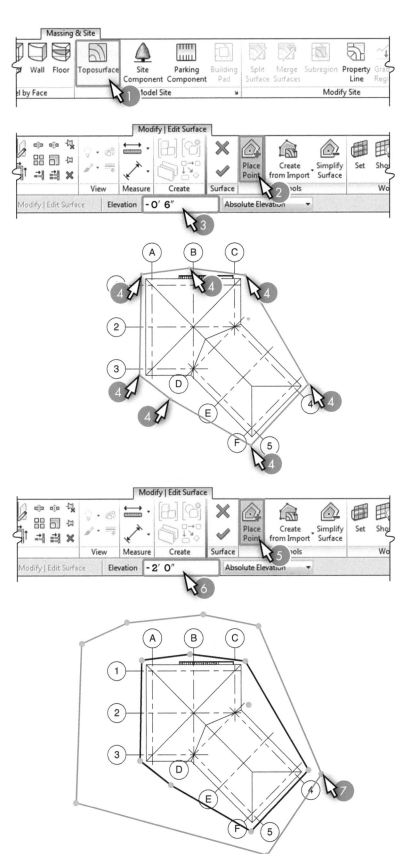

Adding Topography

Site topography is often provided by a civil engineer through a site survey. The Toposurface command allows you to approximate the site topography in the Revit model.

- *Step 1*: **OPEN** the **SITE** plan view and **CLICK** the **TOPOSURFACE** button in the **MASSING & SITE** tab.
- *Step 2*: **CLICK** the **PLACE POINT** button in the **MODIFY | EDIT SURFACE** tab.
- *Step 3*: **SET** the **ELEVATION** value to **-0′ 6″** in the **MODIFY | EDIT SURFACE** tab.

> The SI measurement for this step is **-150**.

- *Step 4*: In the site plan view, **CLICK** around the perimeter of the building as shown in the example. Each click identifies an elevation mark 6″ (or 150mm) below the slab of Level 1 in the Revit project.

- *Step 5*: **CLICK** the **PLACE POINT** button in the **MODIFY | EDIT SURFACE** tab.
- *Step 6*: **SET** the **ELEVATION** value to **-2′ 0″** in the **MODIFY | EDIT SURFACE** tab.

> The SI measurement for this step is **-600**.

- *Step 7*: In the site plan view, **CLICK** around the perimeter of the building as shown in the example. Each click identifies an elevation mark 2′-0″ (or 600mm) below the slab of Level 1 in the Revit project.

> **Guided Discovery 9.3**: Following the exercise to the left, add site topography to a Revit project. The support file is at **WWW.RAFDBOOK.COM/DOWNLOADS**.

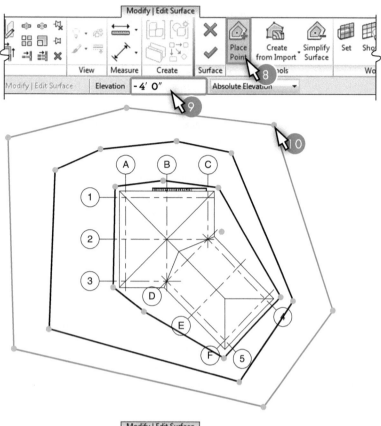

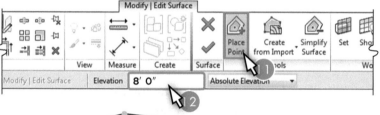

- *Step 8*: **CLICK** the **PLACE POINT** button in the **MODIFY | EDIT SURFACE** tab.
- *Step 9*: **SET** the **ELEVATION** value to **-4' 0"** in the **MODIFY | EDIT SURFACE** tab.

  The SI measurement for this step is **-1200**.

- *Step 10*: In the site plan view, **CLICK** around the perimeter of the building as shown in the example. Each click identifies an elevation mark 4'-0" (or 1200mm) below the slab of Level 1 in the Revit project.

- *Step 11*: **CLICK** the **PLACE POINT** button in the **MODIFY | EDIT SURFACE** tab.
- *Step 12*: **SET** the **ELEVATION** value to **8' 0"** in the **MODIFY | EDIT SURFACE** tab.

  The SI measurement for this step is **-2400**.

- *Step 13*: In the site plan view, **CLICK** at the perimeter of the building as shown in the example. Each click identifies an elevation mark eight feet (or 2400mm) above the slab of Level 1 in the Revit project. This last set of points will create a large hill on the east side of the building.

- *Step 14*: **CLICK** the **FINISH SURFACE** button in the **MODIFY | EDIT SURFACE** tab to complete the toposurface.

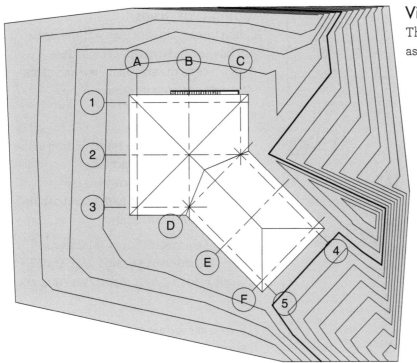

Viewing the Site Topography

The site plan level will display the toposurface as seen in this example.

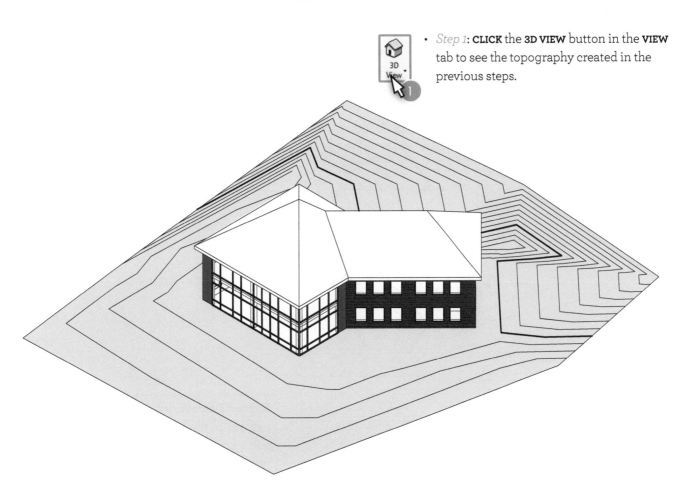

- *Step 1*: **CLICK** the **3D VIEW** button in the **VIEW** tab to see the topography created in the previous steps.

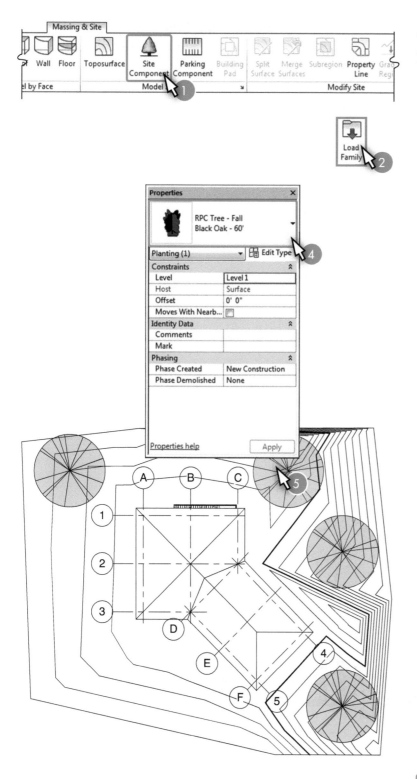

Adding Oak Trees

Adding trees to the site plan will strengthen both interior and exterior perspectives.

- *Step 1*: **OPEN** the **SITE** plan view and **CLICK** the **SITE COMPONENT** button in the **MASSING & SITE** tab.

- *Step 2*: **CLICK** the **LOAD FAMILY** button in the **MODIFY | SITE COMPONENT** tab.

- *Step 3* (*not shown*): **BROWSE** to the **US IMPERIAL>PLANTING** folder and **LOAD** the **RPC TREE - FALL.RFA** family.

  > The SI equivalent family is located in the **ENGLISH>US>PLANTING** folder. The SI equivalent family is **M_RPC TREE - FALL.RFA**

- *Step 4*: **SET** the **RPC TREE** family type to **BLACK OAK - 60'** in the **PROPERTIES** box.

  > The SI equivalent family type is **BLACK OAK - 18.0 METERS.**

- *Step 5*: In the **SITE PLAN** view, **CLICK ONCE** to **ADD** the **BLACK OAK TREES** as shown in this example.

- *Step 6* (*not shown*): **PRESS** the **ESC** key **TWICE** to end the Place Site Component command.

> **Guided Discovery 9.4**: Following the exercise to the left, add site components to a Revit project. The support file is at **WWW.RAFDBOOK.COM/DOWNLOADS.**

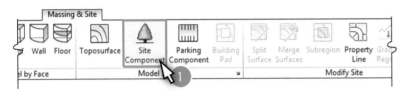

Adding Poplar Trees

Adding trees to the site plan will strengthen both interior and exterior perspectives.

- *Step 1:* **OPEN** the **SITE** plan view and **CLICK** the **SITE COMPONENT** button in the **MASSING & SITE** tab.

- *Step 2:* **SET** the **RPC TREE** family type to **LOMARDY POPLAR - 40'** in the **PROPERTIES** box.

  > The SI equivalent family type is **LOMBARDY POPLAR - 12.2 METERS.**

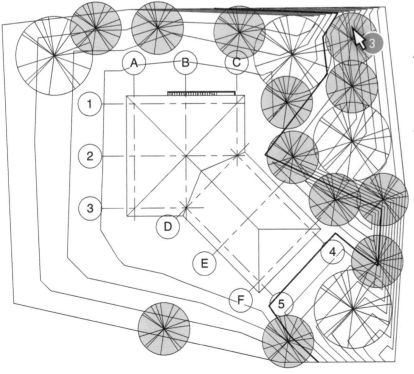

- *Step 3:* In the **SITE PLAN** view, **CLICK ONCE** to **ADD** the **POPLAR TREES** as shown in this example.

- *Step 4 (not shown):* **PRESS** the **ESC** key to end the Place Site Component command.

SITE COMPONENTS AND TREES (continued)

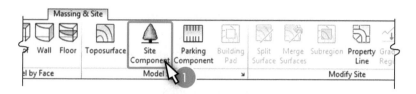

Adding Berry Trees

Adding trees to the site plan will strengthen both interior and exterior perspectives.

- *Step 1*: **OPEN** the **SITE** plan view and **CLICK** the **SITE COMPONENT** button in the **MASSING & SITE** tab.

- *Step 2*: **SET** the **RPC TREE** family type to **SERVICE BERRY - 25'** in the **PROPERTIES** box.

   The SI equivalent family type is **SERVICE BERRY - 7.6 METERS.**

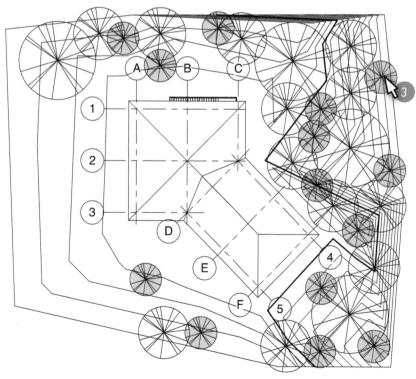

- *Step 3*: In the site plan view, **CLICK ONCE** to **ADD** the **BERRY TREES** as shown in this example.

- *Step 4 (not shown)*: **PRESS** the **ESC** key **TWICE** to end the Place Site Component command.

Viewing the Site Plan with Trees

Click the 3D View button in the View tab to see the trees created in the previous steps.

The default 3D view shows the equivalent of cardboard cutouts for each tree in the plan. As seen in this hidden line view, the hidden line tree graphics are not very impressive.

The strength of RPC (Rich Photorealistic Content) entourage is revealed with photorealistic rendering.

When rendered with Revit's Ray Trace setting, the RPC trees look like real trees.

Revit installs with several RPC libraries. Additional RPC entourage can be purchased from RPC content providers.

Checklist for Site Plans

General

- For interior-based projects, build site information that is visible only from interior perspectives.
- When possible, add RPC entourage to the site plan for realistic exterior environments.
- If you don't know the exact elevations for site contours, estimate the topography based on photographs and site visits.

Checklist for Roofs

General

- For interior-based projects, build roofs only if you anticipate including exterior elevations or exterior perspectives in the design presentation.
- Quickly create flat roofs with a floor slab and parapet walls.
- Rename the roof level to **ROOF** in the **PROJECT BROWSER**.
- Delete the roof ceiling plan view from the **PROJECT BROWSER**.

Guided Discovery Exercises

To complete the guided discovery exercises in this chapter, download support files at **WWW.RAFDBOOK.COM/DOWNLOADS**.

- Sloped Roofs - See page 166
- Flat Roofs - See page 168
- Site Topography - See page 171
- Site Components and Trees - See page 174

Application Exercises

Using an assignment from your instructor or a previously completed studio project, create renderings for the following types of drawings:

- Add a **FLAT ROOF** or a **SLOPED ROOF** to your Revit project.
- Add **SITE TOPOGRAPHY** and **SITE ENTOURAGE** to your Revit project.

chapter 10

ADVANCED MODELING

C hapter 10 introduces custom furniture families. Strong interior perspectives contain realistic representations of the furniture and equipment in a project. Creating custom furniture in Revit will allow you to accurately describe the interior environment.

IN THIS CHAPTER

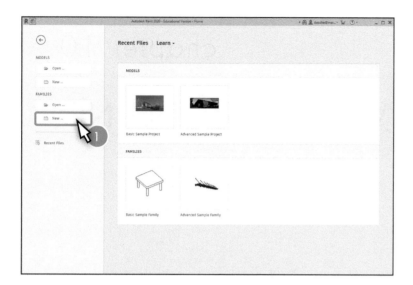

Family Templates and Categories

Families range in scope from furniture to building structure. Revit interacts with families based on their category and parameters. For example, Revit knows that door families need to be hosted by a wall in the project. Revit also knows to include furniture families in furniture schedules. Start each new family with the proper template.

- *Step 1*: **CLICK** the **NEW FAMILY** link on the Revit welcome screen.

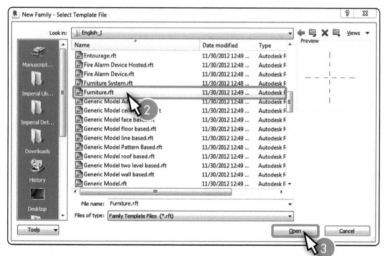

Revit prompts you to select a template file for the new family.

- *Step 2*: **CLICK ONCE** on the **FURNITURE.RFT** file.
- *Step 3*: **CLICK** the **OPEN** button to start the new family.

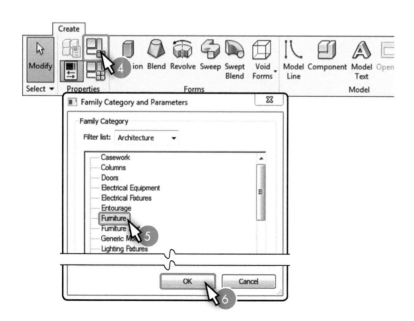

Changing Family Categories

There are times when a family category is incorrect. To verify the family category, complete the following steps:

- *Step 4*: **CLICK** the **FAMILY CATEGORY AND PARAMETERS** button.
- *Step 5*: **SELECT** the **FURNITURE** category.
- *Step 6*: **CLICK** the **OK** button to accept the category changes.

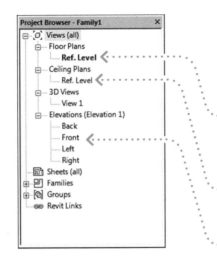

Family Project Browser

Because families usually consist of a single element or object in the building, the standard views are different from what you are used to seeing in the project editor.

- **REF. LEVEL** is the standard **FLOOR PLAN**. Objects visible on this level will show in floor plan views when the family is loaded into a Revit project.

- **REF. LEVEL** is also the standard **CEILING PLAN**. Interior light fixtures are usually attached to this reference plane.

- The standard **ELEVATION** views are **FRONT**, **BACK**, **LEFT**, and **RIGHT**.

- The **CREATE** tab is used to add content to the family.

- The **FORMS** buttons create shapes and the **DATUM** buttons create reference points in the family.

- The **INSERT** tab is used to import two-dimensional and three-dimensional CAD drawings. Imported drawings should be used for reference only and deleted once the geometry is recreated in Revit.

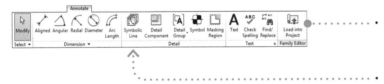

- The **ANNOTATE** tab is used to add **DIMENSIONS** and **DETAIL COMPONENTS** to the family.

- **SYMBOLIC LINES** are lines that are used in architectural drawings, but are not part of the actual geometry. A door swing (shown in plan) is an example of a symbolic line.

- The **MODIFY** tab is used to manipulate geometries in the family. It is almost identical to the Modify tab in the project editor.

- The **VIEW** tab is used to create new views in the family. It is also used to arrange windows in the family editor.

- The **MANAGE** tab is used to adjust settings and parameters for the family.

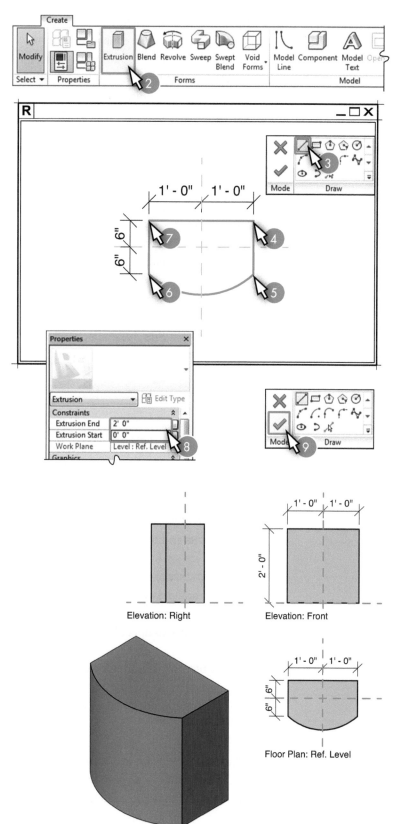

Creating Extrusion Forms

Extrusions are solid forms created with a base shape and an extrusion height. By combining multiple extrusions in a family, you will be able to build almost any furniture.

- *Step 1 (not shown)*: **OPEN** the **FLOOR PLAN: REF. LEVEL** view in the family editor.
- *Step 2*: **CLICK** the **EXTRUSION** button in the **CREATE** tab.
- *Step 3*: **CLICK** the **DRAW: LINE** button in the **MODIFY | CREATE EXTRUSION** tab.

- *Steps 4–7*: **DRAW** the profile of the extrusion using any combination of tools in the draw panel. The profile must be a closed shape.

- *Step 8*: **SET** the **EXTRUSION END** to **2′ 0″** and the **EXTRUSION START** to **0′ 0″** in the **PROPERTIES** box.
- *Step 9*: **CLICK** the **FINISH EDIT MODE** button in the **MODIFY | CREATE EXTRUSION** tab.

Elevation: Right

Elevation: Front

Viewing the Extrusion

Open multiple views in the family editor to see the extrusion. In this example, four different views illustrate the extrusion.

Floor Plan: Ref. Level

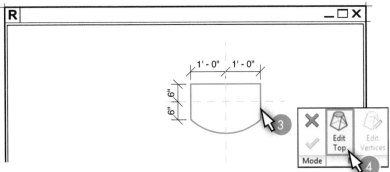

Creating Blend Forms

Blends are solid forms created with a start and end shape that differ from each other. Revit transitions between the two end shapes along the length of the blend.

- *Step 1 (not shown)*: **OPEN** the **FLOOR PLAN: REF. LEVEL** view in the family editor.
- *Step 2*: **CLICK** the **BLEND** button in the **CREATE** tab.
- *Step 3*: **DRAW** the profile of the **BASE BOUNDARY** using any combination of tools in the draw panel.
- *Step 4*: **CLICK** the **EDIT TOP** button in the **MODIFY | CREATE BLEND BASE BOUNDARY** tab.

- *Step 5*: **DRAW** the profile of the **TOP BOUNDARY** using any combination of tools in the draw panel.
- *Step 6*: **SET** the **EXTRUSION END** to **2' 0"** and the **EXTRUSION START** to **0' 0"** in the **PROPERTIES** box.
- *Step 7*: **CLICK** the **FINISH EDIT MODE** button in the **MODIFY | CREATE EXTRUSION** tab.

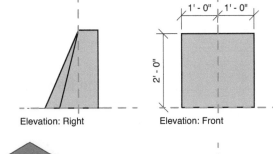

Elevation: Right   Elevation: Front

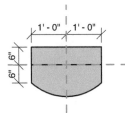

Floor Plan: Ref. Level

Viewing the Blend

Open multiple views in the family editor to see the blend. In this example, four different views illustrate the blend.

CREATING FORMS (continued)

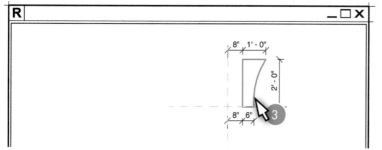

Creating Revolve Forms

Revolves are solid forms created with a profile that is rotated around an axis.

- *Step 1 (not shown):* **OPEN** the **ELEVATION: FRONT** view in the family editor.
- *Step 2:* **CLICK** the **REVOLVE** button in the **CREATE** tab.

- *Step 3:* **DRAW** the revolve **PROFILE** using any combination of tools in the draw panel.

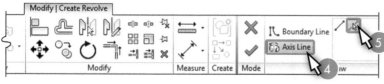

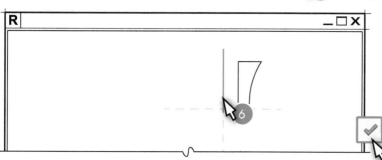

- *Step 4:* **CLICK** the **AXIS LINE** button in the **MODIFY | CREATE REVOLVE** tab.
- *Step 5:* **CLICK** the **PICK LINE** button in the draw panel of the **MODIFY | CREATE REVOLVE** tab.

- *Step 6:* **CLICK ONCE** on the **VERTICAL AXIS** of the reference plane to set it as the **REVOLVE AXIS** line.
- *Step 7:* **CLICK** the **FINISH EDIT MODE** button in the **MODIFY | CREATE EXTRUSION** tab.

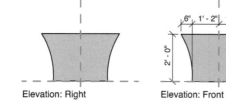

Elevation: Right   Elevation: Front

Viewing the Revolve

Open multiple views in the family editor to see the revolve. In this example, four different views illustrate the created form.

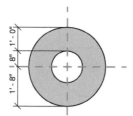

Floor Plan: Ref. Level

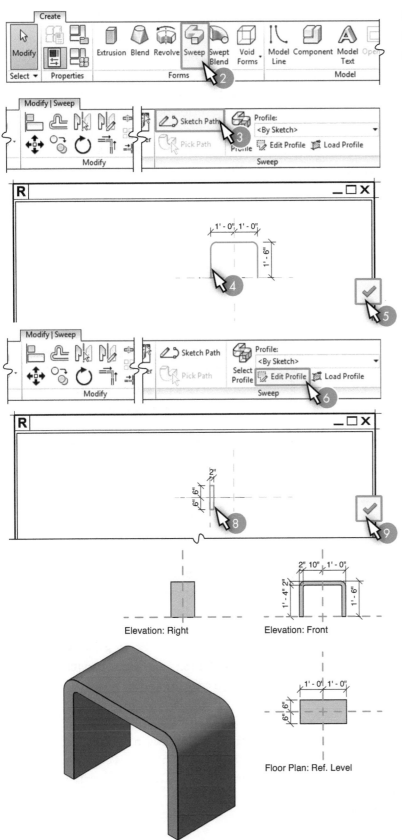

Creating Sweep Forms

Sweeps are solid forms created with a two-dimensional profile extruded along a path.

- *Step 1 (not shown)*: **OPEN** the **ELEVATION: FRONT** view in the family editor.
- *Step 2*: **CLICK** the **SWEEP** button in the **CREATE** tab.
- *Step 3*: **CLICK** the **SKETCH PATH** button in the **MODIFY | SWEEP** tab.

- *Step 4*: **DRAW** the sweep **PATH** using any combination of tools in the draw panel.
- *Step 5*: **CLICK** the **FINISH EDIT MODE** to finish the path sketch.

- *Step 6*: **CLICK** the **EDIT PROFILE** button in the **MODIFY | SWEEP** tab to draw the sweep's profile.

- *Step 7 (not shown)*: **OPEN** the **FLOOR PLAN: REF. LEVEL** view in the family editor.
- *Step 8*: **DRAW** the sweep **PROFILE** using any combination of tools in the draw panel.
- *Step 9*: **CLICK** the **FINISH EDIT MODE** to finish the profile sketch.

- *Step 10 (not shown)*: **CLICK** the **FINISH EDIT MODE** button in the **MODIFY | SWEEP** tab to create the sweep.

Viewing the Sweep

Open multiple views in the family editor to see the sweep. In this example, four different views illustrate the created form.

Elevation: Right

Elevation: Front

Floor Plan: Ref. Level

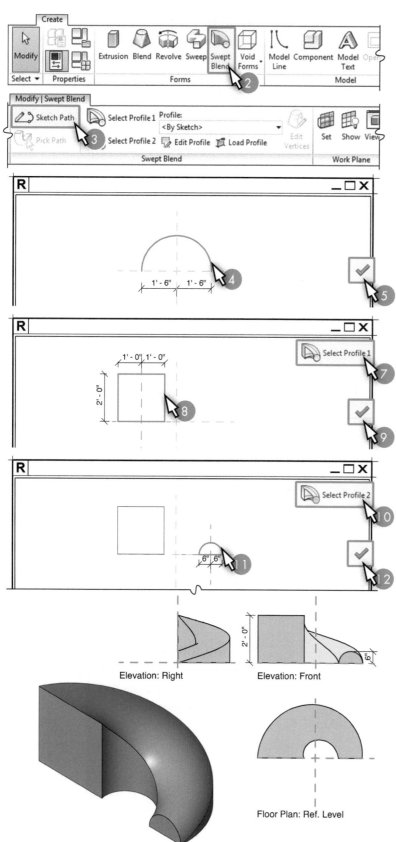

Elevation: Right

Elevation: Front

Floor Plan: Ref. Level

Creating Swept Blend Forms

Swept Blends are a combination of a sweep form and a blend form.

- *Step 1 (not shown)*: **OPEN** the **FLOOR PLAN: REF. LEVEL** view in the family editor.
- *Step 2*: **CLICK** the **SWEPT BLEND** button in the **CREATE** tab.
- *Step 3*: **CLICK** the **SKETCH PATH** button in the **MODIFY | SWEPT BLEND** tab.

- *Step 4*: **DRAW** the swept blend **PATH** using any combination of tools in the draw panel.
- *Note*: Unlike the sweep tool, the swept blend tool allows only a single line or curve segment for the swept blend path.
- *Step 5*: **CLICK** the **FINISH EDIT MODE** to finish the path sketch.

- *Step 6 (not shown)*: **OPEN** the **ELEVATION: FRONT** view.
- *Step 7*: **CLICK** the **SELECT PROFILE 1** button in the **MODIFY | SWEPT BLEND** tab to draw the first profile.
- *Step 8*: **DRAW** the swept blend **PROFILE**.
- *Step 9*: **CLICK** the **FINISH EDIT MODE** to finish the first profile sketch.

- *Step 10*: **CLICK** the **SELECT PROFILE 2** button in the **MODIFY | SWEPT BLEND** tab to draw the second profile.
- *Step 11*: **DRAW** the swept blend **PROFILE**.
- *Step 12*: **CLICK** the **FINISH EDIT MODE** to finish the second profile sketch.

- *Step 13 (not shown)*: **CLICK** the **FINISH EDIT MODE** button in the **MODIFY | SWEPT BLEND** tab to create the swept blend.

Viewing the Swept Blend

Open multiple views in the family editor to see the swept blend. In this example, four different views illustrate the created form.

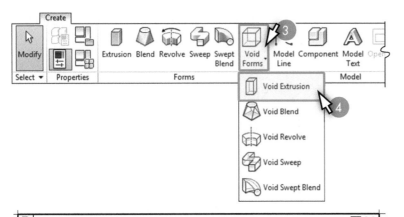

Creating Void Forms

Voids create openings in the solid forms they overlap. Void forms are created the same way as their solid form equivalent shapes.

- *Step 1 (not shown)*: **OPEN** the **FLOOR PLAN: REF. LEVEL** view in the family editor.
- *Step 2 (not shown)*: **CREATE** a **SOLID EXTRUSION** that is **2′ DEEP** by **2′ WIDE** by **2′ TALL**.

- *Step 3*: **CLICK** the **VOID FORMS** button in the **CREATE** tab.
- *Step 4*: **CLICK** the **VOID EXTRUSION** button in the **VOID FORMS** Drop-down menu.

- *Step 5*: **DRAW** a **CIRCLE** similar to this example using the tools in the draw panel.

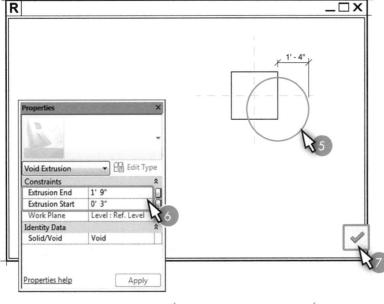

- *Step 6*: **SET** the void's **EXTRUSION END** to **1′ 9″** and the void's **EXTRUSION START** to **0′ 3″** in the **PROPERTIES** box.

- *Step 7*: **CLICK** the **FINISH EDIT MODE** button in the **MODIFY | CREATE EXTRUSION** tab.

Viewing the Sweep

Open multiple views in the family editor to see the sweep. In this example, four different views illustrate the created form. As you can see in these images, combining simple shapes (extrusions with void extrusions) can create complex forms.

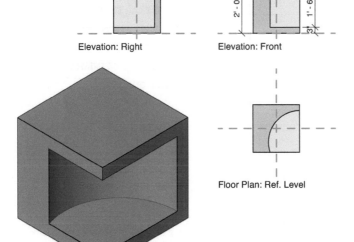

Elevation: Right   Elevation: Front

Floor Plan: Ref. Level

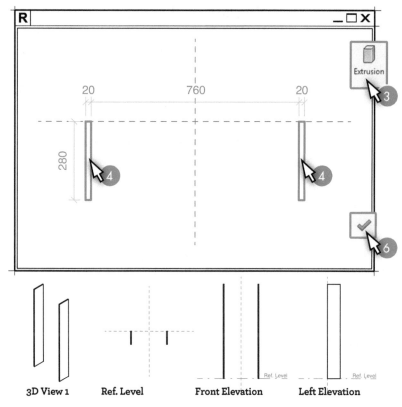

3D View 1   **Ref. Level**   **Front Elevation**   **Left Elevation**

In this step-by-step example we will create a bookshelf furniture family.

Creating the Bookshelf's Left and Right Edge

- *Step 1 (not shown)*: **CREATE** a **NEW FAMILY** with the metric furniture family template.
- *Step 2 (not shown)*: **OPEN** the **REF. LEVEL** plan view.
- *Step 3*: **CLICK** the **EXTRUSION** button.
- *Step 4*: **SKETCH** the left and right edge 20mm x 280mm panels using the dimensions in this example.
- *Step 5*: **SET** the **EXTRUSION END** to **2020mm** and the **EXTRUSION START** to **0mm** in the **PROPERTIES** box.
- *Step 6*: **CLICK** the **FINISH EDIT MODE** to finish the path sketch.

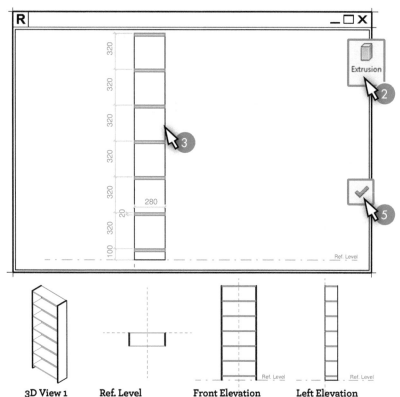

3D View 1   **Ref. Level**   **Front Elevation**   **Left Elevation**

Creating the Bookshelf's Shelves

- *Step 1 (not shown)*: **OPEN** the **LEFT** elevation view.
- *Step 2*: **CLICK** the **EXTRUSION** button.
- *Step 3*: **SKETCH** six 280mm x 20mm shelves using the dimensions in this example.
- *Step 4*: **SET** the **EXTRUSION END** to **380mm** and the **EXTRUSION START** to **-380mm** in the **PROPERTIES** box.
- *Step 5*: **CLICK** the **FINISH EDIT MODE** to finish the path sketch.

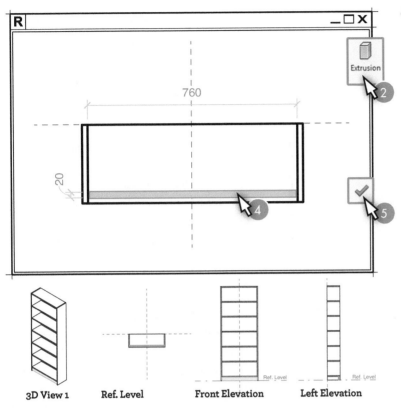

3D View 1   Ref. Level   Front Elevation   Left Elevation

Creating the Bookshelf's Kickplate

- *Step 1 (not shown)*: **OPEN** the **REF. LEVEL** plan view.
- *Step 2*: **CLICK** the **EXTRUSION** button.
- *Step 3*: **SKETCH** the 20mm x 760mm kickplate using the dimensions in this example.
- *Step 4*: **SET** the **EXTRUSION END** to **80mm** and the **EXTRUSION START** to **0mm** in the **PROPERTIES** box.
- *Step 5*: **CLICK** the **FINISH EDIT MODE** to finish the path sketch.

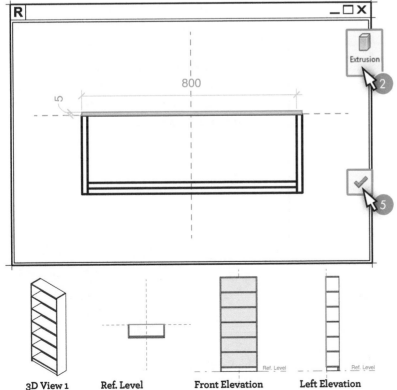

3D View 1   Ref. Level   Front Elevation   Left Elevation

Creating the Bookshelf's Back Panel

- *Step 1 (not shown)*: **OPEN** the **REF. LEVEL** plan view.
- *Step 2*: **CLICK** the **EXTRUSION** button.
- *Step 3*: **SKETCH** the 20mm x 760mm kickplate using the dimensions in this example.
- *Step 4*: **SET** the **EXTRUSION END** to **80mm** and the **EXTRUSION START** to **0mm** in the **PROPERTIES** box.
- *Step 5*: **CLICK** the **FINISH EDIT MODE** to finish the path sketch.

> **Guided Discovery 10.1**: Following the exercise to the left, create a bookshelf furniture family.

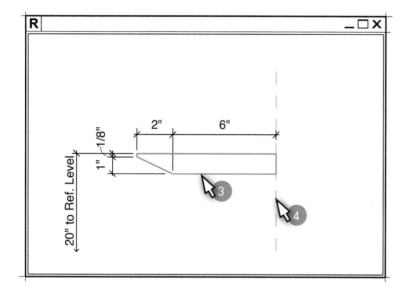

In this step-by-step example we will create a Revit Furniture family of Eero Saarinen's Pedestal Table.

Creating the Table Top

- *Step 1 (not shown)*: **CREATE** a **NEW FAMILY** with the furniture family template.
- *Step 2 (not shown)*: **OPEN** the **FRONT ELEVATION** view.
- *Step 3*: **MAKE** the **TABLE TOP** using the **REVOLVE** button and the dimensions in this example.
- *Step 4*: The **REVOLVE AXIS** is the vertical reference line.

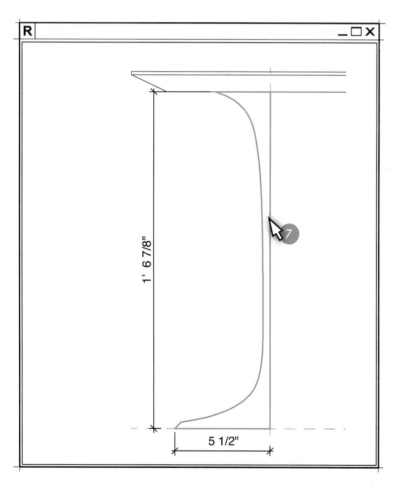

Creating the Table Base

Because the table base is an organic form, reproducing it in Revit with dimensions would be challenging. For this example, you will trace a JPEG image of the table base.

- *Step 5 (not shown)*: **DOWNLOAD** the **SAARINEN PEDESTAL TABLE PROFILE** image from **WWW.RAFDBOOK.COM/DOWNLOADS**.
- *Step 6 (not shown)*: **INSERT CH10-FRONT-PROFILE.JPG** (downloaded in the previous step) into the front elevation view.
- *Step 7*: **MAKE** the **TABLE BASE** using the **REVOLVE** button. **TRACE** over the top of the inserted **IMAGE** using the **LINE** draw tool and the **SPLINE** draw tool.

The Saarinen Pedestal Table was designed by Eero Saarinen in 1957 for Knoll.

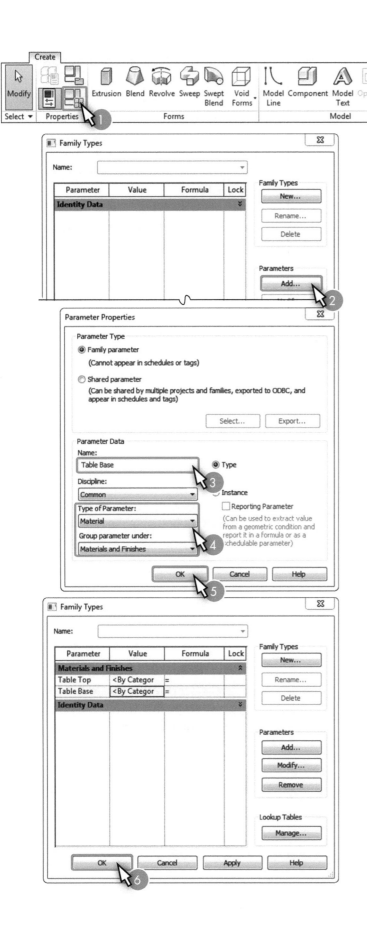

Material Parameters

Material parameters allow you to assign material variables to forms in a family. This allows materials to be updated when the family is added to a project.

- *Step 1*: **CLICK** the **FAMILY TYPES** button in the **CREATE** tab.

- *Step 2*: **CLICK** the **ADD** parameter button in the **FAMILY TYPES** dialog box.

- *Step 3*: **TYPE** a **NAME** for the material parameter. In this example, **TABLE BASE** was typed.
- *Step 4*: **SET** the **TYPE OF PARAMETER** to **MATERIAL** and the **GROUP** to **MATERIALS AND FINISHES**.
- *Step 5*: **CLICK** the **OK** button.

Repeat *Steps 2-5* to create a second material parameter named Table Top.

Both material parameters should be visible in the Materials and Finishes section of the Family Types dialog box.

- *Step 6*: **CLICK** the **OK** button to add the material parameters to the family.

Guided Discovery 10.2: Following the exercise to the left, create a furniture family. The support file is at **WWW.RAFDBOOK.COM/DOWNLOADS**.

MATERIAL PARAMETERS (continued)

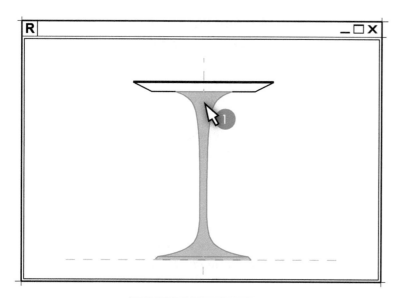

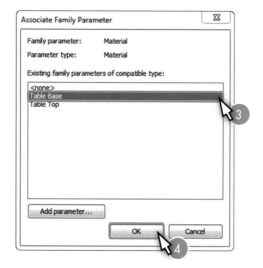

Assigning Material Parameters

Once you have added material parameters to a family, you can assign them to built forms in the family. In this example, two material properties were defined: Table Top and Table Base. In the following steps, the Table Base parameter will be assigned to the bottom Revolve Form.

- *Step 1*: **CLICK ONCE** on the **REVOLVE FORM** that represents the table base.

- *Step 2*: **CLICK** the **ASSOCIATE MATERIAL PARAMETER** button in the **PROPERTIES** box.

- *Step 3*: **SELECT** the **TABLE BASE** parameter in the **ASSOCIATE FAMILY PARAMETER** dialog box.

- *Step 4*: **CLICK** the **OK** button to save the changes.

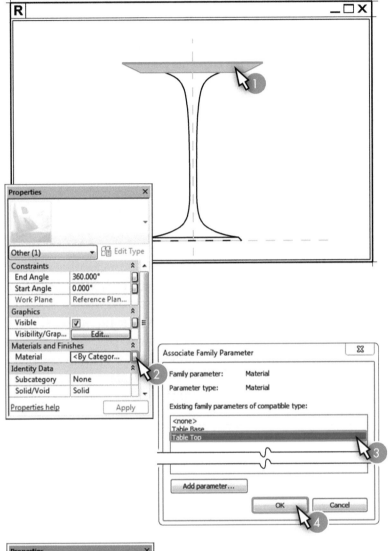

Assigning Material Parameters (continued)

In the following steps, the Table Top parameter will be assigned to the top Revolve Form.

- *Step 1*: **CLICK ONCE** on the **REVOLVE FORM** that represents the table top.

- *Step 2*: **CLICK** the **ASSOCIATE MATERIAL PARAMETER** button in the **PROPERTIES** box.

- *Step 3*: **SELECT** the **TABLE TOP** parameter in the **ASSOCIATE FAMILY PARAMETER** dialog box.

- *Step 4*: **CLICK** the **OK** button to save the changes.

Using Material Parameters in Revit Projects

Once you have assigned material parameters to the furniture family, load the family into a Revit project.

- *Step 1 (not shown)*: **CLICK ONCE** on the **FURNITURE FAMILY** in the Revit project.
- *Step 2*: **CLICK** the **EDIT TYPE** button in the **PROPERTIES** box.
- *Step 3*: Note the **MATERIALS AND FINISHES** section in the **TYPE PROPERTIES** dialog box. Changing the material associated with these parameters updates the material for all instances of the furniture object in the Revit project.

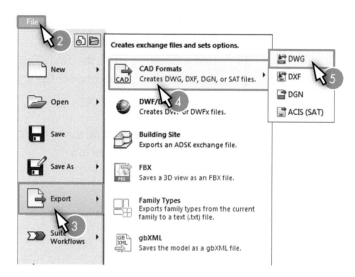

Exporting for CAD

Revit provides export functionality that translates views and sheets in a Revit project to the DWG file format.

- *Step 1 (not shown)*: **OPEN** a Revit **PROJECT** with defined views and sheets.
- *Step 2*: **CLICK** the **FILE TAB**.
- *Step 3*: **SELECT EXPORT**.
- *Step 4*: **SELECT** the **CAD FORMATS** option in the Export menu.
- *Step 5*: **CLICK** the **DWG** button to open the **DWG EXPORT** dialog box.

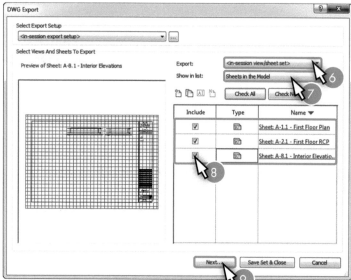

To export sheets to DWG, follow these steps:

- *Step 6*: **SELECT** the **<IN-SESSION VIEW/SHEET SET>** option in the **EXPORT** Drop-down menu.
- *Step 7*: **SELECT** the **SHEETS IN THE MODEL** option in the **SHOW IN LIST** Drop-down menu.
- *Step 8*: **CHECK** each of the **SHEETS** you want to export to the DWG file format.
- *Step 9*: **CLICK** the **NEXT** button.

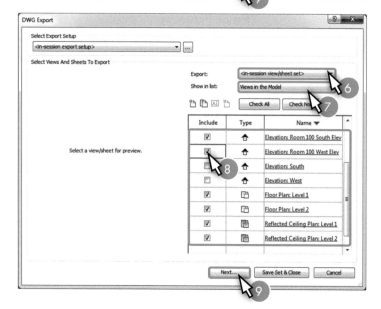

To export views to DWG complete *Steps 1–5* above and then follow these steps:

- *Step 6*: **SELECT** the **<IN-SESSION VIEW/SHEET SET>** option in the **EXPORT** Drop-down menu.
- *Step 7*: **SELECT** the **VIEWS IN THE MODEL** option in the **SHOW IN LIST** Drop-down menu.
- *Step 8*: **CHECK** each of the **VIEWS** you want to export to the DWG file format.
- *Step 9*: **CLICK** the **NEXT** button.

SHORT FILE NAMING

- A-1-1.dwg
- A-1-1.pcp
- A-1-1-View-1.dwg
- A-2-1.dwg
- A-2-1.pcp
- A-8-1.dwg
- A-8-1.pcp
- A-8-1-View-1.dwg
- A-8-1-View-2.dwg

LONG FILE NAMING EXAMPLES

- project1-Sheet - A-1-1 - First Floor Plan.dwg
- project1-Sheet - A-1-1 - First Floor Plan.pcp
- project1-Sheet - A-2-1 - First Floor RCP.dwg
- project1-Sheet - A-2-1 - First Floor RCP.pcp
- project1-Sheet - A-8-1 - Interior Elevations.dwg
- project1-Sheet - A-8-1 - Interior Elevations.pcp
- project1-Sheet-A-1-1-FirstFloorPlan-FloorPlan-Level1.dwg
- project1-Sheet-A-8-1-InteriorElevations-Elevation-Room100EastElev.dwg
- project1-Sheet-A-8-1-InteriorElevations-Elevation-Room100NorthElev.dwg

Exporting for CAD (continued)

Revit allows for long file naming and short file naming conventions.

Long file naming for sheets includes a file name prefix, the sheet number, and the sheet name. Long file naming for views includes a file name prefix, the view type, and the view name.

Short file naming includes the sheet number and sheet name or the view type and view name.

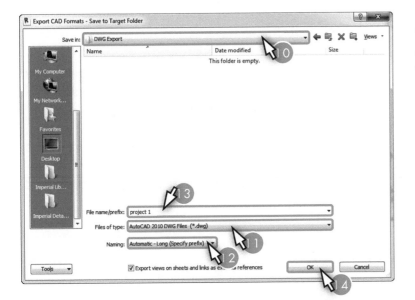

To export with long file naming, complete *Steps 1–9* on the previous page and then follow these steps:

- *Step 10*: **BROWSE** to the folder where you will save the DWG files.
- *Step 11*: **SET** the file format to **AUTOCAD 2010 DWG FILES (*.DWG)**.
- *Step 12*: **SELECT** the **AUTOMATIC - LONG** option in the **NAMING** Drop-down menu.
- *Step 13*: **TYPE** a **FILE NAME/PREFIX** that will be added to the beginning of each exported file.
- *Step 14*: **CLICK** the **OK** button to export the selected views/sheets to DWG format.

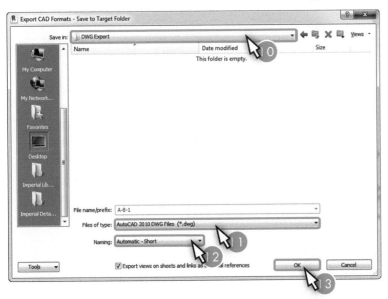

To export with short file naming, complete *Steps 1–9* on the previous page and then follow these steps:

- *Step 10*: **BROWSE** to the folder where you will save the DWG files.
- *Step 11*: **SET** the file format to **AUTOCAD 2010 DWG FILES (*.DWG)**.
- *Step 12*: **SELECT** the **AUTOMATIC - SHORT** option in the **NAMING** Drop-down menu.
- *Step 13*: **CLICK** the **OK** button to export the selected views/sheets to DWG format.

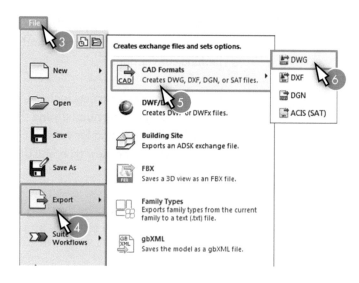

Exporting for SketchUp

Revit provides export functionality that translates views and sheets in a Revit project to the DWG file format.

- *Step 1 (not shown)*: **OPEN** a **REVIT PROJECT** with defined views and sheets.
- *Step 2 (not shown)*: **OPEN** the **3D VIEW** you want to export to **SKETCHUP**.
- *Step 3*: **CLICK** the **FILE TAB** button.
- *Step 4*: **SELECT** the **EXPORT** button.
- *Step 5*: **SELECT** the **CAD FORMATS** option in the **EXPORT** menu.
- *Step 6*: **CLICK** the **DWG** button to open the **DWG EXPORT** dialog box.

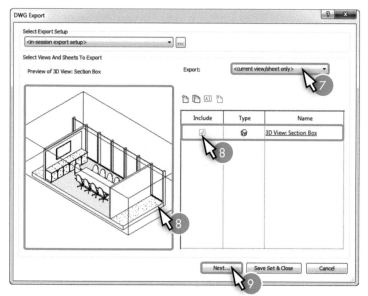

- *Step 7*: **SELECT** the **<CURRENT VIEW/SHEET ONLY>** option in the **EXPORT** Drop-down menu.
- *Step 8*: **VERIFY** the **VIEW NAME** and **PREVIEW** the 3D view you want to export. If you do not see the proper view, **CLICK** the **CANCEL** button and open the correct view from the **PROJECT BROWSER**. Start the export again with *Step 1*.

- *Step 9*: **CLICK** the **NEXT** button.

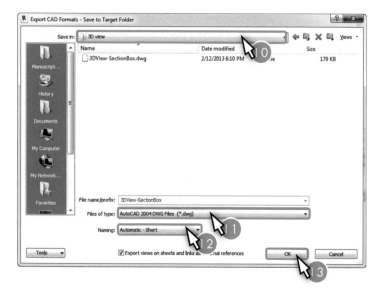

- *Step 10*: **BROWSE** to the folder where you will save the DWG files.
- *Step 11*: **SET** the file format to **AUTOCAD 2004 DWG FILES (*.DWG)**. *Note*: SketchUp cannot import DWG file formats later than 2004.
- *Step 12*: **SELECT** the **AUTOMATIC - SHORT** option in the **NAMING** Drop-down menu.
- *Step 13*: **CLICK** the **OK** button to export the selected 3D views in DWG format.

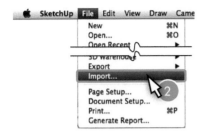

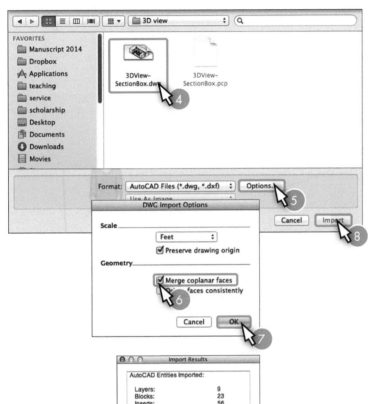

Importing 3D DWG files to SketchUp is a Pro only feature. If you do not have SketchUp Pro, you will not be able to complete these steps.

- *Step 1 (not shown)*: **OPEN** a **NEW SKETCHUP MODEL.**
- *Step 2*: From the **FILE MENU, CLICK** the **IMPORT** option.
- *Step 3 (not shown)*: **BROWSE** to the exported **DWG FILE** on your computer.
- *Step 4*: **CLICK ONCE** on the exported **DWG FILE.**
- *Step 5*: **CLICK** the **OPTIONS** button. This opens the **DWG IMPORT OPTIONS** dialog box.

- *Step 6*: **CHECK** the **MERGE COPLANAR FACES** option box.
- *Step 7*: **CLICK** the **OK** button to close the **OPTIONS** dialog box.
- *Step 8*: **CLICK** the **IMPORT** button to import the Revit model to SketchUp.

- *Step 9*: Once SketchUp has imported the file, you will see an **IMPORT RESULTS** dialog box. **CLICK** the **OK** button to close the **IMPORT RESULTS** dialog box.

- *Step 10 (not shown)*: In SketchUp, explode the imported file to modify its geometry.

Tip: Importing large Revit projects to SketchUp can take several minutes. If you receive a file import error, verify you exported from Revit in the AutoCAD 2004 DWG format.

GUIDED DISCOVERY EXERCISES

Guided Discovery Exercises

To complete the guided discovery exercises in this chapter, download support files at **WWW.RAFDBOOK.COM/DOWNLOADS.**

Follow the step-by-step exercises in the chapter to create a custom **FURNITURE FAMILY:**

- Create a furniture family of the pedestal table designed by Eero Saarinen.
- Add material parameters to the family.
- Insert the family into a Revit project.

Application Exercises

Using an assignment from your instructor or a previously completed studio project do the following:

- Model a furniture family (from a manufacturer) in a Revit furniture family.
- Design and model a custom piece of furniture in a Revit furniture family.

CONSTRUCTION
DOCUMENTS

chapter 11

CONSTRUCTION PLANS AND DETAILS

The previous sections focused on creating drawings for design presentations with a client. Now that you have mastered presentation drawings, it is time to explore advanced skills needed to create drawings for project construction.

The construction plan communicates both the design scope and methods of construction for a contractor. These drawings are the instructions to assemble an interior space or a building. Effective construction plans are often accompanied with schedules that quantify the doors, windows, furniture, and finishes in a project.

Construction details are enlarged drawings that show methods of construction. While Revit won't detail for you, it provides an excellent starting point by generating enlarged views using geometry from the model. Combine the enlarged views with Revit's comprehensive set of detail components and you have a great start to a strong set of details.

IN THIS CHAPTER

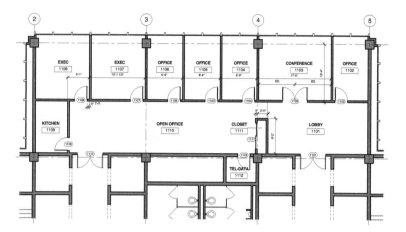

The construction plan is a unique floor plan view that includes room tags, door tags, wall type tags, and construction dimensions. In AutoCAD you might create a construction plan using specific layers and viewports. In Revit, you will create a duplicate plan view and hide the categories of information not present in a construction plan.

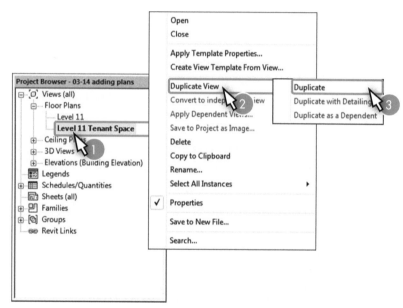

Creating a Construction Plan View

Once you've added walls, doors, and furniture to the Revit project, it is time to create a unique view for the construction plan.

- *Step 1*: **RIGHT-CLICK** on the existing **LEVEL 11 TENANT SPACE** view in the **PROJECT BROWSER**.
- *Step 2*: **SELECT DUPLICATE VIEW** from the context menu.
- *Step 3*: **CLICK** on **DUPLICATE** in the secondary context menu.

This action duplicates the existing plan view as **LEVEL 11 TENANT SPACE COPY 1**.

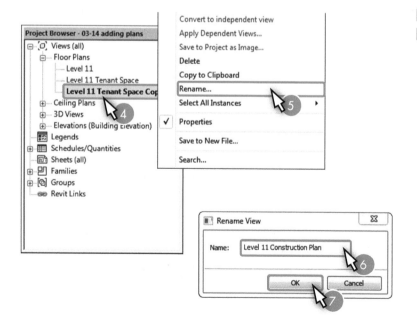

Renaming the Construction Plan View

- *Step 4*: **RIGHT-CLICK** on the new **LEVEL 11 TENANT SPACE COPY 1** view in the **PROJECT BROWSER**.
- *Step 5*: **SELECT RENAME** from the context menu.

- *Step 6*: **RENAME** the plan view to **LEVEL 11 CONSTRUCTION PLAN**.
- *Step 7*: **CLICK** the **OK** button.

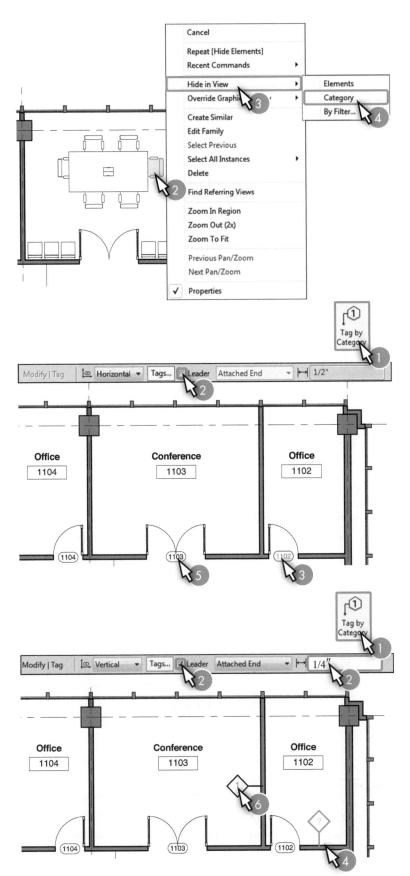

Hiding Furniture in the Construction Plan

Because the construction plan is a unique view, you can hide categories of model elements.

- *Step 1 (not shown)*: **OPEN** the **CONSTRUCTION PLAN** view.
- *Step 2*: **RIGHT-CLICK** any **FURNITURE ELEMENT** in the plan view.
- *Step 3*: **SELECT HIDE IN VIEW** from the context menu.
- *Step 4*: **CLICK** on **CATEGORY** in the secondary context menu. This action hides the furniture category in the current plan view.

Repeat these steps to hide other categories not required in a construction plan.

Adding Door Tags

- *Step 1*: **CLICK** the **TAG BY CATEGORY** button in the **ANNOTATE** tab.
- *Step 2*: **UNCHECK** the leader parameter in the Options bar.
- *Step 3*: **CLICK** on each door in the plan view to add the door tag.
- *Step 4 (not shown)*: **PRESS** the **ESC** key twice to end the Tag command.
- *Step 5*: **DOUBLE-CLICK** the **DOOR NUMBER** to renumber the door.

> **Tip**: In commercial projects, the door number should match the room number.

Adding Wall Tags

- *Step 1*: **CLICK** the **TAG BY CATEGORY** button in the **ANNOTATE** tab.
- *Step 2*: **CHECK** the leader parameter in the Options bar.
- *Step 3*: **SET** the leader length to **1/4″**.
- *Step 4*: **CLICK** on each wall in the plan view to add the wall tag.
- *Step 5 (not shown)*: **PRESS** the **ESC** key twice to end the Tag command.
- *Step 6*: **DOUBLE-CLICK** the **?** in the wall tag to change the wall type number.

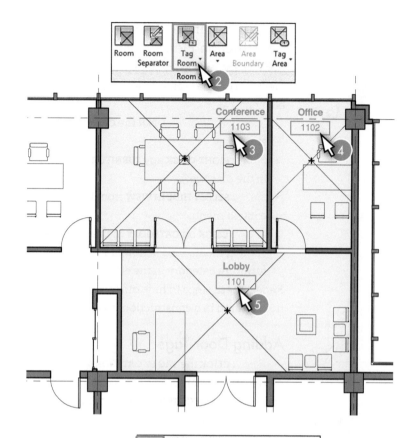

Add Room Tags to Previously Defined Rooms

If room boundaries are already defined in the Revit project, you can tag those rooms in the construction plan view.

- *Step 1 (not shown)*: **OPEN** the **CONSTRUCTION PLAN** view.
- *Step 2*: **CLICK** the **TAG ROOM** button in the **ARCHITECTURE** tab.

- *Step 3*: **CLICK** inside any room to place the room tag. Note that the tag is populated with the room name and number already defined in the project.
- *Steps 4–5*: **ADD** the **ROOM TAG** to the remaining rooms in the plan view.
- *Step 6 (not shown)*: **PRESS** the **ESC** key **TWICE** on the keyboard to end the Tag Room command.

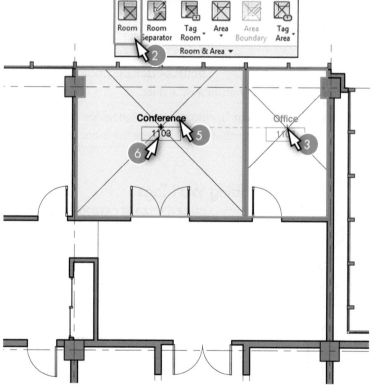

Adding Room Boundaries and Tags

If a room boundary is not defined, use the Room button to creates the room. The button also adds a room tag, which is a view-specific element.

- *Step 1 (not shown)*: **OPEN** the **CONSTRUCTION PLAN** view.
- *Step 2*: **CLICK** the **ROOM** button in the **ARCHITECTURE** tab.
- *Step 3*: **CLICK** inside any room to create both the room boundary and the room tag.

Repeat *Step 3* to add room boundaries to each space in the plan view.

- *Step 4 (not shown)*: **PRESS** the **ESC** key on the keyboard to end the Room command.
- *Step 5*: **DOUBLE-CLICK** the **ROOM NAME** portion of the room tag to name the room. In this example, the room is renamed to **CONFERENCE**.
- *Step 6*: **DOUBLE-CLICK** the **ROOM NUMBER** portion of the room tag to number the room. In this example, the room is renumbered to **1103**.

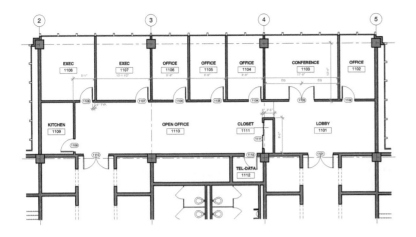

Dimensions on the construction plan are limited to elements unique to new construction. For example, you would dimension new walls and doors in plan, but would not dimension the location of existing doors in the building shell.

Dimension strings need to connect to an existing element for reference during construction. For example, a string of dimensions locating walls should also connect to an existing wall or column line.

Dimensioning Walls

In floor plans, wall dimensions are generally completed in a continuous line. A line of dimensions is referred to as a dimension string.

- *Step 1*: **CLICK** the **ALIGNED DIMENSION** button in the **ANNOTATE** tab.
- *Step 2*: In the **MODIFY | PLACE DIMENSIONS** tab, **SELECT WALL FACES**.

- *Steps 3–5*: Following the example, **CLICK** on each **WALL FACE** in the dimension string.
- *Step 6*: **CLICK ONCE** to **PLACE** the dimension string.

- *Steps 7–10*: Following the example, **CLICK** on each **WALL FACE** in the dimension string.
- *Step 11*: **CLICK ONCE** to **PLACE** the dimension string and end the Dimension command.

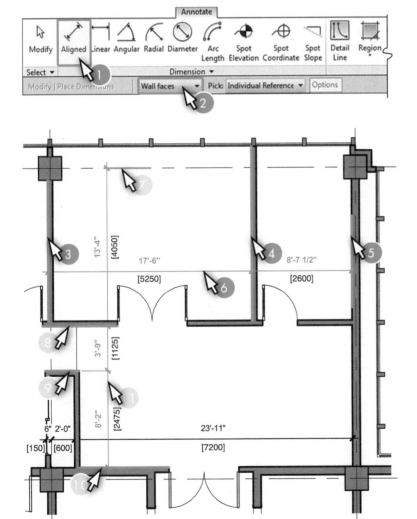

Tip: When dimensioning walls, attempt to dimension to a consistent side of all walls. In the example to the left, the horizontal dimension strings locate the left finish face of all walls. The vertical dimension strings locate the bottom finish face of all walls.

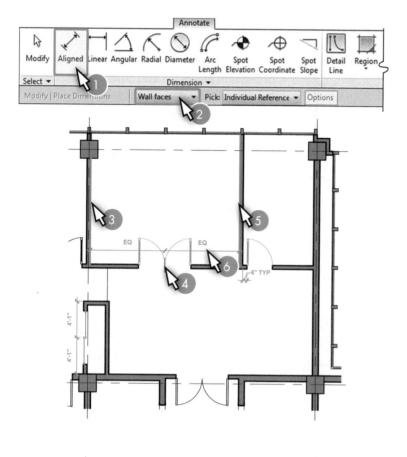

Dimensioning Doors

Doors are most commonly dimensioned to their center line or to the hinge side of the door. The width of a door opening is rarely dimensioned in floor plans because this information is located in the door schedule.

- *Step 1*: **CLICK** the **ALIGNED DIMENSION** button in the **ANNOTATE** tab.
- *Step 2*: In the **MODIFY | PLACE DIMENSIONS** tab, **SELECT WALL FACES.**

- *Steps 3-5*: Following the example, **CLICK** on the **WALL FACE** and **CENTER** of door.
- *Step 6*: **CLICK ONCE** to **PLACE** the dimension string and end the Dimension command.

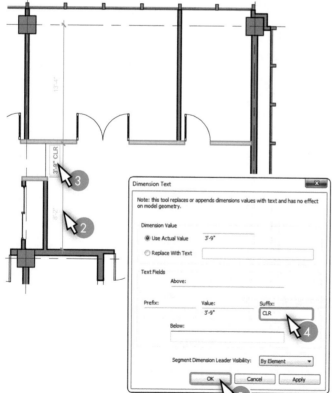

Dimensioning Corridors

Critical dimensions, such as corridor widths, are dimensioned to indicate a clear opening dimension. This helps the contractor understand dimension priorities during construction. Add the word **CLEAR** or the abbreviation **CLR** after any dimension to indicate a clear opening dimension.

Follow the instructions below to add the **CLR** designation to a dimension:
- *Step 1 (not shown)*: Add a dimension string that indicates the dimension between the corridor walls, as shown in this example.
- *Step 2*: **CLICK ONCE** on the dimension string.
- *Step 3*: **CLICK ONCE** on dimension text.
- *Step 4*: **TYPE** the **CLR** abbreviation in the suffix text field.
- *Step 5*: **CLICK** the **OK** button.

Modifying Dimension Strings

Witness Lines connect dimension strings to objects in the Revit model. In this example, we want to add the width of Office 1102 to the existing horizontal dimension string.

- *Step 1*: **CLICK ONCE** on the **DIMENSION STRING**.

- *Step 2*: **CLICK** the **EDIT WITNESS LINES** button in the **MODIFY | DIMENSIONS** tab.

- *Step 3*: **CLICK** the **WALL FACES** that you want to add to the dimension string.

- *Step 4*: **CLICK ONCE** in the drawing area to end the Edit Witness Lines command.

> **Tip**: You can also remove objects from a dimension string in Revit. Following *Steps 1–2* above, click on any wall face currently in the dimension string to remove it from the dimension.

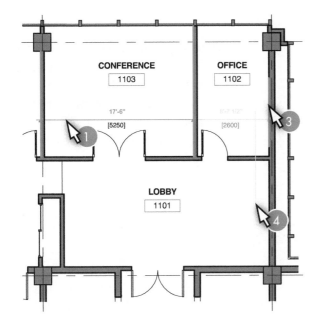

Angular Dimensions

Angular dimension strings display the angle of a wall relative to the horizontal or vertical planes. This type of dimension string is helpful in dimensioning the angle of nonorthogonal (angled) walls.

- *Step 1*: **CLICK** the **ANGULAR DIMENSION** button in the **ANNOTATE** tab.
- *Step 2*: In the **MODIFY | PLACE DIMENSIONS** tab, **SELECT WALL FACES**.

- *Steps 3–4*: Following the example, **CLICK** on the **WALL FACE** of the **ANGLED WALL** and adjacent **VERTICAL WALL**.
- *Step 5*: **CLICK ONCE** to **PLACE** the dimension string and end the Dimension command.

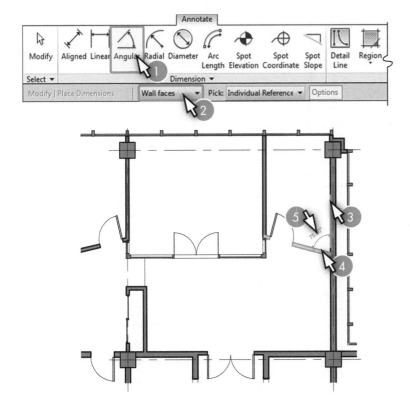

The Callout button creates an enlarged view from a plan, elevation, section, or RCP. Building components updated in the original view will automatically update in callout views.

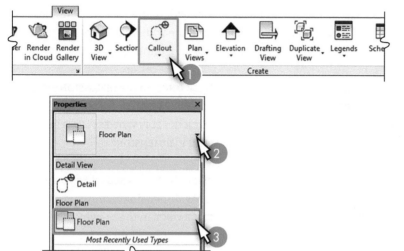

Adding Enlarged Plan Callouts

- *Step 1*: From any plan view, **CLICK** the **CALLOUT** button in the **VIEW** tab.
- *Step 2*: **CLICK** the **CALLOUT TYPE DROP-DOWN ARROW** in the **PROPERTIES** box.
- *Step 3*: **SELECT FLOOR PLAN** as the callout type.

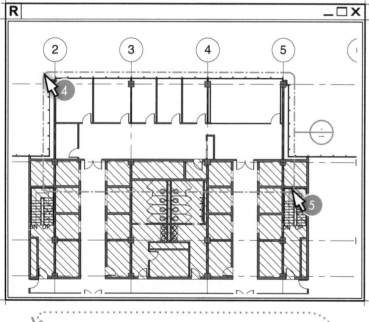

- *Step 4*: **CLICK ONCE** in the floor plan to locate the top-left corner of the callout view's scope. As you move the cursor, the callout box will stretch, indicating the scope of the enlarged view.
- *Step 5*: **CLICK ONCE** on the floor plan to locate the bottom-right corner of the callout view's scope.

Adjusting the Callout Symbol

To adjust the callout symbol, click once on the callout box in the plan view.

- **DRAG** the **ROTATE HANDLE** to rotate the callout.
- **DRAG** the **HEAD HANDLE** to move the callout symbol.
- **DRAG** the **ELBOW HANDLE** to add an elbow to the callout symbol's leader line.
- **DRAG** the **CROP MODEL HANDLE** to adjust the width and height of the callout.

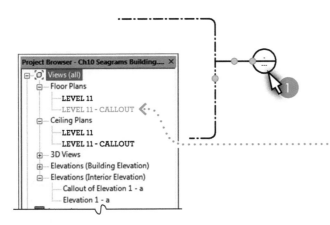

Viewing the Enlarged Plan

- *Step 1*: **RIGHT-CLICK** on the **CALLOUT SYMBOL** and **SELECT GO TO VIEW** from the context menu.

- The enlarged plan view is automatically added to the Floor Plans section of the **PROJECT BROWSER**. In this example, **LEVEL 11 - CALLOUT** is the enlarged view of **LEVEL 11**.

Adjusting the Enlarged Plan's Scope

- *Step 1*: **CLICK** the **SHOW/HIDE CROP REGION** button in the status bar until the **CROP REGION** box is visible in the callout view. When the **CROP REGION** box is visible, you will see a black border around the callout view.

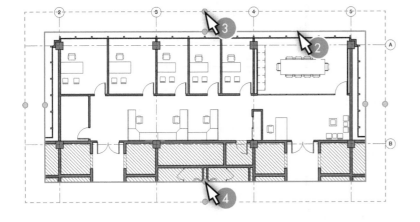

- *Step 2*: **CLICK ONCE** the **CROP REGION BOX** in the callout view.
- *Step 3*: **DRAG** the **ANNOTATION CROP HANDLES** to adjust the width and height of the annotation extents in the callout view.
- *Step 4*: **DRAG** the **CROP MODEL HANDLES** to adjust the width and height of the callout. Changes made to the model crop will adjust the size of the callout rectangle in the original plan view.

Advanced Crop Region Adjustments

- *Step 1 (not shown)*: **CLICK ONCE** the **CROP REGION BOX** in the callout view.

- **CLICK** the **SIZE CROP** button in the **MODIFY | VIEWS** tab to specify the width and height of a crop region when placed on a sheet.
- **CLICK** the **EDIT CROP** button in the **MODIFY | VIEWS** tab to sketch a non-rectangular crop region.

The Callout button can also create detail views from a plan, elevation, section, or RCP. Building components updated in the original view will automatically update in the detail view.

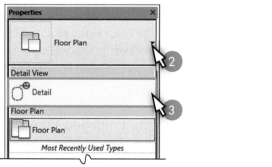

Adding Plan Detail Callouts

- *Step 1*: From any plan view, **CLICK** the **CALLOUT** button in the **VIEW** tab.
- *Step 2*: **CLICK** the **CALLOUT TYPE DROP-DOWN ARROW** in the **PROPERTIES** box.
- *Step 3*: **SELECT DETAIL** as the callout type in the **PROPERTIES** box Drop-down menu.

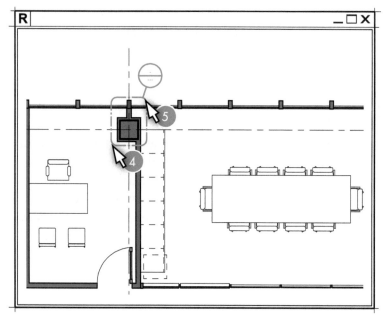

- *Step 4*: **CLICK ONCE** in the floor plan to locate the bottom-left corner of the callout view's scope. As you move the cursor, the callout box will stretch, indicating the scope of the enlarged view.
- *Step 5*: **CLICK ONCE** in the floor plan to locate the top-right corner of the callout view's scope.

Adjusting the Plan Detail Symbol

- *Step 1 (not shown)*: **CLICK ONCE** the **PLAN DETAIL BOX** in the plan view.
- **DRAG** the **ROTATE HANDLE** to rotate the callout.
- **DRAG** the **HEAD HANDLE** to move the callout symbol.
- **DRAG** the **ELBOW HANDLE** to add an elbow to the callout symbol's leader line.
- **DRAG** the **CLIP PLAN HANDLE** to adjust the width and height of the callout.

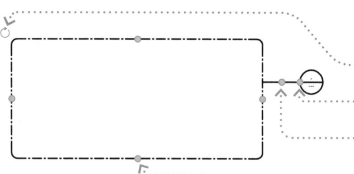

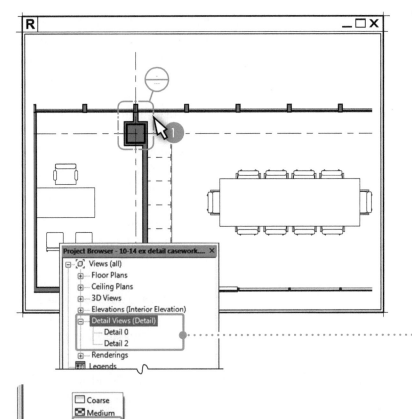

Viewing the Plan Detail

- *Step 1*: **RIGHT-CLICK** on the **DETAIL SYMBOL** in the plan and **SELECT GO TO VIEW** from the context menu.

- The **PLAN DETAIL** view is also available in the **DETAIL VIEWS** section of the **PROJECT BROWSER**.

- *Step 2*: **SET** the **ARCHITECTURAL SCALE** of the detail view to **1-1/2″ = 1′-0″**.

  The equivalent SI scale is **1:10**.

- *Step 3*: **SET** the **DETAIL LEVEL** to **FINE**.

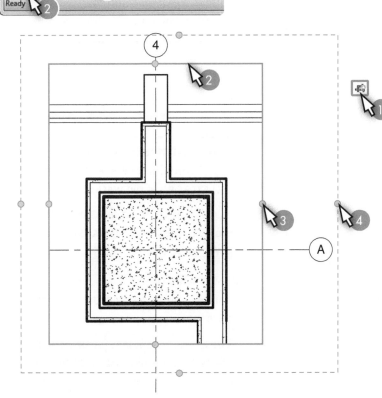

Adjusting the Plan Detail's Scope

- *Step 1*: **CLICK** the **SHOW/HIDE CROP REGION** button in the status bar until the **CROP REGION** box is visible in the detail view.

- *Step 2*: **CLICK ONCE** on the **CROP REGION BOX** in the detail view.

- *Step 3*: **DRAG** the **MODEL CROP HANDLES** to adjust the width and height of the detail. Changes made to the model crop will adjust the size of the plan detail symbol in the original plan view.

- *Step 4*: **DRAG** the **ANNOTATION CROP HANDLES** to adjust the width and height of the annotation extents in the detail.

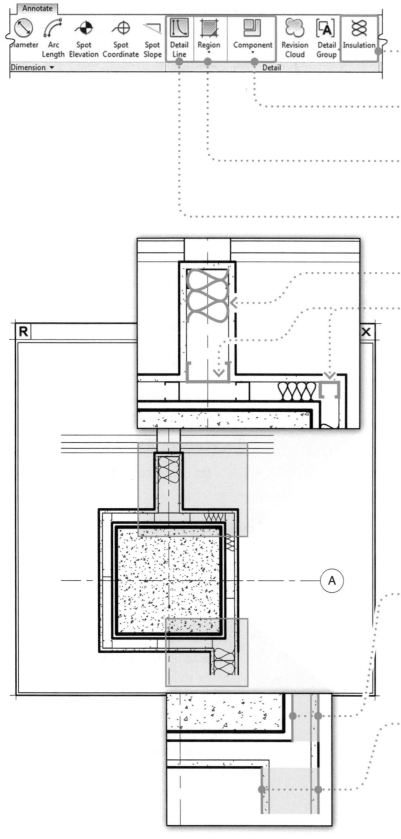

Adding Hatches, Detail Lines, and Detail Components to Plan Details

- **USE** the **INSULATION** button in the **ANNOTATE** tab to draw acoustic and thermal insulation in the detail.
- **USE** the **COMPONENT** button to add detail elements like metal studs and wood framing in the detail.
- **USE** the **REGION** button to add material hatches in the detail. Limit hatching to materials sliced in the drawing.
- **USE** the **DETAIL LINE** button to draw additional lines in the detail.

- The **INSULATION** button is used to add an **ACOUSTIC INSULATION** to walls in the detail.
- The **COMPONENT** button is used to add **1-5/8"** and **3-5/8" INTERIOR METAL STUDS** to the plan detail.

> The SI equivalent metal stud family types are **41MM** and **92MM** respectively.

> **Companion Download 11.1:**
> Download a PDF of commonly used detail components referenced in this exercise at **WWW.RAFDBOOK.COM/DOWNLOADS.**

Two unique walls were used in the plan for this detail.

- A **2-1/4" PARTITION** is created for the column wrap. It contains a **1-5/8" METAL STUD** with **ONE LAYER OF 5/8" DRYWALL** on the interior.

> The SI equivalent **57.5mm PARTITION** is created, with a **42mm METAL STUD** and **ONE LAYER OF 15.5mm DRYWALL** on the interior.

- A **4-7/8" PARTITION** is created, which contains a **3-5/8" METAL STUD** with **ONE LAYER OF 5/8" DRYWALL** on both sides.

> The SI equivalent **123mm PARTITION** is created, with a **92mm METAL STUD** and **ONE LAYER OF 15.5mm DRYWALL** on both sides.

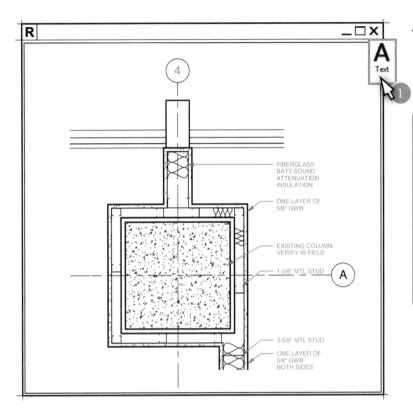

Annotating Plan Details

- *Step 1*: **USE** the **TEXT** button in the **ANNOTATION** tab to add annotation notes to the detail.

> ### Plan Detail Annotation Tips:
> - Limit the annotation text in plan details to information that is not available in other views.
> - Annotate special materials like acoustic insulation.
> - Annotate the location and thickness of gypsum wall board (GWB).
> - Annotate existing structural elements.
> - Annotate metal or wood studs.

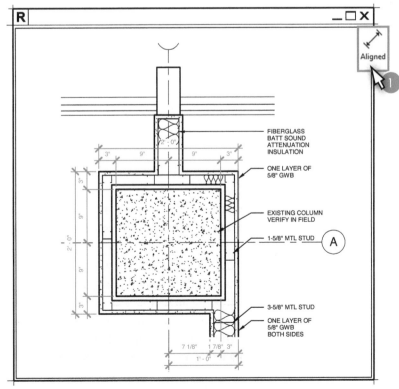

Dimensioning Plan Details

- *Step 1*: **USE** the **ALIGNED DIMENSION** button in the **ANNOTATION** tab to add dimensions to the detail.

> Download an SI example of this detail at:
> **WWW.RAFDBOOK.COM/DOWNLOADS.**

> ### Plan Detail Dimensioning Tips:
> - Dimension the overall width and height of the plan detail.
> - Add a horizontal and vertical dimension string that locates the thickness of walls. When possible, connect this dimension string to the closest column line.

CASEWORK DETAILS

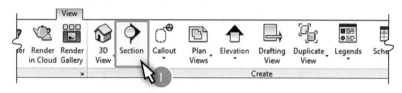

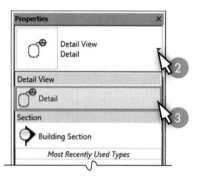

The Section button creates detail sections from a plan, elevation, or RCP view. Building components updated in the original view will automatically update in detail views.

Adding Casework Details

- *Step 1*: From an elevation view, **CLICK** the **SECTION** button in the **VIEW** tab.
- *Step 2*: In the **PROPERTIES** box, **CLICK** the **SECTION TYPE DROP-DOWN ARROW.**
- *Step 3*: **SELECT DETAIL** as the section type.

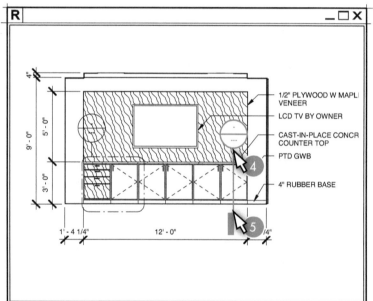

- *Step 4*: **CLICK ONCE** in the elevation to locate the top of the casework section. As you move the cursor, the detail section symbol will stretch, indicating the scope of the detail.
- *Step 5*: **CLICK ONCE** to locate the bottom of the casework section.

Adjusting the Section Detail Symbol

- *Step 1 (not shown)*: **CLICK ONCE** on a **DETAIL SYMBOL** to adjust its visual properties.
- **CLICK** the **FLIP SECTION** symbol to flip to the direction of the detail view.
- **CLICK** the **CYCLE SECTION TAIL** symbol to change the graphics for each section tail.
- **CLICK** the **GAPS IN SEGMENTS** symbol to remove the portion of the section line that overlaps the casework plan.
- **DRAG** the **ARROWS** to adjust the width and depth of the building section.

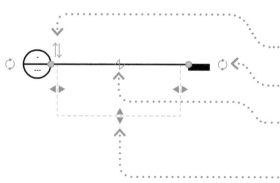

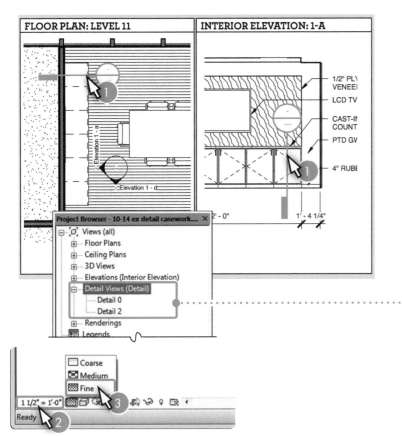

Viewing the Casework Detail

When you add a detail symbol in an elevation, Revit also adds a detail symbol to the corresponding plan view.

- *Step 1*: **RIGHT-CLICK** on the **DETAIL SYMBOL** in a plan or elevation view and **SELECT GO TO VIEW** from the context menu.

- The **CASEWORK DETAIL** view is also available in the **DETAIL VIEWS** section of the **PROJECT BROWSER**.

- *Step 2*: **SET** the **ARCHITECTURAL SCALE** of the detail view to **1-1/2″ = 1′-0″**.

  The equivalent SI scale is **1:10**.

- *Step 3*: **SET** the **DETAIL LEVEL** to **FINE**.

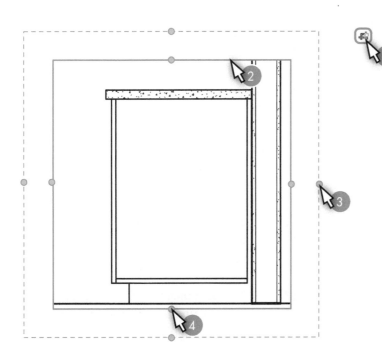

Adjusting the Detail's Scope

- *Step 1*: **CLICK** the **SHOW/HIDE CROP REGION** button in the status bar until the **CROP REGION** box is visible in the detail view.

- *Step 2*: **CLICK ONCE** on the **CROP REGION** box in the detail view.

- *Step 3*: **DRAG** the **ANNOTATION CROP HANDLES** to adjust the width and height of the annotation extents in the detail.

- *Step 4*: **DRAG** the **MODEL CROP HANDLES** to adjust the width and height of the detail. Changes made to the model crop will adjust the size of the detail symbol in the original elevation and plan view.

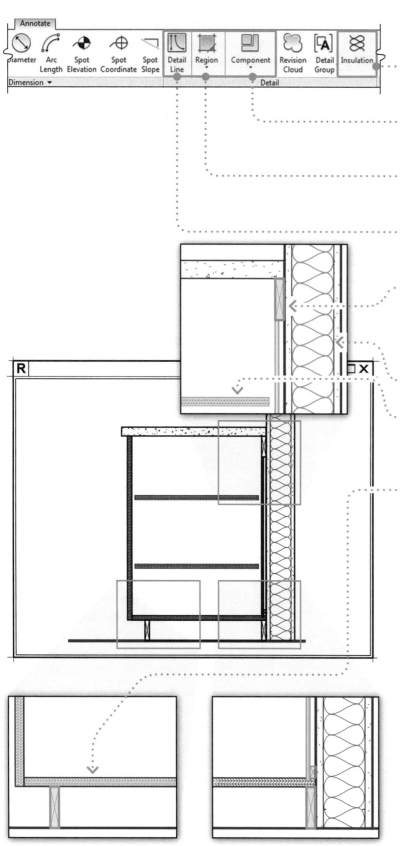

Adding Hatches, Detail Lines, and Detail Components to Casework Details

- **USE** the **INSULATION** button in the **ANNOTATE** tab to draw acoustic and thermal insulation in the detail.
- **USE** the **COMPONENT** button to add detail elements, such as metal studs and wood framing, in the detail.
- **USE** the **REGION** button to add material hatches in the detail. Limit hatching to materials sliced in the drawing.
- **USE** the **DETAIL LINE** button to draw additional lines in the detail.

- The **COMPONENT** button is used to add a **NOMINAL 1″ X 4″** to the casework detail.

  The SI equivalent nominal cut lumber family type is **25 X 100MM NOMINAL**.

- The **INSULATION** button is used to add an **ACOUSTIC INSULATION** to walls in the detail.
- The **COMPONENT** and **REGION** buttons are used to add adjustable shelves to the casework detail.
- The **REGION** button is used to hatch the plywood in the detail.

Note the direction of the plywood hatch in the enlarged view. The sample Revit project for this chapter includes the Plywood - Aligned hatch pattern, which aligns with the orientation of the plywood in the detail. To rotate the plywood hatch pattern, add a hatch region to the detail and then rotate the completed hatch region. Each horizontal line represents 1/4″ (or 6mm) of thickness. The diagonal lines are symbolic of the alternating wood strands.

- **DETAIL LINES** were used to draw the back interior panel in the cabinet.
- **DETAIL LINES** were used to draw the 1″ x 1/2″ (or 25mm x 12.5mm) wood blocking.
- The **COMPONENT** button was used to add a **NOMINAL 1″ X 4″** for the base of the casework detail.

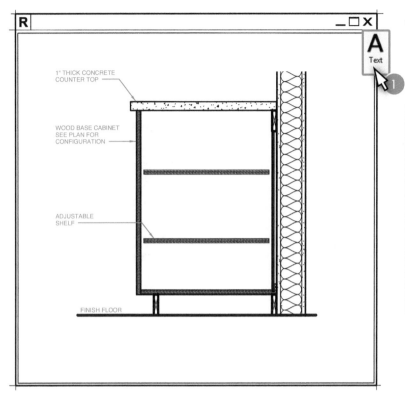

Annotating Casework Details

- *Step 1*: **USE** the **TEXT** button in the **ANNOTATION** tab to add annotation notes to the detail.

Casework Detail Annotation Tips:
- Limit the annotation text in casework details to information that is not available in other views.
- Annotate the countertop material and thickness.
- Annotate special hardware such as locks.
- Adjustable shelves should be noted in the detail.
- Annotate the finish floor.

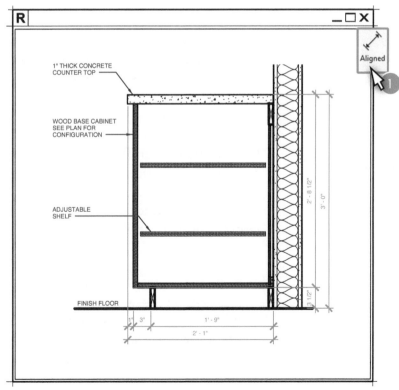

Dimensioning Casework Details

- *Step 1*: **USE** the **ALIGNED DIMENSION** button in the **ANNOTATION** tab to add dimensions to the detail.

Download an SI example of this detail at: **WWW.RAFDBOOK.COM/DOWNLOADS.**

Casework Detail Dimensioning Tips:
- Dimension the overall height of the cabinet including the countertop.
- Dimension the overall depth of the cabinet and countertop.
- Dimension the depth and height of the toe kick.

Companion Download 11.2:
Download a PDF of commonly used detail components referenced in this exercise at **WWW.RAFDBOOK.COM/DOWNLOADS.**

PROJECT PHASING

Project phasing in Revit allows you to identify when elements like doors and walls are added to or removed from the project. Common phases include Existing, Demolished, and New.

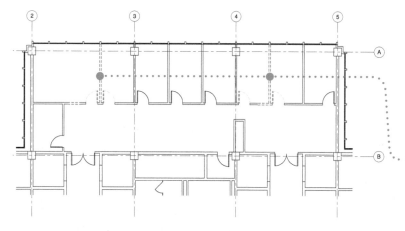

Existing Conditions Plan

The existing conditions floor plan describes the interior conditions prior to construction. See page 219 for instructions on phase filtering an existing conditions plan view.

- Walls and doors have the **PHASE CREATED** parameter set to **EXISTING**.

Demolition Plan

The demolition plan indicates interior elements demolished during construction. See page 220 for instructions on phase filtering a demolition plan view.

- Walls and doors to be demolished have the **PHASE CREATED** parameter set to **EXISTING**.
- Walls and doors to be demolished have the **PHASE DEMOLISHED** set to **NEW CONSTRUCTION**.

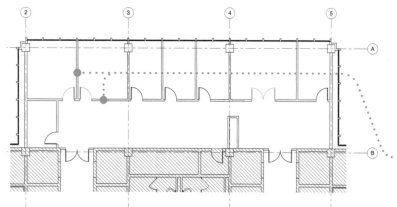

New Construction Plan

The new construction plan indicates elements added to the space during construction. See page 221 for instructions on phase filtering a new construction plan view.

- Walls and doors have the **PHASE CREATED** parameter set to **NEW CONSTRUCTION**.
- Walls and doors have the **PHASE DEMOLISHED** set to **NONE**.

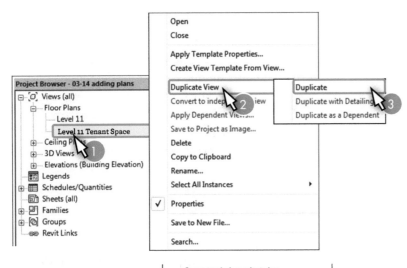

Creating an Existing Conditions Plan View

Once you've added existing walls and doors to the Revit project, it is time to create a unique view for the existing conditions plan.

- *Step 1*: **RIGHT-CLICK** on the existing **LEVEL 11 TENANT SPACE** view in the **PROJECT BROWSER**.
- *Step 2*: **SELECT DUPLICATE VIEW** from the context menu.
- *Step 3*: **CLICK** on **DUPLICATE** in the secondary context menu.

Renaming the Existing Conditions Plan View

- *Step 4*: **RIGHT-CLICK** on the new **LEVEL 11 TENANT SPACE COPY 1** view in the **PROJECT BROWSER**.
- *Step 5*: **SELECT RENAME** from the context menu.

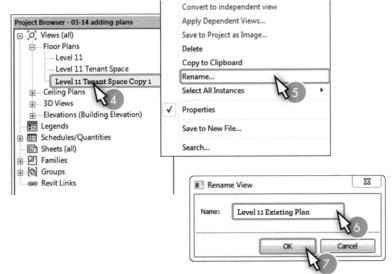

- *Step 6*: **RENAME** the plan view to **LEVEL 11 EXISTING PLAN**.
- *Step 7*: **CLICK** the **OK** button.

Phasing the Existing Conditions Plan View

The phase filters in the plan's Properties palette control the visibility to model elements in the view.

- *Step 1*: **CHANGE** the **PHASE CREATED** for existing walls and doors to **EXISTING**.
- *Step 2*: **CHANGE** the view's **PHASE FILTER** to **SHOW COMPLETE**.
- *Step 3*: **CHANGE** the view's **PHASE** to **EXISTING**.

Applying these filters will hide all model elements, like doors and walls, that are phased as demolished or new construction.

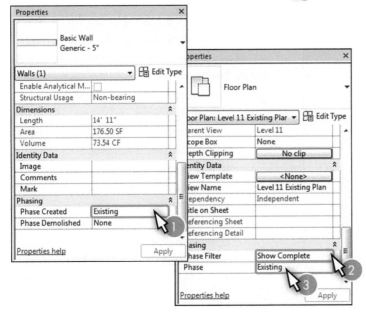

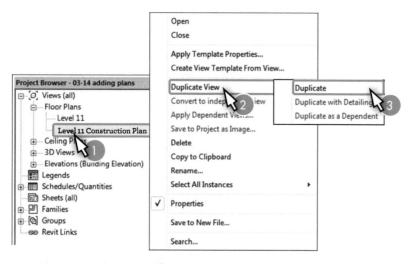

Creating a Demolition Plan View

Once you've added existing walls, doors, and furniture to the Revit project, it is time to create a unique view for the demolition plan.

- *Step 1*: **RIGHT-CLICK** on the existing **LEVEL 11 CONSTRUCTION** view in the **PROJECT BROWSER**.
- *Step 2*: **SELECT DUPLICATE VIEW** from the context menu.
- *Step 3*: **CLICK** on **DUPLICATE** in the secondary context menu.

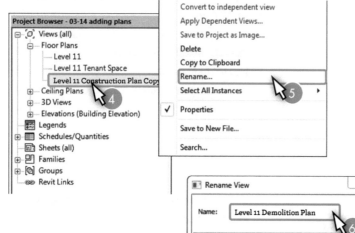

Renaming the Demolition Plan View

- *Step 4*: **RIGHT-CLICK** on the new **LEVEL 11 TENANT SPACE COPY 1** view in the **PROJECT BROWSER**.
- *Step 5*: **SELECT RENAME** from the context menu.
- *Step 6*: **RENAME** the plan view to **LEVEL 11 CONSTRUCTION PLAN**.
- *Step 7*: **CLICK** the **OK** button.

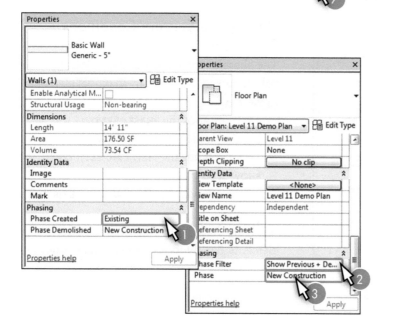

Phasing the Demolition Plan View

The phase filters in the plan's Properties palette control the visibility to model elements in the view.

- *Step 1*: **CHANGE** the **PHASE CREATED** for demolished walls and doors to **EXISTING**.
- *Step 2*: **CHANGE** the **PHASE DEMOLISHED** for demolished walls and doors to **NEW CONSTRUCTION**.
- *Step 3*: **CHANGE** the view's **PHASE FILTER** to **SHOW PREVIOUS + DEMOLISHED**.
- *Step 4*: **CHANGE** the view's **PHASE** to **NEW CONSTRUCTION**.

Applying these filters will hide all model elements that are phased as demolished.

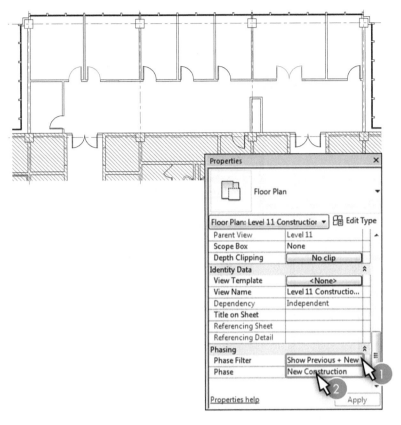

New Construction Plan View

In a new construction plan, model elements are indicated with a heavy line weight. Demolished model elements are hidden. The following instructions will filter a plan view's phasing to show existing conditions and new construction:

- *Step 1*: **CHANGE** the view's **PHASE FILTER** to **SHOW PREVIOUS + NEW**.
- *Step 2*: **CHANGE** the view's **PHASE** to **NEW CONSTRUCTION**.

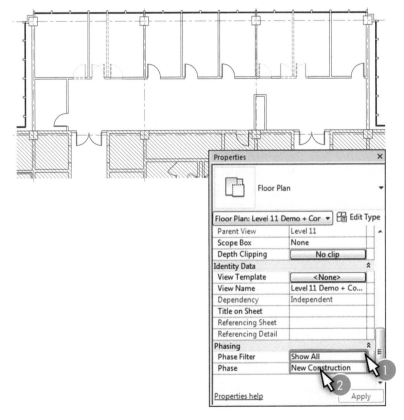

Demo + New Construction Plan View

In this type of floor plan, new construction model elements are indicated with a heavier line weight. Demolished model elements are indicated with a dashed line. The following instructions will filter a plan view's phasing to show existing conditions, demolished elements, and new construction:

- *Step 1*: **CHANGE** the view's **PHASE FILTER** to **SHOW ALL**.
- *Step 2*: **CHANGE** the view's **PHASE** to **NEW CONSTRUCTION**.

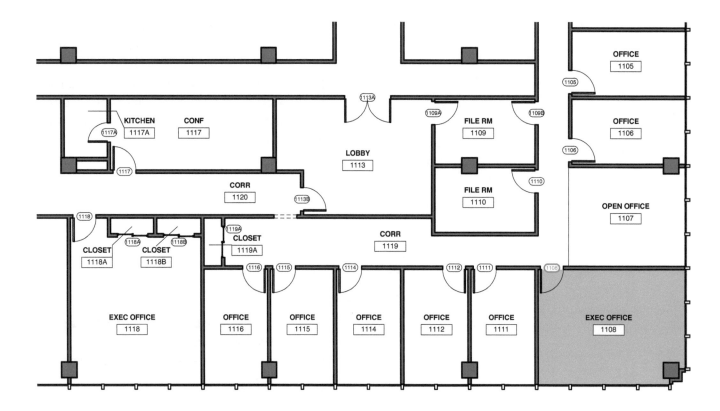

In commercial interiors, the door schedule is a table that identifies new interior doors in the project.

- **DOOR SCHEDULES** are sorted by **DOOR NUMBER** and include abbreviated material references for the door's material and finish.

The partial floor plan (above) includes **ROOM NUMBERS** and **ROOM NAMES** for each space in the project.

- In the plan, each door also contains a tag with a **DOOR NUMBER.**
- In commercial interiors, it is common for the **DOOR NUMBER** to match the **ROOM NUMBER.**
- Instructions for adding door tags to a Revit project begin on page 203.

The door schedule (facing page) uses **MATERIAL ABBREVIATIONS** to identify the finish specification for each door.

- The schedule specified the following finishes for **DOOR 1108: DOOR FINISH: WD/GLS** (wood and glass) and **FRAME FINISH: WD** (wood).

Door Schedules in Revit

Revit simplifies the scheduling process by automatically generating the door schedule from the floor plan. Each door in a Revit project will appear in the door schedule.

- The **MARK** field is synced between the **DOOR SCHEDULE** and the **DOOR TAG** in the floor plan. When you change the door mark in a plan view, the door schedule is automatically updated. Changes made in the schedule view are updated in the plan view.
- The **WIDTH**, **HEIGHT**, and **THICKNESS** fields are calculated by Revit for each door.
- **FIRE RATING** and **HARDWARE SET** fields are added directly in the schedule view or in the floor plan.

Door Schedule									
Mark	**Type Mark**	**Door**				**Frame Material**	**Fire Rating**	**Hardware Set**	**Comments**
		Width	**Height**	**Thickness**	**Finish**				
1105	A	3' - 0"	7' - 0"	0' - 2"	WD/GLS	WD		5	
1106	A	3' - 0"	7' - 0"	0' - 2"	WD/GLS	WD		5	
1108	A	3' - 0"	7' - 0"	0' - 2"	WD/GLS	WD		5	
1109A	F	3' - 0"	7' - 0"	0' - 2"	MTL/PT1	MTL/PT3		2	
1109B	F	3' - 0"	7' - 0"	0' - 2"	MTL/PT1	MTL/PT3		2	
1110	F	3' - 0"	7' - 0"	0' - 2"	MTL/PT1	MTL/PT3		2	
1111	A	3' - 0"	7' - 0"	0' - 2"	WD/GLS	WD		5	
1112	A	3' - 0"	7' - 0"	0' - 2"	WD/GLS	WD		5	
1113A	B	6' - 0"	7' - 0"	0' - 2"	WD/GLS	WD		1	
1113B	A	3' - 0"	7' - 0"	0' - 2"	WD/GLS	WD		3	
1114	A	3' - 0"	7' - 0"	0' - 2"	WD/GLS	WD		5	
1115	A	3' - 0"	7' - 0"	0' - 2"	WD/GLS	WD		5	
1116	A	3' - 0"	7' - 0"	0' - 2"	WD/GLS	WD		5	
1117	A	3' - 0"	7' - 0"	0' - 2"	WD/GLS	WD		3	
1117A	E	2' - 6"	7' - 0"	0' - 2"	MTL/PT1	MTL/PT3		3	

Door Schedule									
Mark	**Type Mark**	**Door**				**Frame Material**	**Fire Rating**	**Hardware Set**	**Comments**
		Width	**Height**	**Thickness**	**Finish**				
1105	A	900mm	2100mm	50mm	WD/GLS	WD		5	
1106	A	900mm	2100mm	50mm	WD/GLS	WD		5	
1108	A	900mm	2100mm	50mm	WD/GLS	WD		5	
1109A	F	900mm	2100mm	50mm	MTL/PT1	MTL/PT3		2	
1109B	F	900mm	2100mm	50mm	MTL/PT1	MTL/PT3		2	
1110	F	900mm	2100mm	50mm	MTL/PT1	MTL/PT3		2	
1111	A	900mm	2100mm	50mm	WD/GLS	WD		5	

Door Material Abbreviations

Material abbreviations used in door schedules are intentionally generic. Paint materials, for example, are listed as PT1, PT2, PT3, etc. Specific information about each paint designation (including manufacturer, finish, color, etc.) is noted in a material legend or in the written project specifications.

Using abbreviations saves time preparing the schedule and space in the construction documents. If a finish is changed mid-project, the designer updates the finish legend or specifications in a project. The abbreviations used in the schedule remain unchanged.

This second door schedule indicates the appropriate SI dimension for the door's width, height, and thickness.

The following is a list of common finish and material abbreviations for doors and door frames:

- **W** or **WD** – wood
- **MTL** – metal
- **P** or **PT** – paint

DOOR SCHEDULES (continued)

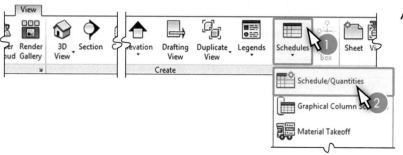

Adding the Door Schedule

- *Step 1*: **CLICK** the **SCHEDULES DROP-DOWN ARROW** in the **VIEW** tab.
- *Step 2*: **CLICK** the **SCHEDULE/QUANTITIES** option in the Drop-down menu.

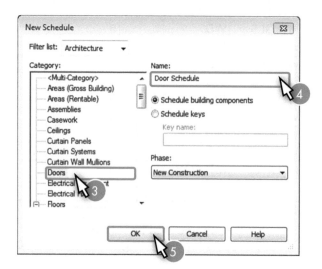

- *Step 3*: **SELECT** the **DOORS** category in the **NEW SCHEDULE** dialog box.

- *Step 4*: **CHANGE** the schedule name to **DOOR SCHEDULE**.

- *Step 5*: **CLICK** the **OK** button.

Adding Fields

- *Step 1*: **CLICK ONCE** on the **MARK** field in the **FIELDS** tab.
- *Step 2*: **CLICK** the **ADD** button.

Repeat *Steps 1* and *2* to add the following fields to the schedule (in this order):
- **MARK**
- **TYPE MARK**
- **WIDTH**
- **HEIGHT**
- **THICKNESS**
- **FINISH**
- **FRAME MATERIAL**
- **FIRE RATING**
- **COMMENTS**

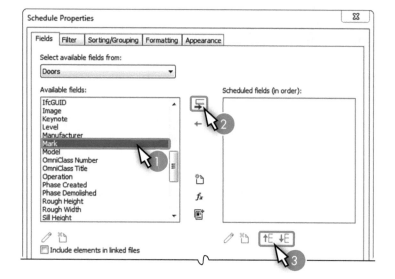

- *Step 3*: Use the **MOVE UP** and **MOVE DOWN** buttons to change the order of the fields in the schedule to match the order listed above.

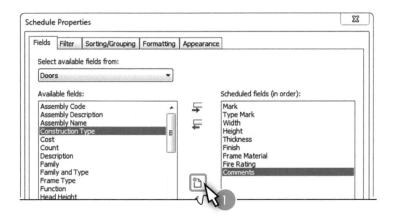

Adding Custom Fields

Revit allows you to create custom fields for a schedule. In the instance of a door schedule, you may want to create a Hardware Set field to note the specific hardware for each door in a project.

- *Step 1*: **CLICK** the **ADD PARAMETER** button to **OPEN** the **PARAMETER PROPERTIES** dialog box.

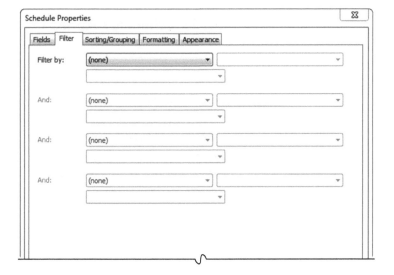

- *Step 2*: **TYPE HARDWARE SET** in the parameter data **NAME** field.
- *Step 3*: **CHANGE** the **TYPE OF PARAMETER** to **TEXT**.
- *Step 4*: **CHANGE** the **GROUP PARAMETER UNDER** value to **TEXT**.
- *Step 5*: **CLICK** the **OK** button to add the new parameter to the door schedule.
- *Step 6 (not shown)*: In the **SCHEDULE PROPERTIES** dialog box, **CLICK** the **MOVE UP** button to position the newly created **HARDWARE SET** field just under the **FIRE RATING** field.

Filtering the Schedule

The Filter tab provides an opportunity to limit the number of doors that appear in the schedule. For example, you could add a filter that shows only doors on the 11th floor of this project by filtering doors with marks between 1100 and 1199.

Do not make any changes to this tab at this time.

Door schedule instructions continue on the next page.

DOOR SCHEDULES (continued)

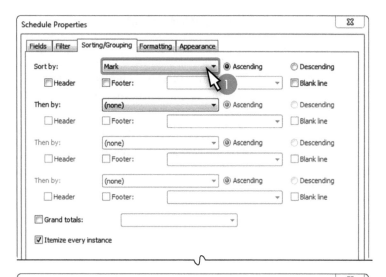

Sorting the Schedule

The Sorting/Grouping tab contains multiple sort criteria for the schedule. Door schedules are sorted by door number. In Revit, the door number is the mark variable.

- *Step 1*: **CHANGE** the **SORT BY** parameter to **MARK**.

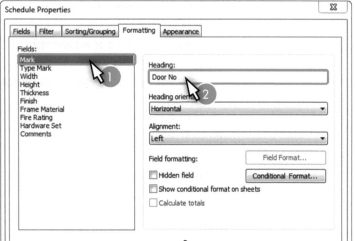

Formatting the Schedule

The Formatting tab contains individual format settings for each column in the schedule.

- *Step 1*: **CLICK ONCE** on the **MARK** field to change its format properties.
- *Step 2*: Change the **HEADING** field from **MARK** to **DOOR NO**.

Repeat *Steps 1–2* to rename the Type Mark field to Door Type.

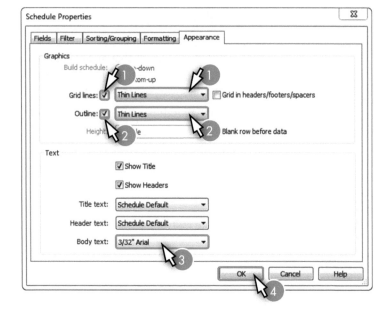

Changing the Schedule's Appearance

The Appearance tab contains font and line weight settings for the schedule.

- *Step 1*: **CHECK** the **GRID LINES BOX** and **SET** the **LINE THICKNESS** to **THIN LINES**.
- *Step 2*: **CHECK** the **OUTLINE BOX** and **SET** the **LINE THICKNESS** to **THIN LINES**.
- *Step 3*: **SET** the **BODY TEXT** to **3/32" ARIAL**.
- *Step 4*: **CLICK** the **OK** button to save the schedule's settings. The schedule view will automatically open.

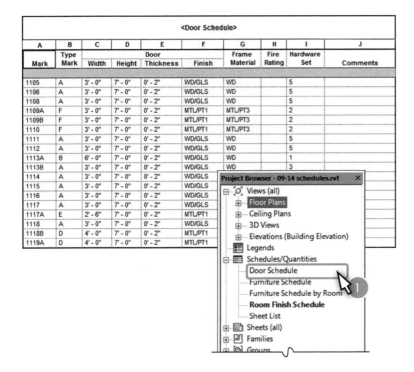

A	B	C	D	E	F	G	H	I	J
				Door		**Frame**	**Fire**	**Hardware**	
Mark	**Type Mark**	**Width**	**Height**	**Thickness**	**Finish**	**Material**	**Rating**	**Set**	**Comments**
1105	A	3' - 0"	7' - 0"	0' - 2"	WD/GLS	WD		5	
1106	A	3' - 0"	7' - 0"	0' - 2"	WD/GLS	WD		5	
1108	A	3' - 0"	7' - 0"	0' - 2"	WD/GLS	WD		5	
1109A	F	3' - 0"	7' - 0"	0' - 2"	MTL/PT1	MTL/PT3		2	
1109B	F	3' - 0"	7' - 0"	0' - 2"	MTL/PT1	MTL/PT3		2	
1110	F	3' - 0"	7' - 0"	0' - 2"	MTL/PT1	MTL/PT3		2	
1111	A	3' - 0"	7' - 0"	0' - 2"	WD/GLS	WD		5	
1112	A	3' - 0"	7' - 0"	0' - 2"	WD/GLS	WD		5	
1113A	B	6' - 0"	7' - 0"	0' - 2"	WD/GLS	WD		1	
1113B	A	3' - 0"	7' - 0"	0' - 2"	WD/GLS	WD		3	
1114	A	3' - 0"	7' - 0"	0' - 2"	WD/GLS				
1115	A	3' - 0"	7' - 0"	0' - 2"	WD/GLS				
1116	A	3' - 0"	7' - 0"	0' - 2"	WD/GLS				
1117	A	3' - 0"	7' - 0"	0' - 2"	WD/GLS				
1117A	E	2' - 6"	7' - 0"	0' - 2"	MTL/PT1				
1118	A	3' - 0"	7' - 0"	0' - 2"	WD/GLS				
1118B	D	4' - 0"	7' - 0"	0' - 2"	MTL/PT1				
1119A	D	4' - 0"	7' - 0"	0' - 2"	MTL/PT1				

<Door Schedule>

Viewing the Schedule

The Door Schedule view is used to update door properties in a project.

- *Step 1*: **DOUBLE-CLICK** on the **SCHEDULE NAME** in the **PROJECT BROWSER.**

Right-click on a schedule name in the Project Browser to delete or duplicate the schedule.

To add a schedule to a sheet, drag the schedule name from the Project Browser onto a sheet in the Revit project.

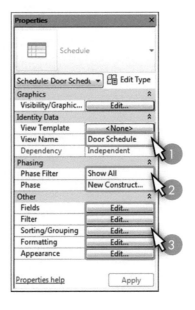

Adjusting the Schedule

The Schedule Properties palette contains several editable properties for the active schedule view.

- *Step 1*: **CHANGE** the **SCHEDULE NAME** in the **VIEW NAME** field.
- *Step 2*: **SET** the appropriate **CONSTRUCTION PHASE FILTER** for the schedule.

For example, by selecting New Construction, all doors phased as existing will be removed from the schedule. Door phases are defined by the Phase setting in the door's Properties palette in the plan view.

- *Step 3*: **CLICK** the **EDIT** button to modify the schedule's **FIELDS, FILTER, SORTING/ GROUPING, FORMATTING,** or **APPEARANCE** settings.

DOOR SCHEDULES (continued)

<Door Schedule>									
A	**B**	**C**	**D**	**E**	**F**	**G**	**H**	**I**	**J**
Mark	Type Mark	Width	Height	Door Thickness	Finish	Frame Material	Fire Rating	Hardware Set	Comments
1105	A	3' - 0"	7' - 0"	0' - 2"	WD/GLS	WD		5	
1106	A	3' - 0"	7' - 0"	0' - 2"	WD/GLS	WD		5	
1108	A	3' - 0"	7' - 0"	0' - 2"	WD/GLS	WD		5	
1109A	F	3' - 0"	7' - 0"	0' - 2"	MTL/PT1	MTL/PT3		2	
1109B	F	3' - 0"	7' - 0"	0' - 2"	MTL/PT1	MTL/PT3		2	
1110	F	3' - 0"	7' - 0"	0' - 2"	MTL/PT1	MTL/PT3		2	
1111	A	3' - 0"	7' - 0"	0' - 2"	WD/GLS	WD		5	
1112	A	3' - 0"	7' - 0"	0' - 2"	WD/GLS	WD		5	
1113A	B	6' - 0"	7' - 0"	0' - 2"	WD/GLS	WD		1	
1113B	A	3' - 0"	7' - 0"	0' - 2"	WD/GLS	WD		3	
1114	A	3' - 0"	7' - 0"	0' - 2"	WD/GLS	WD		5	
1115	A	3' - 0"	7' - 0"	0' - 2"	WD/GLS	WD		5	
1116	A	3' - 0"	7' - 0"	0' - 2"	WD/GLS	WD		5	
1117	A	3' - 0"	7' - 0"	0' - 2"	WD/GLS	WD		3	
1117A	E	2' - 6"	7' - 0"	0' - 2"	MTL/PT1	MTL/PT3		3	
1118	A	3' - 0"	7' - 0"	0' - 2"	WD/GLS	WD		5	
1118B	D	4' - 0"	7' - 0"	0' - 2"	MTL/PT1	MTL/PT3		4	
1119A	D	4' - 0"	7' - 0"	0' - 2"	MTL/PT1	MTL/PT3		4	

Adjusting the Schedule's Appearance

- *Step 1:* **USE** the **HIDE COLUMNS** button to hide a column in the schedule view. This is useful when you add a column to the schedule for a calculation but do not want the column visible in the schedule view.
- *Step 2:* **USE** the **DELETE ROWS** button to remove a row from the schedule. When you delete a door's row from the schedule view, the door is also deleted in the floor plan view.
- *Step 3:* **USE** the **GROUP** button to combine multiple columns under a header column.
- *Step 4:* **USE** the **APPEARANCE** buttons to adjust the **TEXT FONT** and **TEXT ALIGNMENT** in the schedule.
- *Step 5:* **CLICK** the **HIGHLIGHT IN MODEL** button to jump to a plan view of the selected door.

Grouping Columns

In this example, the **WIDTH, HEIGHT, THICKNESS,** and **FINISH** columns are grouped under a **DOOR** group column.

- *Steps 1–2:* **CLICK ONCE** on the **WIDTH** column header and **DRAG** to the **FINISH** column header.
- *Step 3:* **CLICK** the **GROUP** header button.
- *Step 4:* **CLICK ONCE** in the new group heading and rename it **DOOR**.

Editing the Schedule

There are two primary methods to update the contents in a door schedule: updating content in the schedule view and updating content in the floor plan view.

Editing: Schedule View

Updates in the schedule view are synced with the door definition in the floor plan view. For example, when you change the finish of a door in the schedule view the door's properties are automatically updated in the floor plan view.

- *Step 1*: **CLICK** on any **CELL** and **UPDATE** the content in the **SCHEDULE** view.

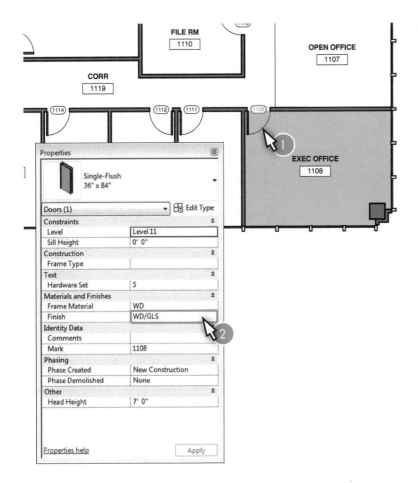

		Door				F
						Door Schedule
Mark	Type Mark	Width	Height	Thickness	Finish	M
1105	A	3' - 0"	7' - 0"	0' - 2"	WD/GLS	WD
1106	A	3' - 0"	7' - 0"	0' - 2"	WD/GLS	WD
1108	A	3' - 0"	7' - 0"	0' - 2"	WD/GLS	WD
1109A	F	3' - 0"	7' - 0"	0' - 2"	MTL/PT1	
1109B	F	3' - 0"	7' - 0"	0' - 2"	MTL/PT1	MT
1110	F	3' - 0"	7' - 0"	0' - 2"	MTL/PT1	MT

Editing: Plan View

- *Step 1*: **CLICK ONCE** on the **DOOR** in **PLAN** view.

- *Step 2*: Change the value of any field in the **PROPERTIES** box to update the door's properties. Changes are automatically updated in the **DOOR SCHEDULE** view.

Revit Tips

- Floor plans are commonly drawn at 1/8″ = 1′-0″.

  > The equivalent SI scale is **1:100**.

- Use annotation detail lines to indicate major overhead architectural conditions.
- Revit will automatically cross-reference elevation and detail symbols in the floor plan when you place each view on a sheet.

Annotation Tips

- Set an appropriate architectural scale before dimensioning a floor plan.
- Add room tags to every room in the project.
- Add door tags to construction plans.
- Add furniture and equipment tags to furniture plans.
- Use text annotations to identify special conditions in the floor plan.

Dimension Tips

- Set an appropriate architectural scale before dimensioning a floor plan.
- Dimension strings should start at the nearest column line or structural column and connect to every wall and wall opening.
- Provide an angle dimension for walls not placed at 90 degrees in the plan.
- Provide radial dimensions for all curved walls. Dimension the center of the curved wall and the wall's start and end points.

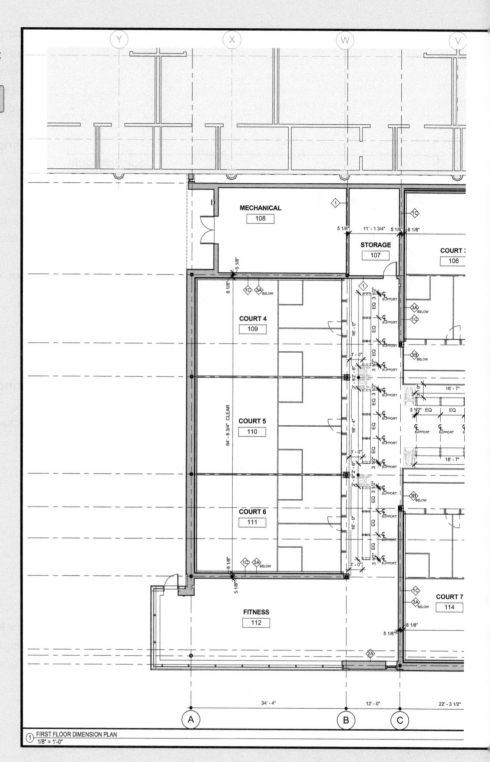

FIRST FLOOR DIMENSION PLAN
1/8″ = 1′-0″

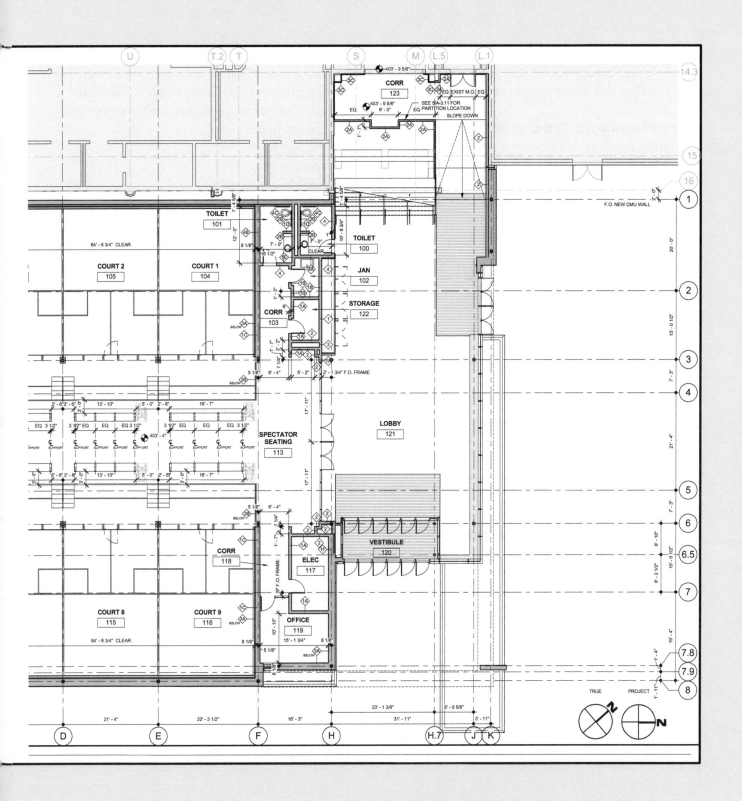

Construction Plan
Middlebury College Squash Center
ARC/Architectural Resources Cambridge

LEARNING EXERCISES

Learning Exercises

These exercises are intended to help you improve your understanding of construction plans and details in Revit.

Learning Exercise 11.1: Construction Plan

To begin this exercise, open the Revit project completed in Learning Exercises 5.3 at the end of Chapter 5. You can also download a support file and a sample solution for this exercise at WWW.RAFDBOOK.COM/DOWNLOADS.

Follow the step-by-step exercises in the chapter to add a CONSTRUCTION PLAN to the companion Revit project:
- Duplicate the LEVEL 11 PRESENTATION PLAN view and rename it to LEVEL 11 CONSTRUCTION PLAN.
- Set the Architectural Scale.
- Add ROOM TAGS to the construction plan.
- Add DOOR TAGS to the construction plan.
- Add DIMENSIONS to the construction plan.

Learning Exercise 11.2: Door Schedule

To begin this exercise, open the Revit project completed in Learning Exercises 11.1. Download a sample solution in PDF format at WWW.RAFDBOOK.COM/DOWNLOADS.

Follow the step-by-step exercises in the chapter to add a DOOR SCHEDULE to the companion Revit project.

Learning Exercise 11.3: Details

To begin this exercise, open the Revit project completed in Learning Exercises 11.2. Download a sample solution in PDF format at WWW.RAFDBOOK.COM/DOWNLOADS.

Follow the step-by-step exercises in the chapter to add the following DETAILS to the companion Revit project:
- Column Surround/Plan Detail
- Casework Detail

Application Exercises

Using an assignment from your instructor or a previously completed studio project, convert a building shell to a Revit project. Add the following items to the new project:
- Existing conditions plan
- Demolition plan
- Construction plan
- Door schedule
- Construction details

chapter 12

FURNITURE AND FINISH PLANS

F urniture and Finish plans communicate scope of the interior design in a project. In addition to these plans, construction documents also include schedules that quantify the furniture, materials, and finishes in a project. Revit syncs changes between the plan and schedule views.

IN THIS CHAPTER

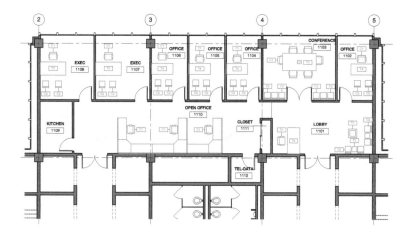

The furniture plan is a unique floor plan view that includes furniture, furniture tags, and room tags.

In AutoCAD you might create a furniture plan using specific layers and viewports. In Revit, you will create a duplicate plan view and hide the categories of information not present in a furniture plan.

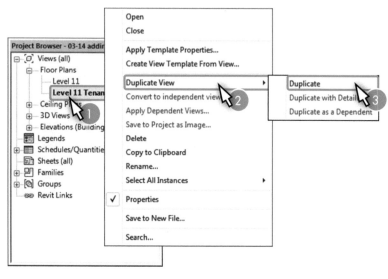

Creating a Furniture Plan View

- *Step 1*: **RIGHT-CLICK** on the existing **LEVEL 11 TENANT SPACE** view in the **PROJECT BROWSER**.
- *Step 2*: **SELECT DUPLICATE VIEW** from the context menu.
- *Step 3*: **CLICK** on **DUPLICATE** in the secondary context menu.

This action duplicates the existing plan view as **LEVEL 11 TENANT SPACE COPY 1**.

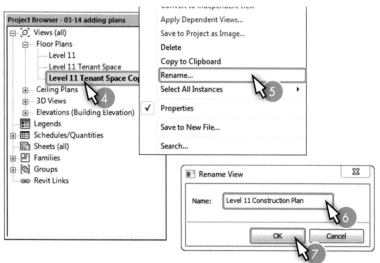

Renaming the Furniture Plan View

- *Step 4*: **RIGHT-CLICK** on the new **LEVEL 11 TENANT SPACE COPY 1** in the **PROJECT BROWSER**.
- *Step 5*: **SELECT RENAME** from the context menu.
- *Step 6*: **RENAME** the plan view to **LEVEL 11 FURNITURE PLAN**.
- *Step 7*: **CLICK** the **OK** button.

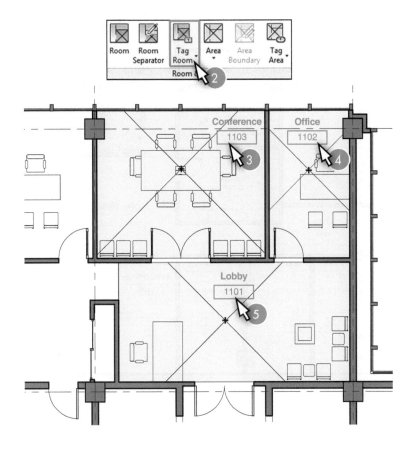

Tagging Rooms in the Furniture Plan

If room boundaries are already defined in the Revit project, you can tag those rooms in the construction plan view.

- *Step 1 (not shown)*: **OPEN** the **FURNITURE PLAN** view.
- *Step 2*: **CLICK** the **TAG ROOM** button in the **ARCHITECTURE** tab.
- *Step 3*: **CLICK** inside any room to place the room tag. Note that the tag is populated with the room name and number set in the construction plan.
- *Steps 4–5*: **ADD** the **ROOM TAG** to the remaining rooms in the furniture plan view.
- *Step 6 (not shown)*: **PRESS** the **ESC** key **TWICE** on the keyboard to end the Tag Room command.

Tagging Furniture in the Furniture Plan

Like doors in the construction plan, each furniture element needs to be tagged in the furniture plan.

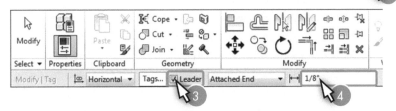

- *Step 1 (not shown)*: **OPEN** the **FURNITURE PLAN** view.
- *Step 2*: **CLICK** the **TAG BY CATEGORY** button in the **ANNOTATE** tab.
- *Step 3*: **CHECK** the **LEADER** box in the **MODIFY | TAG** ribbon.
- *Step 4*: **SET** the **LEADER LENGTH** to **1/8″**.

The SI measurement for this step is **3**.

- *Step 5*: **CLICK** on any furniture element to place the furniture tag. If prompted to load a furniture tag, **CLICK** the **YES** button. **NAVIGATE** to the **US IMPERIAL>ANNOTATIONS>ARCHITECTURAL** folder and load the **FURNITURE TAG.RFA** family.
- *Step 6*: **DOUBLE-CLICK** the **FURNITURE TAG "?"** to number the furniture. Furniture numbering conventions are discussed on page 237.

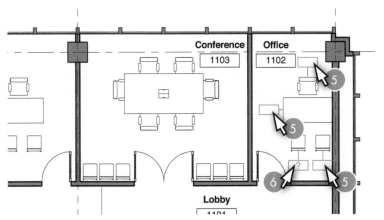

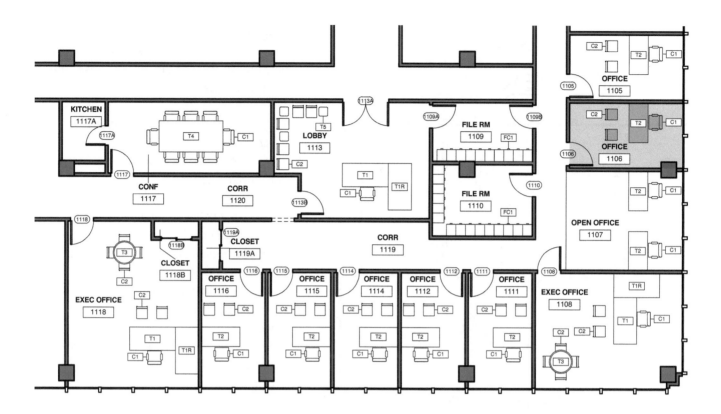

In commercial interiors, the furniture schedule is a table that identifies all furniture in the design project.

- **FURNITURE SCHEDULES** are sorted by **FURNITURE MARK** and include abbreviated material references for the furniture's material and finish.

The partial floor plan (above) includes room numbers and room names for each space in the project.

- In the plan, each room contains furniture with a connected tag annotating the **FURNITURE NUMBER.**
- In commercial interiors, it is common for the furniture number to start with a letter followed by a number.
- Instructions for adding furniture tags to a Revit project begin on page 235.

Furniture Schedules in Revit

Revit simplifies the scheduling process by automatically generating the furniture schedule from the floor plan.

- Each furniture item in a Revit project will appear in the furniture schedule.
- The **TYPE MARK** field (also known as the furniture number) is synced between the schedule view and the furniture tag in the floor plan view. When you change the furniture mark in a plan view, the furniture schedule is automatically updated. Changes made in the schedule view are updated in the plan view.
- The **COUNT** field is a calculated field that displays the total quantity of each furniture type in the project. The count field updates as you add and remove furniture from the project.
- **MANUFACTURER, DESCRIPTION, FABRIC/FINISH,** and **COMMENT** fields are typed directly in the schedule view or in the floor plan.

Types of Furniture Schedules

Because Revit creates the furniture schedule based on the information in the project, there is an opportunity to create multiple furniture schedules to represent the data for specific tasks. This section of the text reviews both the furniture schedule and the furniture schedule by room.

Quantity Furniture Schedule					
Type Mark	Count	Manufacturer	Description	Fabric / Finish	C
C1	20	Herman Miller	Task Chair	Leather / Black	
C2	31	Vitra	Breuer Chair	Chrome / Leather	
FC1	25	HON	5 Drawer File	Black	

Furniture Schedule by Room						
Room: Number	Room: Name	Type Mark	Count	Manufacturer	Descri
1105	OFFICE	C1	1	Herman Miller	Task Cha
1105	OFFICE	C2	2	Vitra	Breuer C
1105	OFFICE	T2	1	HON	Office De
1106	OFFICE	C1	1	Herman Miller	Task Cha
1106	OFFICE	C2	2	Vitra	Breuer C
1106	OFFICE	T2	1	HON	Office De

Quantity Furniture Schedule

The Quantity Furniture Schedule (above) quantifies every furniture item in the project. In addition, manufacturer information and the fabric and finishes are listed with each item.

- Chairs **C1** and **C2** located in **ROOM 1106** are represented in the count field of this schedule.

Furniture Schedule by Room

The Furniture Schedule by Room (above) sorts the furniture by its location in the project. In the example above, each room is separated in the schedule with the corresponding furniture items.

- According to this schedule, **ROOM 1106** has three unique furniture items: **C1, C2,** and **T2.**
- Each of these furniture items is also visible in room 1106 on the facing page.

Furniture Numbers/Marks

The furniture schedules use standard abbreviations to identify the furniture mark for each item in the project. The initial letter is an abbreviation of the furniture type.

- **C** – chair
- **T** – table
- **S** – sofa
- **FC** – file cabinet

The number following the letter changes incrementally for each unique furniture item in the category. For example, **C1** and **C2** are unique chairs in the project. A third chair type would receive the **C3** mark. Furniture marks used in plans and schedules are intentionally generic. Using these abbreviations saves time preparing the schedule and space in the construction documents.

QUANTITY FURNITURE SCHEDULES

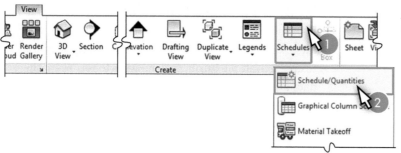

Adding the Quantity Furniture Schedule

- *Step 1*: **CLICK** the **SCHEDULES DROP-DOWN ARROW** in the **VIEW** tab.
- *Step 2*: **CLICK** the **SCHEDULE/QUANTITIES** option in the Drop-down menu.

- *Step 3*: **SELECT** the **FURNITURE** category in the **NEW SCHEDULE** dialog box.
- *Step 4*: **CHANGE** the schedule name to **QUANTITY FURNITURE SCHEDULE**.
- *Step 5*: **CLICK** the **OK** button.

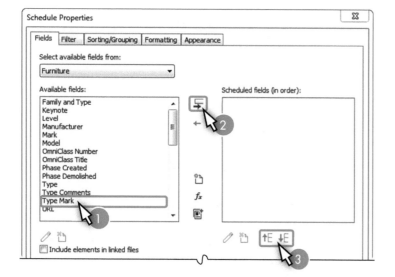

Adding Fields

The Fields tab determines which columns appear in the schedule.

- *Step 1*: **CLICK ONCE** on the **TYPE MARK** field in the **FIELDS** tab.
- *Step 2*: **CLICK** the **ADD** button.

Repeat *Steps 1* and *2* to add the following fields to the schedule (in this order):

- **TYPE MARK**
- **COUNT**
- **MANUFACTURER**
- **DESCRIPTION**
- **COMMENTS**

- *Step 3*: Use the **MOVE UP** and **MOVE DOWN** buttons to change the order of the fields in the schedule to match the order listed above.

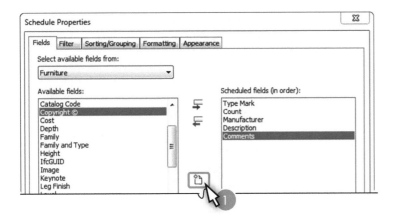

Adding Custom Fields

Revit allows you to create custom fields for a schedule. In the instance of a furniture schedule, you may want to create a Fabric/Finish field to note the specific fabric and finish for each furniture item in a project.

- *Step 1*: **CLICK** the **ADD PARAMETER** button to open the **PARAMETER PROPERTIES** dialog box.

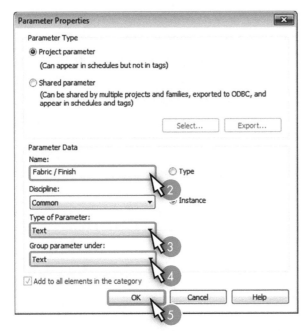

- *Step 2*: **TYPE FABRIC/FINISH** in the parameter data **NAME** field.
- *Step 3*: Change the **TYPE OF PARAMETER** to **TEXT**.
- *Step 4*: Change the **GROUP PARAMETER UNDER** value to **TEXT**.
- *Step 5*: **CLICK** the **OK** button to add the new parameter to the door schedule.
- *Step 6 (not shown)*: In the **SCHEDULE PROPERTIES** dialog box, **CLICK** the **MOVE UP** button to position the **FABRIC/FINISH** field just under the **DESCRIPTION** field.

Filtering the Schedule

The Filter tab provides an opportunity to limit the furniture that appears in the schedule. For example, you could add a filter that shows only chairs in a project by filtering furniture with marks that start with the letter C.

Do not make any changes to this tab at this time.

Quantity furniture schedule instructions continue on the next page.

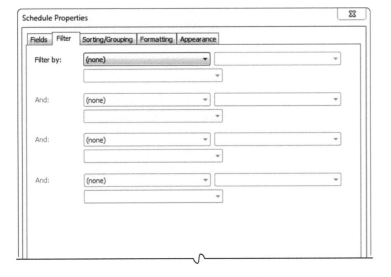

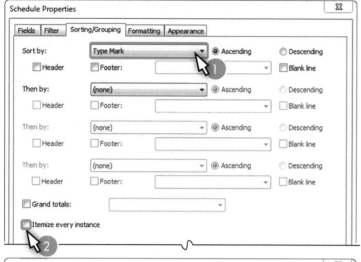

Sorting the Schedule

The Sorting/Grouping tab contains multiple sort criteria for the schedule. Furniture schedules are sorted by furniture number. In Revit, the furniture number is the Type Mark variable.

- *Step 1*: **CHANGE** the **SORT BY** parameter to **TYPE MARK**.
- *Step 2*: **UNCHECK** the **ITEMIZE EVERY INSTANCE** box.

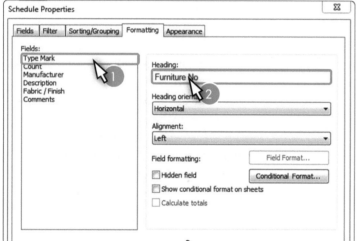

Formatting the Schedule

The Formatting tab contains individual format settings for each column in the schedule.

- *Step 1*: **CLICK ONCE** on the **TYPE MARK** field to change its format properties.
- *Step 2*: Change the **HEADING** field from **TYPE MARK** to **FURNITURE NO**.

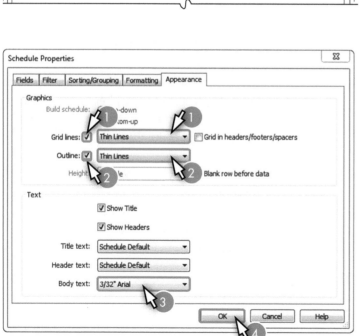

Changing the Schedule's Appearance

The Appearance tab contains font and line weight settings for the schedule.

- *Step 1*: **CHECK** the **GRID LINES BOX** and **SET** the **LINE THICKNESS** to **THIN LINES**.
- *Step 2*: **CHECK** the **OUTLINE BOX** and **SET** the **LINE THICKNESS** to **THIN LINES**.
- *Step 3*: **SET** the **BODY TEXT** to **3/32" ARIAL**.
- *Step 4*: **CLICK** the **OK** button to save the schedule's settings. The **SCHEDULE** view will automatically open.

Viewing the Schedule

The Furniture Schedule view is used to update furniture properties in a project.

- *Step 1:* **DOUBLE-CLICK** on the **SCHEDULE NAME** in the **PROJECT BROWSER.**

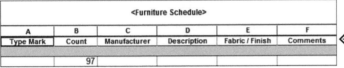

<Furniture Schedule>					
A	B	C	D	E	F
Type Mark	Count	Manufacturer	Description	Fabric / Finish	Comments
	97				

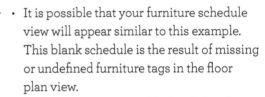

<Furniture Schedule>					
A	B	C	D	E	F
Type Mark	Count	Manufacturer	Description	Fabric / Finish	Comments
C1	20	Herman Miller	Task Chair	Leather / Black	
C2	31	Vitra	Breuer Chair	Chrome / Leath	
FC1	25	HON	5 Drawer File	Black	
T1	3	HON	Executive Desk	Metal / Mahoga	
T1R	3	HON	Exec Desk Ret	Metal / Mahoga	
T2	9	HON	Office Desk	Metal / Mahoga	
T3	2	HON	Small Conferen	Metal / Mahoga	
T4	1	Vitra	Conference Ta	Metal / Mahoga	
T5	3	Vitra	Breuer Side Ta	Chrome	

- It is possible that your furniture schedule view will appear similar to this example. This blank schedule is the result of missing or undefined furniture tags in the floor plan view.
- As furniture tags are added or defined in the plan view, the furniture schedule will automatically add a row for each furniture type.

Adjusting the Schedule

The Schedule Properties palette contains several editable properties for the active schedule view.

- *Step 1:* **CHANGE** the **SCHEDULE NAME** in the **VIEW NAME** field.
- *Step 2:* **CLICK** the **EDIT** button to modify the schedule's **FIELDS, FILTER, SORTING/GROUPING, FORMATTING,** or **APPEARANCE** settings.

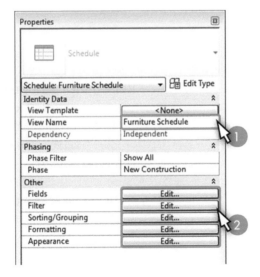

					<Furniture Schedule by Room>		
A	B	C	D	E	F	G	H
Room	Room: Name	Type Mark	Count	Manufacturer	Description	Fabric / Finish	Comments
1105	OFFICE	C1	1	Herman Miller	Task Chair	Leather / Black	
1105	OFFICE	C2	2	Vitra	Breuer Chair	Chrome / Leather	
1105	OFFICE	T2	1	HON	Office Desk	Metal / Mahogany	
1106	OFFICE	C1	1	Herman Miller	Task Chair	Leather / Black	
1106	OFFICE	C2	2	Vitra	Breuer Chair	Chrome / Leather	
1106	OFFICE	T2	1	HON	Office Desk	Metal / Mahogany	
1107	OPEN OFFICE	C1	2	Herman Miller	Task Chair	Leather / Black	
1107	OPEN OFFICE	T2	2	HON	Office Desk	Metal / Mahogany	
1108	EXEC OFFICE	C1	1	Herman Miller	Task Chair	Leather / Black	
1108	EXEC OFFICE	C2	6	Vitra	Breuer Chair	Chrome / Leather	
1108	EXEC OFFICE	T1	1	HON	Executive Desk	Metal / Mahogany	
1108	EXEC OFFICE	T1R	1	HON	Exec Desk Ret	Metal / Mahogany	
1108	EXEC OFFICE	T3	1	HON	Small Conferen	Metal / Mahogany	

The Furniture Schedule by Room sorts the furniture by its location in the project. Each room is listed separately in the schedule with the corresponding furniture items assigned to the room. This type of schedule is useful for furniture installations and client meetings where the furniture and room relationships are critical.

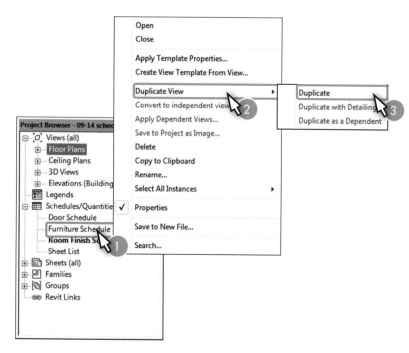

Duplicating Schedules

Because the Quantity Furniture Schedule we just created shares many properties with the Furniture Schedule by Room, duplicating the existing schedule will save setup time.

- *Step 1*: **RIGHT-CLICK** on the existing **FURNITURE SCHEDULE** in the **PROJECT BROWSER.**
- *Step 2*: **SELECT DUPLICATE VIEW** from the context menu.
- *Step 3*: **CLICK** on **DUPLICATE** in the secondary context menu. This action duplicates the existing schedule including all of its settings.

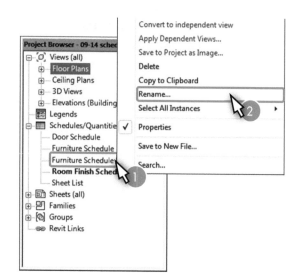

Renaming Schedules

- *Step 1*: **RIGHT-CLICK** on the new **FURNITURE SCHEDULE COPY** in the **PROJECT BROWSER.**
- *Step 2*: **SELECT RENAME** from the context menu.
- *Step 3 (not shown)*: **RENAME** the schedule to **FURNITURE SCHEDULE BY ROOM** and **CLICK OK.**

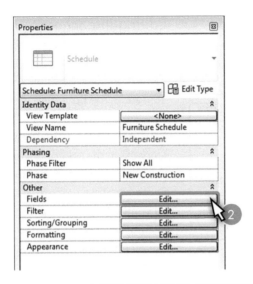

Edit the Schedule's Properties

- *Step 1*: **OPEN** the **FURNITURE SCHEDULE BY ROOM** view from the **PROJECT BROWSER**.
- *Step 2*: **CLICK** the **FIELDS EDIT** button in the **PROPERTIES** box.

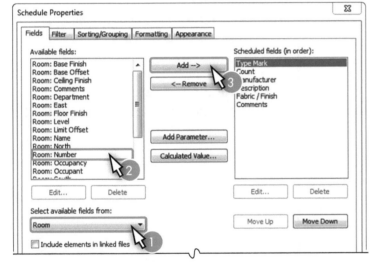

Adding Fields

- *Step 1*: **CHANGE** the **AVAILABLE FIELDS** Drop-down menu to **ROOM**.
- *Step 2*: **CLICK ONCE** on the **ROOM: NUMBER** field in the **FIELDS** tab.
- *Step 3*: **CLICK** the **ADD** button.

Repeat *Steps 2* and *3* to add the following fields to the schedule (in this order):

- **ROOM: NUMBER**
- **ROOM: NAME**
- **TYPE MARK**
- **COUNT**
- **MANUFACTURER**
- **DESCRIPTION**
- **COMMENTS**

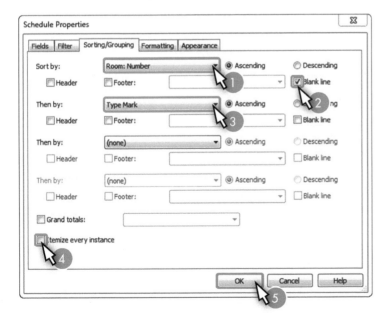

Sorting the Schedule

Use the Sorting/Grouping tab to tell Revit how to sort the schedule.

- *Step 1*: **SET** the **SORT BY** parameter to **ROOM: NUMBER**.
- *Step 2*: **CHECK** the **BLANK LINE** box in the **SORT BY** parameter.
- *Step 3*: **SET** the first **THEN BY** parameter to **TYPE MARK**.
- *Step 4*: **UNCHECK** the **ITEMIZE EVERY INSTANCE** box.
- *Step 5*: **CLICK** the **OK** button to close the **SCHEDULE PROPERTIES** dialog box and return to the **SCHEDULE** view.

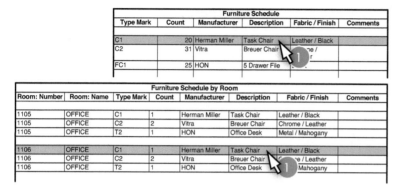

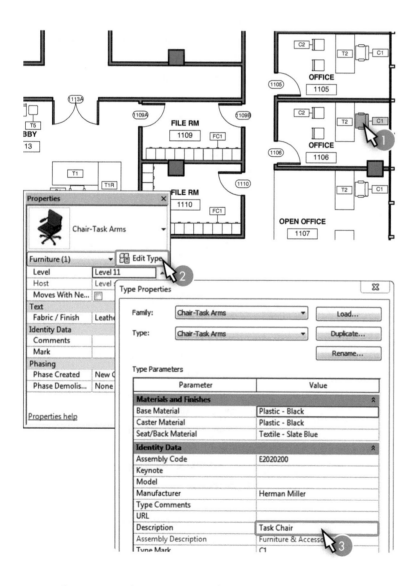

Editing the Schedule

There are two primary methods to update the contents in a furniture schedule: updating content in the schedule view and updating content in the floor plan view.

Editing: Schedule View

Updates in the schedule view are synced with the furniture's definition in the floor plan view. Some furniture properties are synced across all similar furniture types in a project. For example, when you change the type mark in the schedule view, the furniture tag for every instance of that furniture is automatically updated in the floor plan view.

- *Step 1:* **CLICK** on any **CELL** to update the content in the **SCHEDULE** view.

Editing: Plan View

- *Step 1:* **CLICK ONCE** on the **FURNITURE** item in the **PLAN** view.

- *Step 2:* **CLICK** the **EDIT TYPE** button in the **PROPERTIES** box.

- *Step 3:* **UPDATE** furniture **DESCRIPTION** in the **TYPE PROPERTIES** dialog box. Changes are automatically updated in the furniture schedule.

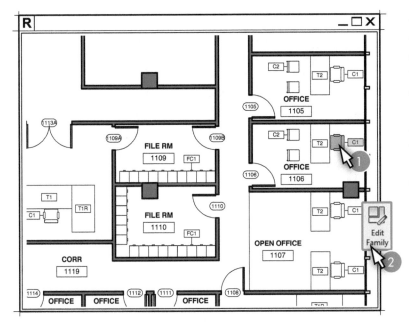

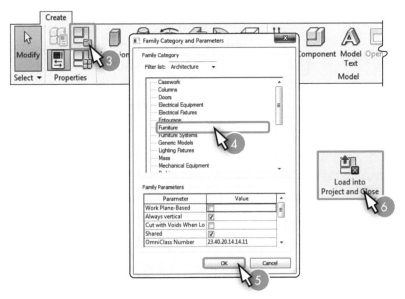

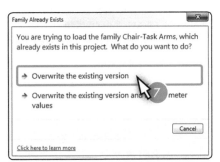

Schedules and Family Categories

Schedules only list Revit families of the corresponding family category. For example, a furniture schedule only lists families that are categorized as furniture. If a furniture family is not showing up in a furniture schedule, changing its category to furniture often solves the problem.

Changing a Family Category

- *Step 1*: In plan view, **CLICK ONCE** on the miscategorized furniture.
- *Step 2*: **CLICK** the **EDIT FAMILY** button in the **MODIFY | FURNITURE** tab. This opens the family editor.

- *Step 3*: **CLICK** the **FAMILY CATEGORY AND PARAMETERS** button in the **CREATE** tab.

- *Step 4*: **CLICK** the **FURNITURE** category in the **FAMILY CATEGORY AND PARAMETERS** dialog box.
- *Step 5*: **CLICK** the **OK** button.

- *Step 6*: **CLICK** the **LOAD INTO PROJECT AND CLOSE** button in the **CREATE** tab.

- *Step 7*: Revit warns you that the family already exists in the project. **CLICK** the **OVERWRITE THE EXISTING VERSION** button to replace the existing family with the modified category.

Open the Furniture Schedule view to verify that the furniture family is now listed in the schedule.

FINISH PLANS

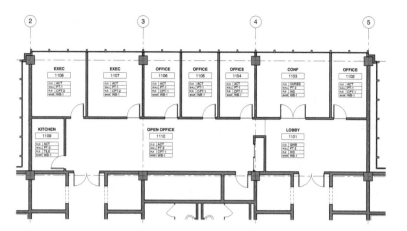

The finish plan is a plan view that includes information about interior finishes in the project. Room finish information is stored within the room definition. In Revit, you will use special room tags and schedules to display the room finish information.

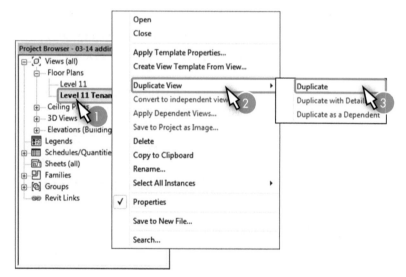

Creating a Finish Plan View

- *Step 1*: **RIGHT-CLICK** on the existing **LEVEL 11 TENANT SPACE** view in the **PROJECT BROWSER**.
- *Step 2*: **SELECT DUPLICATE VIEW** from the context menu.
- *Step 3*: **CLICK** on **DUPLICATE** in the secondary context menu.

This action duplicates the existing plan view as **LEVEL 11 TENANT SPACE COPY 1**.

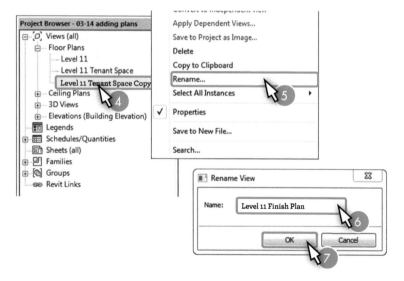

Renaming the Finish Plan View

- *Step 4*: **RIGHT-CLICK** on the new **LEVEL 11 TENANT SPACE COPY 1** in the **PROJECT BROWSER**.
- *Step 5*: **SELECT RENAME** from the context menu.

- *Step 6*: **RENAME** the plan view to **LEVEL 11 FINISH PLAN**.
- *Step 7*: **CLICK** the **OK** button.

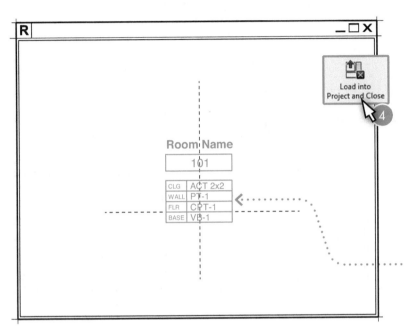

Tagging Rooms in the Finish Plan

If room boundaries are already defined in the Revit project, you can tag those rooms in the finish plan view. The room finish tag displays ceiling, wall, floor, and base materials for each room.

- *Step 1 (not shown)*: **DOWNLOAD** the **ROOM TAG W FINISH.RFA** Revit family from **WWW.RAFDBOOK.COM/DOWNLOADS.**

- *Step 2 (not shown)*: **OPEN** the **FINISH PLAN** view.

- *Step 3*: **OPEN** the **ROOM TAG W FINISH.RFA** family.

- *Step 4*: **CLICK** the **LOAD INTO PROJECT AND CLOSE** button in the **CREATE** tab of the family editor.

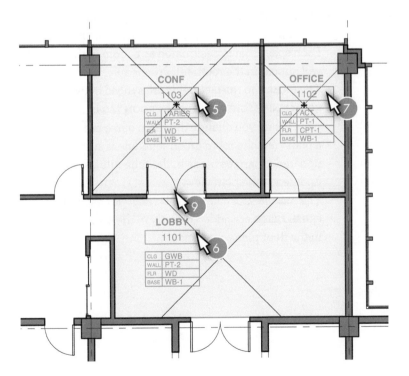

- *Step 5*: **CLICK** inside any room to place the room tag. Note that the tag populates with the room name and number set in the construction plan. Room finishes also populate if they are present in the room definition.

- *Steps 6–7*: **ADD** the **ROOM TAG** to the remaining rooms in the finish plan view.

- *Step 8 (not shown)*: **PRESS** the **ESC** key **TWICE** on the keyboard to end the Tag Room command.

- *Step 9*: **CLICK TWICE** on a **MATERIAL ABBREVIATION** in the room finish tag to modify the finish.

A list of standard finish abbreviations is provided on page 249. Learn more about how these finishes sync with a room finish schedule on page 254.

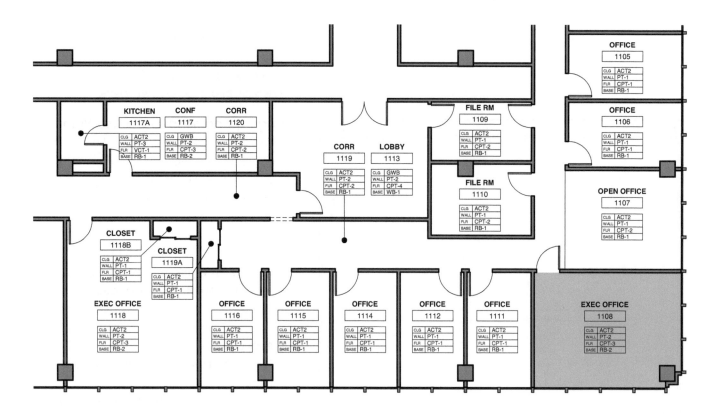

In commercial interiors, the room finish schedule is a table that identifies the interior finish for every room (or space) in the project.

- Finish schedules are sorted by room number and include abbreviated material references for the floor, walls, and ceiling finish in each room.
- The **PARTIAL FLOOR PLAN** (above) includes **ROOM NUMBERS** and **ROOM NAMES** for each space in the project.
- The **ROOM FINISH SCHEDULE** (facing page) uses standard **MATERIAL ABBREVIATIONS** to identify the finish specification for each room.
- Instructions for adding room boundaries begin in Chapter 4 on page 77
- Instructions for adding room finish tags begin on page 247.

For example, the schedule specified the following finishes for **EXECUTIVE OFFICE 1108** (bottom-right corner of floor plan):

- **FLOOR FINISH: C3** (carpet)
- **BASE FINISH: RB2** (rubber base)
- **WALL FINISH: WT1** (wall treatment) and **PT1** (paint)
- **CEILING FINISH: ACT2** (acoustic ceiling tile)

Schedules in Revit

Revit simplifies the scheduling process by automatically generating the room finish schedule from the floor plan.

- Each space that is designated as a room in the project will appear in the room finish schedule.
- The **NAME** and **NUMBER** fields are synced between the **ROOM FINISH SCHEDULE** and the **ROOM TAG** in the floor plan. When you change the room name or number in a plan view, the room finish schedule is automatically updated. Changes made in the schedule view are updated in the plan view.
- The **AREA** field is calculated by Revit for each room.
- **FINISH FIELDS** are added directly in the schedule view or in the floor plan.

Room Finish Schedule

Room No	Name	Floor Finish	Base Finish	Wall Finish	Ceiling Finish	Area	Comments
1105	OFFICE	CPT-1	RB-1	PT-1	ACT2	124 SF	
1106	OFFICE	CPT-1	RB-1	PT-1	ACT2	123 SF	
1107	OPEN OFFICE	CPT-2	RB-1	PT-1	ACT2	193 SF	
1108	EXEC OFFICE	CPT-3	RB-2	PT-2	ACT2	281 SF	
1109	FILE RM	CPT-2	RB-1	PT-1	ACT2	98 SF	
1110	FILE RM	CPT-2	RB-1	PT-1	ACT2	116 SF	
1111	OFFICE	CPT-1	RB-1	PT-1	ACT2	123 SF	
1112	OFFICE	CPT-1	RB-1	PT-1	ACT2	123 SF	
1113	LOBBY	CPT-4	WB-1	PT-2	GWB	282 SF	
1114	OFFICE	CPT-1	RB-1	PT-1	ACT2	125 SF	
1115	OFFICE	CPT-1	RB-1	PT-1	ACT2	123 SF	
1116	OFFICE	CPT-1	RB-1	PT-1	ACT2	123 SF	
1117	CONF	CPT-3	RB-2	PT-2	GWB	193 SF	
1117A	KITCHEN	VCT-1	RB-1	PT-3	ACT2	42 SF	
1118	EXEC OFFICE	CPT-3	RB-2	PT-2	ACT2	351 SF	
1118B	CLOSET	CPT-1	RB-1	PT-1	ACT2	12 SF	
1119	CORR	CPT-2	RB-1	PT-2	ACT2	366 SF	
1119A	CLOSET	CPT-1	RB-1	PT-1	ACT2	14 SF	
1120	CORR	CPT-2	RB-1	PT-2	ACT2	248 SF	

Finish Material Abbreviations

Material abbreviations used in room finish schedules are intentionally generic. Different carpet styles, for example, are listed as **CPT1**, **CPT2**, **CPT3**, etc. Specific information about each carpet style (including manufacturer, finish, color, etc.) is noted in the written project specifications or a material legend.

Using abbreviations saves time preparing the schedule. If a finish is changed mid-project, the designer updates the finish legend or specifications in a project. The abbreviations used in the schedule remain unchanged.

The following is a list of common interior finish material abbreviations:

Floor finish abbreviations
- **CPT** or **C** – carpet
- **CT** – ceramic tile
- **ST** – stone
- **QT** – quarry tile
- **W** or **WD** – wood
- **VCT** – vinyl composite tile

Wall base abbreviations
- **CB** – ceramic tile base
- **QB** – quarry tile base
- **STB** – stone base
- **VB** – vinyl base
- **WB** – wood base

Wall finish abbreviations
- **P** or **PT** – paint
- **VWC** – vinyl wall covering
- **WC** – wall covering
- **WT** – wall treatment

ROOM FINISH SCHEDULES (continued)

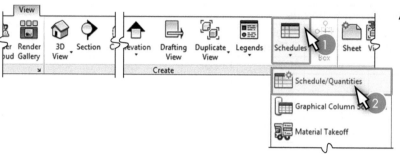

Adding Room Finish Schedules

- *Step 1*: **CLICK** the **SCHEDULES DROP-DOWN ARROW** in the **VIEW** tab.
- *Step 2*: **CLICK** the **SCHEDULES/QUANTITIES** option in the Drop-down menu.

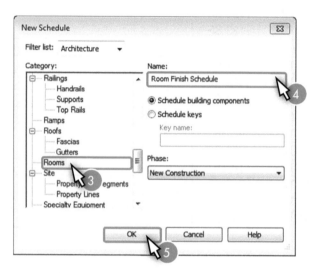

- *Step 3*: **SELECT** the **ROOMS** category in the **NEW SCHEDULE** dialog box.
- *Step 4*: **CHANGE** the schedule name to **ROOM FINISH SCHEDULE**.
- *Step 5*: **CLICK** the **OK** button.

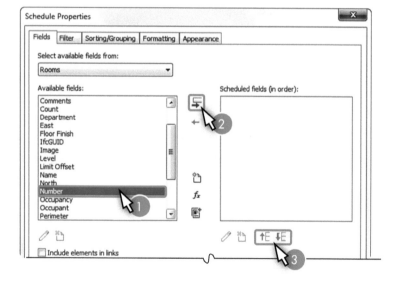

Adding Fields

- *Step 1*: **CLICK ONCE** on the **NUMBER** field in the **AVAILABLE FIELDS** column.
- *Step 2*: **CLICK** the **ADD** button.

Repeat *Steps 1* and *2* to add the following fields to the schedule (in this order):

- **NUMBER**
- **NAME**
- **FLOOR FINISH**
- **BASE FINISH**
- **WALL FINISH**
- **CEILING FINISH**
- **AREA**
- **COMMENTS**

- *Step 3*: Use the **MOVE UP** and **MOVE DOWN** buttons to change the order of the fields in the schedule to match the order listed above.

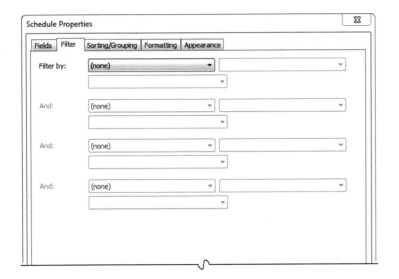

Filtering the Schedule

The Filter tab provides the ability to limit the rooms that appear in the schedule. For example, filtering rooms with numbers between 1100 and 1199 would show rooms on the 11th floor in the schedule.

Do not make any changes to this tab at this time.

Room finish schedule instructions continue on the next page.

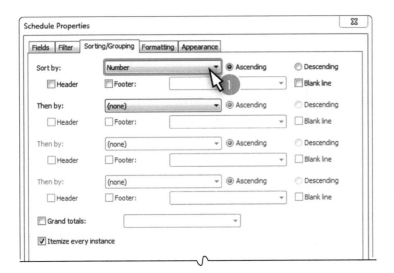

Sorting the Schedule

The Sorting/Grouping tab contains multiple sort criteria for the schedule. Room finish schedules are sorted by room number.

- *Step 1*: **CHANGE** the **SORT BY** parameter to **NUMBER.**

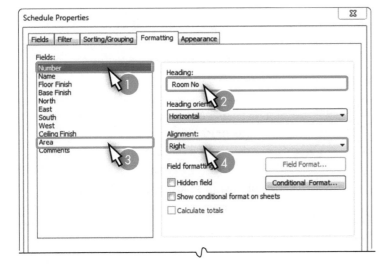

Formatting the Schedule

The Formatting tab contains individual format settings for each column in the schedule.

- *Step 1*: **CLICK ONCE** on the **NUMBER** field to change its format properties.
- *Step 2*: Change the **HEADING** field from **NUMBER** to **ROOM NO.**
- *Step 3*: **CLICK ONCE** on the **AREA** field to change its format properties.
- *Step 4*: **CHANGE** the **ALIGNMENT** field to **ALIGN RIGHT.**

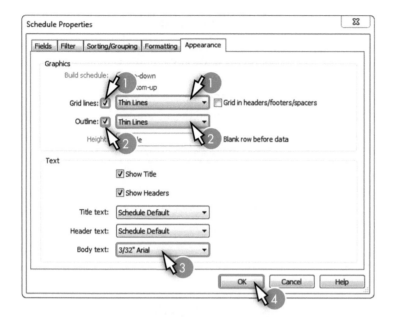

Changing the Schedule's Appearance

The Appearance tab contains font and line weight settings for the schedule.

- *Step 1*: **CHECK** the **GRID LINES BOX** and **SET** the **LINE THICKNESS** to **THIN LINES**.
- *Step 2*: **CHECK** the **OUTLINE BOX** and **SET** the **LINE THICKNESS** to **THIN LINES**.

- *Step 3*: **SET** the **BODY TEXT** to **3/32" ARIAL**.
- *Step 4*: **CLICK** the **OK** button to save the schedule's settings. The schedule view will automatically open.

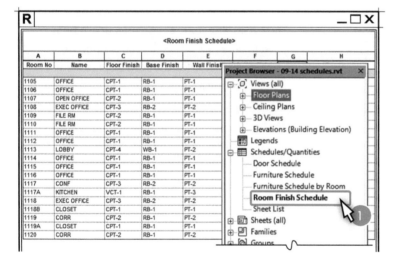

Viewing the Schedule

The room finish schedule view is used to update room finish properties in a project.

- *Step 1*: **DOUBLE-CLICK** on the **SCHEDULE NAME** in the **PROJECT BROWSER**.

Right-click on a schedule name in the **PROJECT BROWSER** to delete or duplicate the schedule.

To add a schedule to a sheet, drag the schedule name from the **PROJECT BROWSER** onto a sheet in the Revit project.

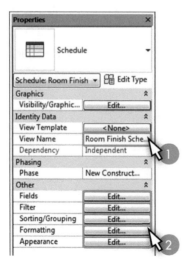

Adjusting the Schedule

The Schedule Properties palette contains several editable properties for the active schedule view.

- *Step 1*: **CHANGE** the **SCHEDULE NAME** in the **VIEW NAME** field.
- *Step 2*: **CLICK** the **EDIT** buttons to modify the schedule's **FIELDS, FILTER, SORTING/ GROUPING, FORMATTING**, or **APPEARANCE** settings.

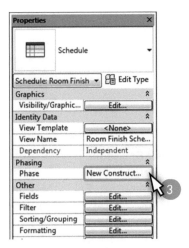

Adjusting the Schedule (continued)

- *Step 3*: **SET** the appropriate **CONSTRUCTION PHASE** for the schedule.

For example, by selecting New Construction, all rooms phased as existing will be removed from the schedule. Room phases are defined by the phase setting in the floor plan's view properties. If a floor plan's view is phased as New Construction, all room definitions in that view will also be phased as New Construction.

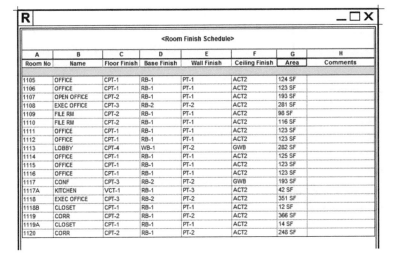

Adjusting the Schedule's Appearance

- *Step 1*: **USE** the **HIDE COLUMNS** button to hide a column in the schedule view. This is useful when you add a column to the schedule for a calculation but do not want the column visible in the schedule view.
- *Step 2*: **USE** the **DELETE ROWS** button to remove a row from the schedule. When you delete a room's row from the schedule view, the room is also deleted in the floor plan view.
- *Step 3*: **USE** the **GROUP** button to combine multiple columns under a header column.
- *Step 4*: **USE** the **APPEARANCE** buttons to adjust the text font and text alignment in the schedule.
- *Step 5*: **USE** the **NOT PLACED/UNENCLOSED** buttons to quickly **SHOW**, **HIDE**, or **ISOLATE** all schedule items that are not placed in the Revit project.

> **Tip:** Not placed rooms contain the words **NOT PLACED** in the area column. Use the **DELETE ROW** button to permanently remove these rooms from the schedule view.

ROOM FINISH SCHEDULES (continued)

Editing the Schedule

There are two primary methods to update the contents in a room finish schedule: updating content in the schedule view and updating content in the floor plan view.

Room Finish Schedule					
Room No	Name	Floor Finish	Base Finish	Wall Finish	Ce Fi
1105	OFFICE	CPT-1	RB-1	PT-1	ACT
1106	OFFICE	CPT-1	RB-1	PT-1	ACT
1107	OPEN OFFICE	CPT-2	RB-1	PT-1	ACT
1108	EXEC OFFICE	CPT-3	RB-2	PT-2	ACT
1109	FILE RM	CPT-2	RB-1	T-1	ACT
1110	FILE RM	CPT-2	RB-1	PT-1	ACT

Editing: Schedule View

Updates in the schedule view are synced with the room area definitions in the floor plan view. For example, when you change the name of a room in the schedule view, the room tag is automatically updated in the floor plan view.

- *Step 1:* **CLICK** on any **CELL** and **UPDATE** the content in the schedule view.

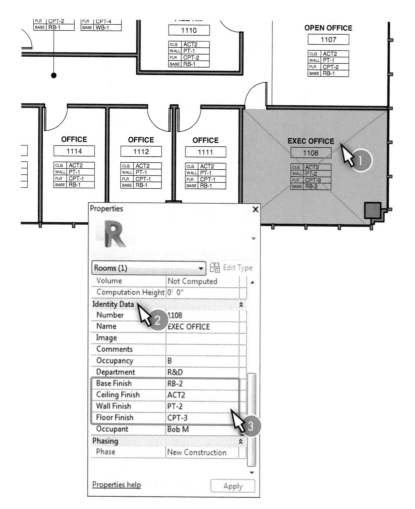

Editing: Plan View

- *Step 1:* **MOVE** the **CURSOR** over the room until you see the **BLUE X** and the **SHADED ROOM BOUNDARY**. **CLICK ONCE** on the **BLUE X**.

- *Step 2:* **SCROLL DOWN** to the **IDENTITY DATA** section of the **PROPERTIES** box.
- *Step 3:* **CHANGE** the **VALUE** of **ANY FIELD** in the **PROPERTIES** box to update the finishes for the selected room. Changes are automatically updated in the room finish schedule view.

Learning Exercise/Checklists: Furniture Plans

These exercises are intended to help you improve your understanding of furniture plans and schedule in Revit.

Learning Exercise 12.1: Furniture Plan

To begin this exercise, open the Revit project completed in Learning Exercises 11.3 at the end of Chapter 11. You can also download a support file for this exercise at **WWW.RAFDBOOK.COM/DOWNLOADS**.

Follow the step-by-step exercises in the chapter to add a **FURNITURE PLAN** to the companion Revit project:

- Duplicate the **LEVEL 11 CONSTRUCTION PLAN** view and rename it to **LEVEL 11 FURNITURE PLAN**.
- Set the Architectural Scale.
- Add **ROOM TAGS** to the plan view.
- Hide the **DOOR TAGS** and **WALL TAGS** in the plan view.
- Tag all **FURNITURE** in the plan view.

Revit Tips: Furniture Plans

- Furniture plans are commonly drawn at 1/8″ = 1′-0″.

  > The equivalent SI scale is **1:100**.

- Check the family category for furniture elements that you cannot tag.

Annotation Tips: Furniture Plans

- Set an appropriate architectural scale before adding room tags and furniture tags to the plan.
- Add room tags to every room in the plan.
- Hide door tags and wall tags.
- Use text annotations to identify special conditions in the plan.

Learning Exercise/Checklists: Furniture Schedules

Learning Exercise 12.2: Furniture Schedules

To begin this exercise, open the Revit project completed in Learning Exercises 12.1.

Follow the step-by-step exercises in the chapter to add the following **SCHEDULES** to the companion Revit project:

- Quantity Furniture Schedule
- Furniture Schedule by Room

Revit Tips: Furniture Schedules

- If a furniture family is not showing up in a furniture schedule, changing its category to furniture often solves the problem. Learn more on page 245.

Checklist: Quantity Furniture Schedules

- The first **FIELD/COLUMN** in the schedule should be **TYPE MARK**. (Do not use the **MARK** field.)
- Set the schedule's **PRIMARY SORT** to **TYPE MARK**. Schedules are typically sorted by the first column.
- Verify the proper **FIELDS** are added in the proper order:
  - **TYPE MARK**
  - **COUNT**
  - **MANUFACTURER**
  - **DESCRIPTION**
  - **COMMENTS**

Checklist: Quantity Furniture Schedules (continued)

- **UNCHECK** the **ITEMIZE EVERY INSTANCE** box in the **SORTING/GROUPING** tab.
- Use schedule **FILTERS** to limit the information presented in a schedule.

Checklist: Furniture Schedules by Room

- The first **FIELD/COLUMN** in the schedule should be **ROOM: NUMBER**.
- Set the schedule's **PRIMARY SORT** to **ROOM NUMBER**.
- Set the schedule's **SECONDARY SORT** to **TYPE MARK**.
- Verify the proper **FIELDS** are added in the proper order:
  - **ROOM: NUMBER**
  - **ROOM: NAME**
  - **TYPE MARK**
  - **COUNT**
  - **MANUFACTURER**
  - **DESCRIPTION**
  - **COMMENTS**
- **CHECK** the **ITEMIZE EVERY INSTANCE** box in the **SORTING/GROUPING** tab.
- Use schedule **FILTERS** to limit the information presented in a schedule.

Learning Exercise/Checklists: Finish Plans

These exercises are intended to help you improve your understanding of finish plans and schedule in Revit.

Learning Exercise 12.3: Finish Plan

To begin this exercise, open the Revit project completed in Learning Exercises 12.2.

Follow the step-by-step exercises in the chapter to add a **FURNITURE PLAN** to the companion Revit project:

- Duplicate the **LEVEL 11 CONSTRUCTION PLAN** view and rename it to **LEVEL 11 FURNITURE PLAN**.
- Set the Architectural Scale.
- Add **ROOM TAGS** to the plan view.
- Hide the **DOOR TAGS** and **WALL TAGS** in the plan view.
- Tag all **FURNITURE** in the plan view.

Revit Tips: Finish Plans

- Finish plans are commonly drawn at 1/8″ = 1′-0″.

> The equivalent SI scale is **1:100**.

- Use the finish schedule to assign materials to the walls, floors, and ceilings in the project. These finishes will automatically populate in the room finish tag.

Annotation Tips: Finish Plans

- Set an appropriate architectural scale before adding room finish tags to the finish plan.
- Add room finish tags to every room in the finish plan.
- Hide door tags and wall tags in the finish plan.
- Hide furniture in the finish plan.
- Use text annotations to identify special conditions in the finish plan.

Learning Exercise/Checklists: Finish Schedules

Learning Exercise 12.4: Room Finish Schedule

To begin this exercise, open the Revit project completed in Learning Exercises 12.3.

Follow the step-by-step exercises in the chapter to add the following **SCHEDULE** to the companion Revit project:
- Quantity Furniture Schedule
- Furniture Schedule by Room

Revit Tips: Room Finish Schedules

- To remove extra rooms in the schedule identified as "not placed" in the area column, use the Delete Row button or the Hide Not Placed button. Learn more on page 253.

Checklist: Room Finish Schedule

- The first **FIELD/COLUMN** in the schedule should be the room **NUMBER**.
- Set the schedule's **PRIMARY SORT** to **NUMBER**. Schedules are typically sorted by the first column.
- Verify the proper **FIELDS** are added in the proper order:
  - **NUMBER**
  - **NAME**
  - **FLOOR FINISH**
  - **BASE FINISH**
  - **WALL FINISH**
  - **CEILING FINISH**
  - **AREA**
  - **COMMENTS**
- **CHECK** the **ITEMIZE EVERY INSTANCE** box in the **SORTING/ GROUPING** tab.
- If needed, use schedule **FILTERS** to limit the information presented in the schedule.

chapter 13

CONSTRUCTION RCPS AND DETAILS

Reflected ceiling plans (RCPs) for construction documents contain additional information not included on presentation ceiling plans. In design and construction, these drawings are used to coordinate ceiling-mounted building systems including lighting, HVAC, fire sprinklers, and egress signage.

IN THIS CHAPTER

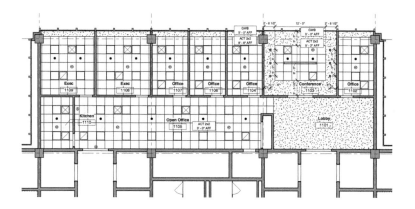

The construction RCP is used to identify the location of all ceiling-mounted building systems including lighting, HVAC, fire sprinklers, and egress signage.

In AutoCAD you might create a construction RCP using specific layers and viewports. In Revit, you will duplicate the presentation ceiling plan view created in Chapter 5.

Duplicating a Ceiling Plan View

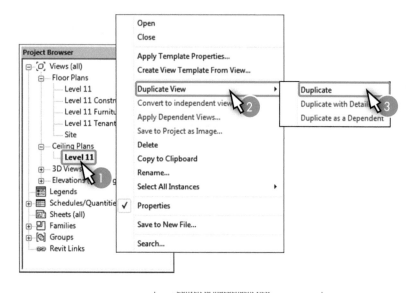

- *Step 1*: **RIGHT-CLICK** on the existing **CEILING PLAN > LEVEL 11** view in the **PROJECT BROWSER**.
- *Step 2*: **SELECT DUPLICATE VIEW** from the context menu.
- *Step 3*: **CLICK** on **DUPLICATE** in the secondary context menu.

This action duplicates the existing ceiling plan view as **LEVEL 11 COPY 1**.

Renaming the Ceiling Plan View

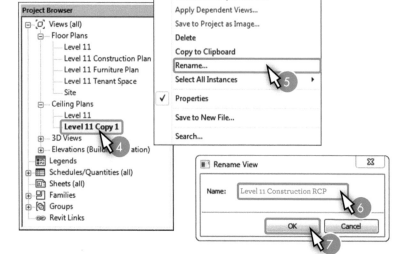

- *Step 4*: **RIGHT-CLICK** on the new **LEVEL 11 COPY 1** in the **PROJECT BROWSER**.
- *Step 5*: **SELECT RENAME** from the context menu.

- *Step 6*: **RENAME** the plan view to **LEVEL 11 CONSTRUCTION RCP**.
- *Step 7*: **CLICK** the **OK** button.

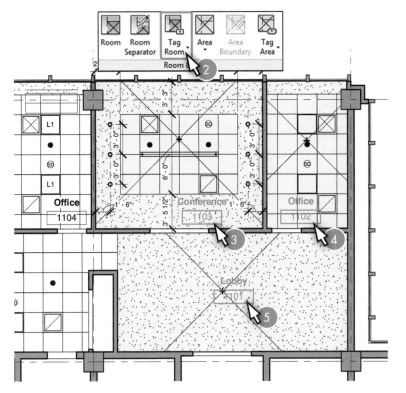

Tagging Rooms in the RCP

If room boundaries are already defined in the Revit project, you can tag those rooms in the ceiling plan view.

- *Step 1 (not shown)*: **OPEN** the **CEILING PLAN** view.
- *Step 2*: **CLICK** the **TAG ROOM** button in the **ARCHITECTURE** tab.
- *Step 3*: **CLICK** inside any room to place the room tag. Note that the tag is populated with the room name and number set in the construction plan.
- *Steps 4–5*: **ADD** the **ROOM TAG** to the remaining rooms in the furniture plan view.
- *Step 6 (not shown)*: **PRESS** the **ESC** key **TWICE** on the keyboard to end the Tag Room command.

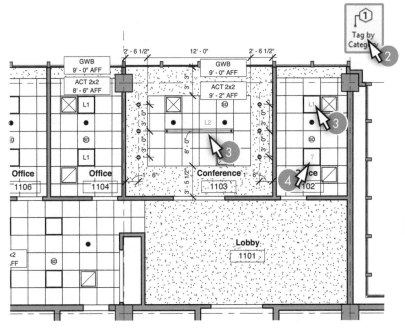

Tagging Light Fixtures in the RCP

Like doors in the construction plan, each light fixture needs to be tagged in the RCP.

- *Step 1 (not shown)*: **OPEN** the **CEILING PLAN** view.
- *Step 2*: **CLICK** the **TAG BY CATEGORY** button in the **ANNOTATE** tab.
- *Step 3*: **CLICK** on any light fixture to place the fixture tag.

Tip: If prompted to load a light fixture tag, **CLICK** the **YES** button. **NAVIGATE** to the **US IMPERIAL>ANNOTATIONS>ELECTRICAL** folder and load the **LIGHTING FIXTURE TAG.RFA** family.

- *Step 4*: **DOUBLE-CLICK** the **LIGHT FIXTURE TAG** "**?**" to number the light fixture.

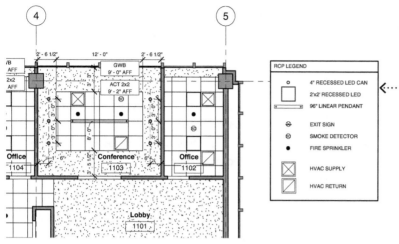

In a set of construction documents, legends identify what each symbol represents in the corresponding plan. Legends are drawn at the same scale as the corresponding plan.

- The ceiling plan legend typically includes light fixtures, exit signs, smoke detectors, fire sprinklers, and HVAC symbols.

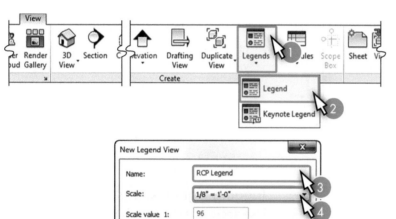

Creating the Legend

- *Step 1*: **CLICK** the **LEGENDS DROP-DOWN ARROW** in the **VIEW** tab.
- *Step 2*: **CLICK** the **LEGEND** option in the Drop-down menu.

- *Step 3*: Set the legend **NAME** to **RCP LEGEND** category in the **NEW LEGEND VIEW** dialog box.
- *Step 4*: Set the legend **SCALE** to **1/8″ = 1′-0″** in the **NEW LEGEND VIEW** dialog box.
- *Step 5*: **CLICK** the **OK** button.

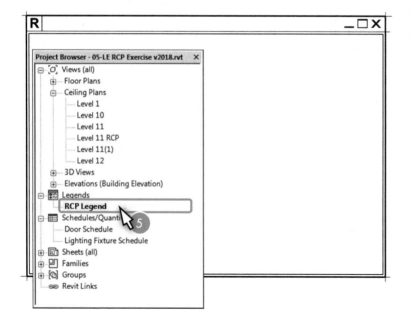

Viewing the Legend

Legends are a scaled drafting view where you can combine detail lines, annotative text, and families. Like other views in Revit, legends are dragged onto sheets where they can be combined with corresponding plan view.

- *Step 1*: **DOUBLE-CLICK** on the **SCHEDULE NAME** in the **PROJECT BROWSER**. When you initially open a new legend view, you will see an empty drawing area.

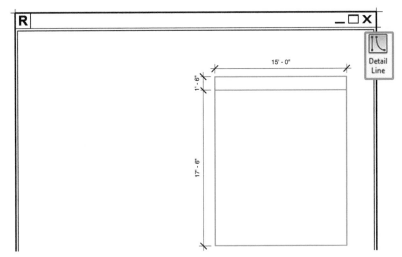

Adding Detail Lines

- **USE** the **DETAIL LINE** button in the **ANNOTATE** tab to draw the perimeter of the legend. These lines will need to be adjusted as you add symbols and text to the legend.

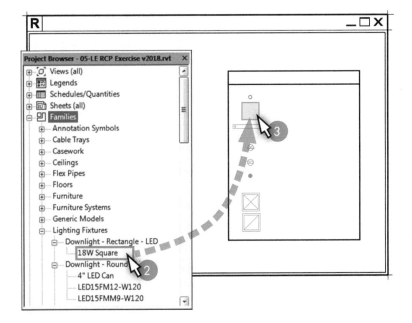

Adding Families/Symbols

Family symbols must be dragged from the Project Browser into the legend view.

- *Step 1*: In the **PROJECT BROWSER**, navigate to the **FAMILIES>LIGHTING FIXTURES> DOWNLIGHT - RECTANGLE - LED>18W SQUARE** family type.
- *Step 2*: **DRAG** the **LEVEL 1 FLOOR PLAN** view from the **PROJECT BROWSER** to the **A-1.1** sheet view.
- *Step 3*: When the **LEVEL 1 PLAN** view is centered on the sheet, drop it on the sheet by **RELEASING** the mouse button.

Repeat *Steps 1–3* to add additional family types to the legend.

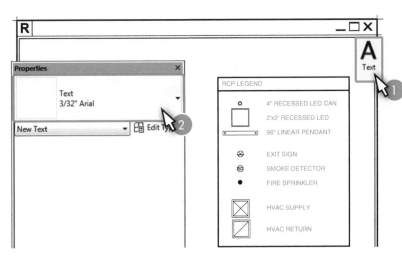

Adding Annotative Text

- *Step 1*: **USE** the **TEXT** button in the **ANNOTATION** tab to add text notes to the detail.
- *Step 2*: **USE** the **3/32″ ARIAL** text style for text annotations.

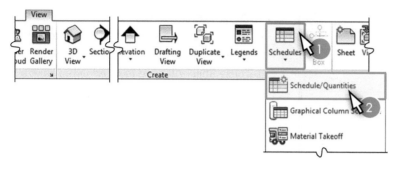

The Lighting Fixture Schedule is useful to identify the type and quantity of light fixtures in the project. This schedule should be customized to include fields important to the current project.

- *Step 1*: **CLICK** the **SCHEDULES DROP-DOWN ARROW** in the **VIEW** tab.
- *Step 2*: **CLICK** the **SCHEDULES/QUANTITIES** option in the Drop-down menu.

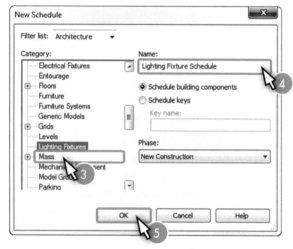

- *Step 3*: **SELECT** the **LIGHTING FIXTURES** category in the **NEW SCHEDULE** dialog box.

- *Step 4*: **CHANGE** the schedule name to **LIGHTING FIXTURE SCHEDULE.**

- *Step 5*: **CLICK** the **OK** button.

Adding Fields

- *Step 1*: **CLICK ONCE** on the **TYPE MARK** field in the available fields column.
- *Step 2*: **CLICK** the **ADD** button.

Repeat *Step 1* and *Step 2* to add the following fields to the schedule (in this order):

- **TYPE MARK**
- **COUNT**
- **DESCRIPTION**
- **MANUFACTURER** (optional)
- **COMMENTS**

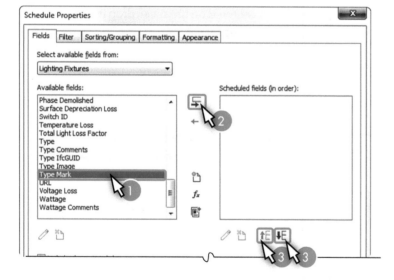

- *Step 3*: Use the **MOVE UP** and **MOVE DOWN** buttons to change the order of the fields in the schedule to match the order listed above.

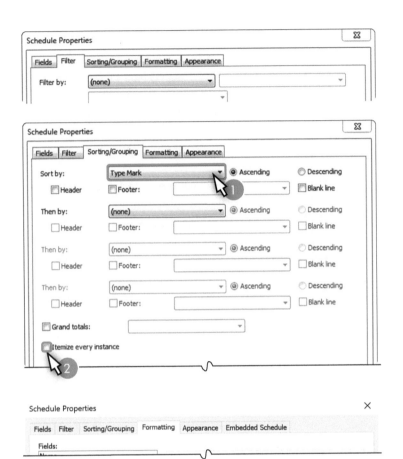

Filtering the Schedule
The Filter tab provides the ability to limit the light fixtures that appear in the schedule. Do not make any changes to this tab at this time.

Sorting the Schedule
The Sorting/Grouping tab contains multiple sort criteria for the schedule.
- *Step 1:* **CHANGE** the primary **SORT BY** parameter to **TYPE MARK**.
- *Step 2:* **UNCHECK** the **ITEMIZE EVERY INSTANCE** box.

Formatting the Schedule
The Formatting tab contains individual format settings for each column in the schedule. Do not make any changes to this tab at this time.

Viewing the Schedule
The Lighting Fixture Schedule view is used to update light fixture properties in a project.
- It is possible that your lighting fixture schedule view will appear similar to this example. The blank row at the top of this schedule is the result of missing or undefined light fixture tags in the floor plan view.
- As light fixture tags are added or defined in the ceiling plan view, the schedule will automatically add a row for each family type.

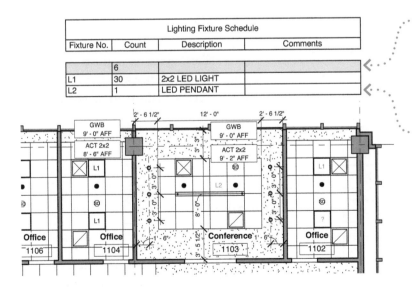

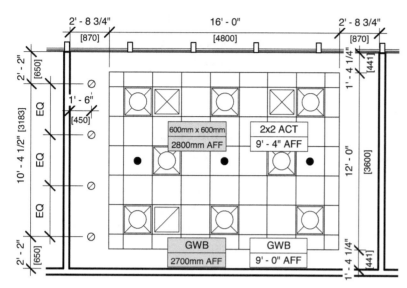

Ceiling plans are typically drawn to the same architectural scale as the floor plan. Dimensions on the ceiling plan are limited to elements unique to the ceiling plan. For example, you would dimension lights in the RCP while you would not dimension walls because they should be dimensioned in the floor plan.

- Changes in ceiling material are often dimensioned in the ceiling plan.
- Items located within a gypsum wallboard (GWB) ceiling are dimensioned.
- Items located within an acoustic ceiling tile (ACT) system are not dimensioned, as their location can be easily determined based on the symbol's location in the ACT grid.

> The SI equivalent dimensions are provided in brackets. SI ceiling tags are rendered with a light grey background.

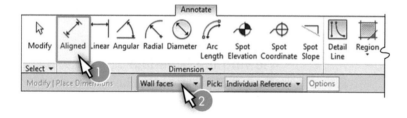

Adding Dimension Strings

- *Step 1*: **CLICK** the **ALIGNED DIMENSION** button in the **ANNOTATE** tab.
- *Step 2*: In the **MODIFY | PLACE DIMENSIONS** tab, **SELECT WALL FACES**. This allows you to start dimension strings from the faces of walls in the ceiling plan.

- *Step 3*: Following the example to the left, **CLICK** on the **INTERIOR WALL** in the room.
- *Steps 4–5*: **CLICK** on the **CENTER LINES** for the recessed lights.
- *Step 6*: **CLICK** on the **INTERIOR WALL** in the room.

As you move the mouse you will see the dimension string following the cursor position.

- *Step 7*: Position the dimension string outside the room as shown in this drawing and **CLICK ONCE** to **PLACE** the dimension string and end the Dimension command.

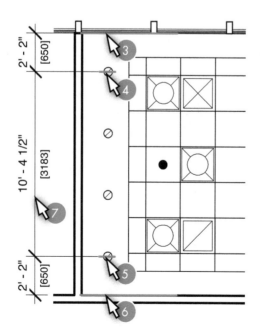

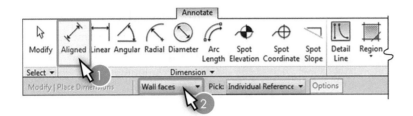

Adding EQ Dimension Strings

The dimension equality icon (**EQ**) equally distributes all items in the dimension string and replaces the actual dimension with the **EQ** symbol.

- *Step 1*: **CLICK** the **ALIGNED DIMENSION** button in the **ANNOTATE** tab.
- *Step 2*: In the **MODIFY | PLACE DIMENSIONS** tab, **SELECT WALL FACES.**

- *Steps 3–6*: Following the example to the left, **CLICK** on the **CENTER LINE** for each recessed light.
- *Step 7*: Position the dimension string outside the room as shown in this example. **CLICK ONCE** to **PLACE** the dimension string and end the Dimension command.
- *Step 8*: **CLICK** the **EQ ICON** to distribute the lights in this dimension string.

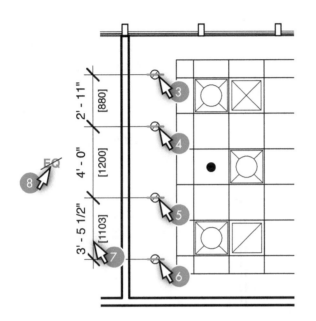

This drawing shows the redistributed lights after the dimension equality icon is clicked.

- *Step 9 (optional)*: **CLICKING** the **DIMENSION EQUALITY** icon a second time will replace the **EQ** symbol in the dimension string with the actual dimension between each item.

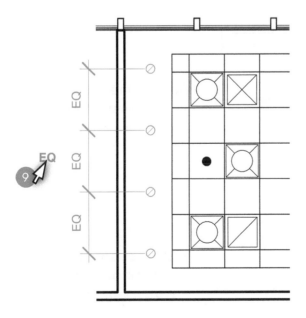

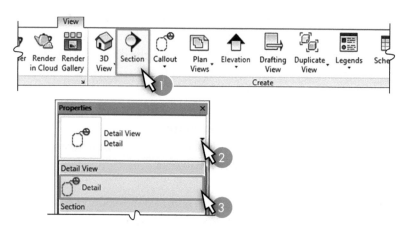

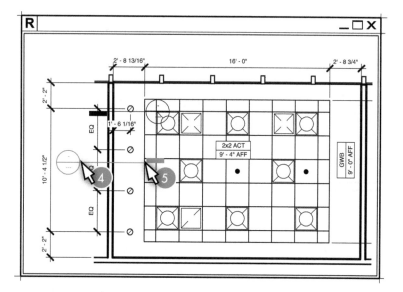

Adding Ceiling Details

Ceiling details are used to document unique conditions in a ceiling system. Details can include soffit conditions, changes in material, and ceiling clouds.

- *Step 1*: From a **CEILING PLAN** view, **CLICK** the **SECTION** button in the **VIEW** tab.
- *Step 2*: In the **PROPERTIES** box, **CLICK** the **SECTION TYPE DROP-DOWN ARROW**.
- *Step 3*: **SELECT DETAIL** as the section type.

- *Step 4*: **CLICK ONCE** in the elevation to locate one end of the ceiling section. As you move the cursor, the detail section symbol will stretch, indicating the scope of the detail.
- *Step 5*: **CLICK ONCE** to locate the bottom of the casework section.

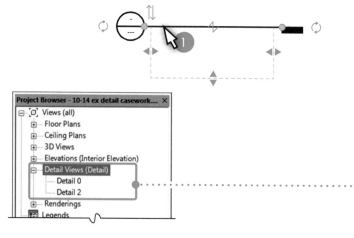

Viewing the Ceiling Detail

- *Step 1*: **RIGHT-CLICK** on the **DETAIL SYMBOL** in the ceiling plan and **SELECT GO TO VIEW** from the context menu.

- The **CEILING DETAIL** view is also available in the **DETAIL VIEWS** section of the **PROJECT BROWSER**.

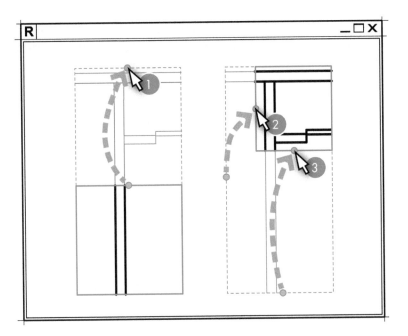

Adjusting the Detail's Scope

In most instances, Revit creates the detail section view between 3'-0" and 6'-0" above the finish floor. As shown in this example, the resulting view is two lines representing the wall in the detail.

- *Step 1*: **STRETCH** the top of the **CROP REGION** box to reveal the ceiling and structural floor above.
- *Steps 2–3*: **STRETCH** the left and bottom of the **CROP REGION** box to crop the soffit detail as shown in this example.

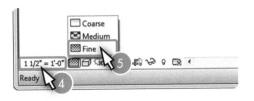

- *Step 4*: **SET** the **ARCHITECTURAL SCALE** of the detail view to **1-1/2" = 1'-0"**.

  The equivalent SI scale is **1:10**.

- *Step 5*: **SET** the **DETAIL LEVEL** to **FINE**.

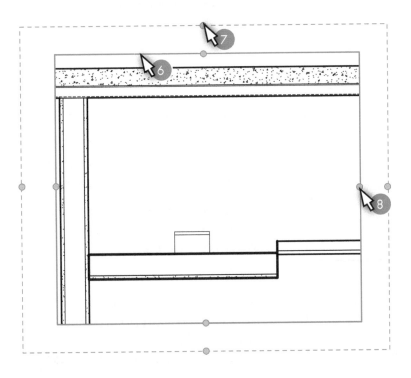

- *Step 6*: **CLICK ONCE** on the **CROP REGION BOX** in the detail view.
- *Step 7*: **DRAG** the **ANNOTATION CROP HANDLES** to adjust the width and height of the annotation extents in the detail.
- *Step 8*: **DRAG** the **MODEL CROP HANDLES** to adjust the width and height of the detail.

> **Guided Discovery 13.1**: Following the exercise on this and the following pages, create a ceiling detail. The support file is at **WWW.RAFDBOOK.COM/DOWNLOADS.**

CEILING DETAILS (continued)

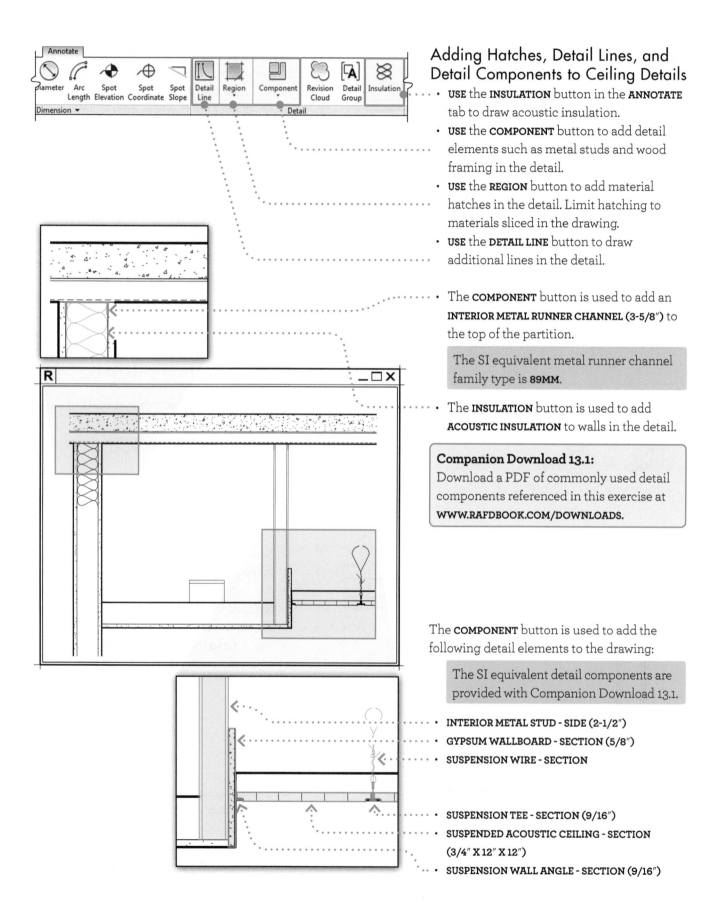

Adding Hatches, Detail Lines, and Detail Components to Ceiling Details

- **USE** the **INSULATION** button in the **ANNOTATE** tab to draw acoustic insulation.
- **USE** the **COMPONENT** button to add detail elements such as metal studs and wood framing in the detail.
- **USE** the **REGION** button to add material hatches in the detail. Limit hatching to materials sliced in the drawing.
- **USE** the **DETAIL LINE** button to draw additional lines in the detail.

- The **COMPONENT** button is used to add an **INTERIOR METAL RUNNER CHANNEL (3-5/8")** to the top of the partition.

  The SI equivalent metal runner channel family type is **89MM**.

- The **INSULATION** button is used to add **ACOUSTIC INSULATION** to walls in the detail.

  Companion Download 13.1:
  Download a PDF of commonly used detail components referenced in this exercise at **WWW.RAFDBOOK.COM/DOWNLOADS**.

The **COMPONENT** button is used to add the following detail elements to the drawing:

  The SI equivalent detail components are provided with Companion Download 13.1.

- **INTERIOR METAL STUD - SIDE (2-1/2")**
- **GYPSUM WALLBOARD - SECTION (5/8")**
- **SUSPENSION WIRE - SECTION**

- **SUSPENSION TEE - SECTION (9/16")**
- **SUSPENDED ACOUSTIC CEILING - SECTION (3/4" X 12" X 12")**
- **SUSPENSION WALL ANGLE - SECTION (9/16")**

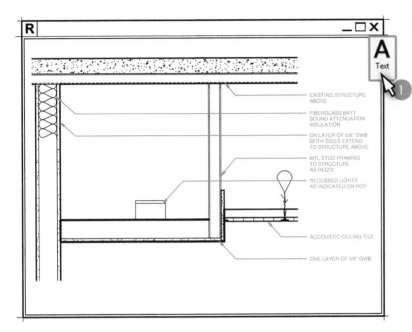

Annotating Ceiling Details

- *Step 1*: **USE** the **TEXT** button in the **ANNOTATION** tab to add annotation notes to the detail.

Ceiling Detail Annotation Tips:

- Limit the annotation text in ceiling details to information that is not available in other views.
- Annotate special materials like acoustic insulation.
- Annotate the location and thickness of gypsum wallboard (GWB) and acoustic ceiling tile (ACT).
- Annotate existing structural elements.
- Annotate metal or wood studs.

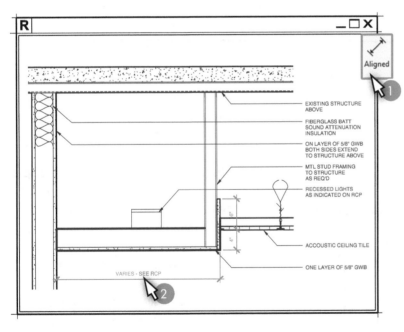

Dimensioning Ceiling Details

- *Step 1*: **USE** the **ALIGNED DIMENSION** button in the **ANNOTATION** tab to add dimensions to the detail.
- *Step 2*: **DOUBLE-CLICK** on a **DIMENSION** to change the measured value to text. In this example, the measured dimension was changed to **VARIES - SEE RCP**.

Download an SI example of this detail at:
WWW.RAFDBOOK.COM/DOWNLOADS

Ceiling Detail Dimensioning Tips:

- Add vertical dimension strings at changes in ceiling height.
- Add horizontal dimensions to indicate the width of ceiling materials. In this example, the dimension was overridden with text because the dimension changes at different positions in the ceiling.

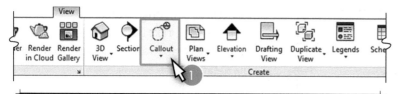

Adding Enlarged RCP Callouts

- *Step 1*: From any RCP view, **CLICK** the **CALLOUT** button in the **VIEW** tab.
- *Step 2 (not shown)*: **CLICK** the **CALLOUT TYPE DROP-DOWN ARROW** in the **PROPERTIES** box and **SELECT CEILING PLAN** as the callout type.

- *Step 3*: **CLICK ONCE** in the RCP to locate the top-left corner of the callout view's scope. As you move the cursor, the callout box will stretch, indicating the scope of the enlarged view.
- *Step 4*: **CLICK ONCE** in the RCP to locate the bottom-right corner of the callout view's scope.

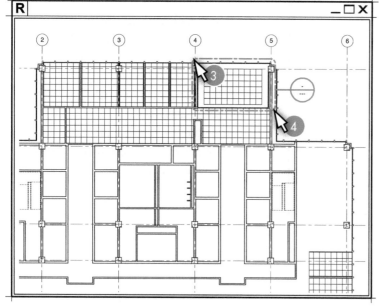

> **Guided Discovery 13.2**: Following the exercise on this and the following pages, create a ceiling callout. The support file is at **WWW.RAFDBOOK.COM/DOWNLOADS.**

Viewing the Enlarged RCP

- *Step 1*: **RIGHT-CLICK** on the **CALLOUT SYMBOL** and **SELECT GO TO VIEW** from the context menu.

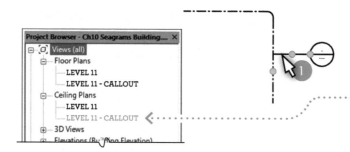

- The **ENLARGED RCP** view is also available in the **CEILING PLANS** section of the **PROJECT BROWSER.**

Adjusting the Enlarged Plan's Scope

- *Step 1 (not shown)*: **CLICK** the **SHOW/HIDE CROP REGION** button in the status bar until the **CROP REGION** box is visible in the callout view.
- *Step 2*: **CLICK ONCE** the **CROP REGION BOX** in the callout view.
- *Step 3*: **DRAG** the **ANNOTATION CROP HANDLES** to adjust the width and height of the annotation extents in the callout.
- *Step 4*: **DRAG** the **CROP MODEL HANDLES** to adjust the width and height of the callout. Changes made to the model crop will adjust the size of the callout rectangle in the original RCP view.

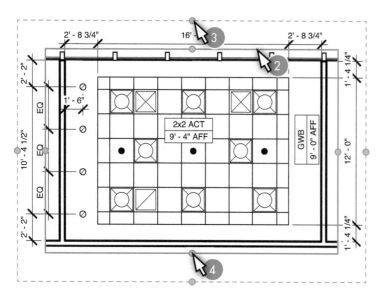

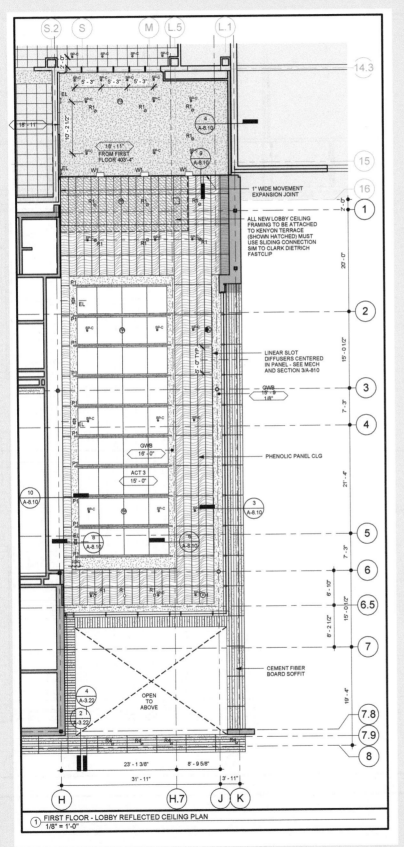

Revit Tips

- Enlarged views are commonly drawn at 1/4" = 1'-0" scale.

  > The equivalent SI scale is **1:50.**

- Revit will automatically cross-reference the Callout symbol in the floor plan, elevation, or ceiling plan when you place the callout view on a sheet.

Annotation Tips

- In Revit, set an appropriate architectural scale before annotating each enlarged view.
- Add room labels to each space in the callout view.
- Add text labels to identify materials not annotated in the original view.

Dimension Tips

- In Revit, set an appropriate architectural scale before dimensioning an interior elevation.
- Limit dimensions to objects and elements that are not already dimensioned in the referenced view.
- Start dimension strings from the column grid.

Companion Download 13.2:

Download a professional example of ceiling details at **WWW.RAFDBOOK.COM/DOWNLOADS.**

Partial Ceiling Plan

Middlebury College Squash Center

ARC/Architectural Resources Cambridge

REFLECTED CEILING PLAN (RCP) CHECKLIST

Revit Tips

- RCPs are commonly drawn at the same architectural scale as the floor plan.
- Revit automatically hides furniture in the RCP view.
- In Revit, the default cut plane for RCPs is 7' or 2300mm above the finish floor.

Annotation Tips

- Ceiling components must be hosted by a ceiling. This means you must add ceilings to the ceiling plan before you can add light fixtures, HVAC symbols, or life safety symbols.
- Use the Ceiling Tag w Height symbol to annotate each ceiling surface in the RCP.
- Use text annotations to identify special conditions in the RCP.
- Building systems located in acoustic ceiling tile (ACT) ceilings should be positioned in the center of a ceiling tile.

Dimension Tips

- Set an appropriate architectural scale before dimensioning a ceiling plan.
- Dimensions on the ceiling plan are limited to elements unique to the ceiling plan.
- Changes in ceiling material are often dimensioned in the ceiling plan.
- Building systems located in gypsum wallboard (GWB) ceilings should be dimensioned to the closest wall.
- Building systems located in ACT ceilings are usually not dimensioned because their position can be located with the ceiling grid.

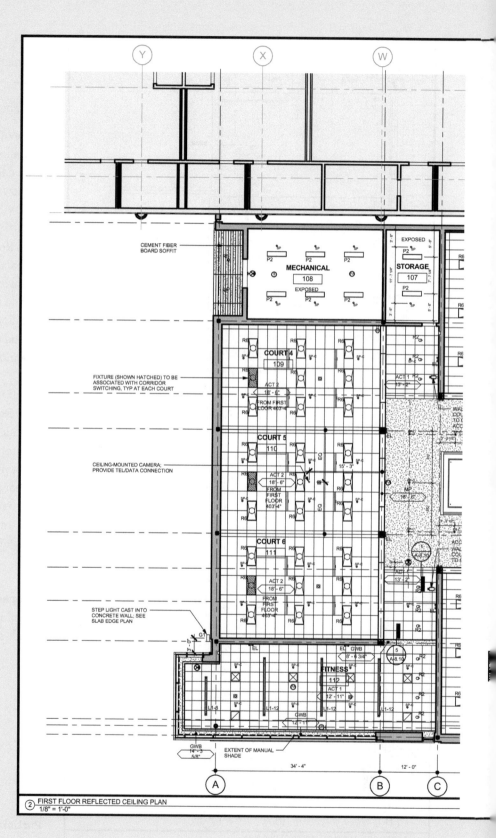

FIRST FLOOR REFLECTED CEILING PLAN
1/8" = 1'-0"

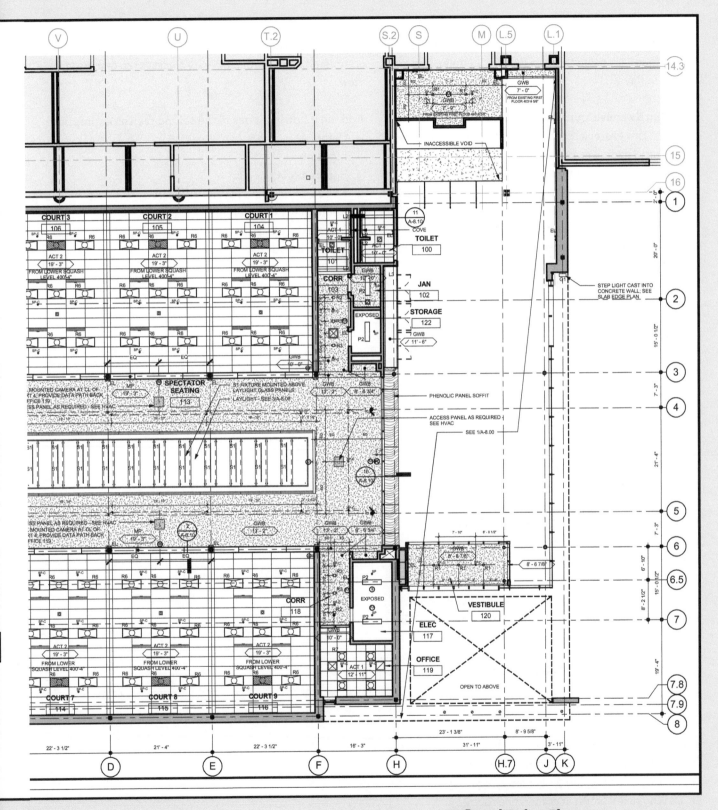

Reflected Ceiling Plan

Middlebury College Squash Center

ARC/Architectural Resources Cambridge

LEARNING EXERCISES

Learning Exercises

These exercises are intended to help you improve your understanding of construction RCPs, schedules, and details in Revit.

Learning Exercise 13.1: Construction RCPs

To begin this exercise, open the Revit project completed in Learning Exercises 12.4 at the end of Chapter 12. You can also download a support file and a sample solution for this exercise at **WWW.RAFDBOOK.COM/DOWNLOADS.**

Follow the step-by-step exercises in the chapter to add a **CONSTRUCTION REFLECTED CEILING PLAN** to the companion Revit project:

- Duplicate the **LEVEL 11 RCP** view and rename it to **LEVEL 11 CONSTRUCTION RCP.**
- Set the Architectural Scale.
- Add the following elements to the RCP:
  - Ceilings
  - Lighting
  - Egress signage
  - Fire sprinklers and HVAC diffusers
  - Ceiling tags with height
  - Light fixture tags
  - Dimensions and annotations

Learning Exercise 13.2: Light Fixture Schedule

Download a sample solution in PDF format at **WWW.RAFDBOOK.COM/DOWNLOADS.**

Follow the step-by-step exercises in the chapter to add a **LIGHT FIXTURE SCHEDULE** to the companion Revit project.

Learning Exercise 13.3: Enlarged RCPs and Details

Download a sample solution in PDF format at **WWW.RAFDBOOK.COM/DOWNLOADS.**

Follow the step-by-step exercises in the chapter to add the following **DETAILS** to the companion Revit project:

- Enlarged ceiling plan (at conference room)
- Ceiling detail (soffit at conference room)
- Plan detail (column detail)
- Casework detail

Application Exercises

Using an assignment from your instructor or a previously completed studio project, create a **REFLECTED CEILING PLAN** view.

Add the following items to the ceiling plan as appropriate:
- Ceilings
- Lighting
- Egress signage
- Fire sprinklers and HVAC diffusers
- Ceiling tags with height
- Light fixture tags
- Dimensions and annotations

chapter 14

SHEETS AND PRINTING

Revit excels in sheet creation, organization, and printing because it automates many of the tedious and error-prone tasks required with CAD drawings and hand drawings. This chapter explains how to create and organize sheets for construction drawings. Creating custom title blocks is also reviewed in the chapter.

IN THIS CHAPTER

CREATING SHEETS

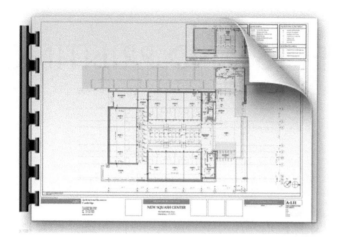

Organizing Drawings

The order and appearance of sheets is crucial when creating drawings for a design presentation or for construction documents. Revit excels in this part of project delivery because it automates many of the tedious and error-prone tasks that were manually completed in AutoCAD.

The title block (or title border) should be consistent across all presentation sheets. Drawing sheets should be organized with a logical numbering scheme.

Drawing symbols (like elevation and section tags) should properly link the plan and elevation or section drawing.

NO.	SHEET NAME	NO.	SHEET NAME
A-000	TITLE SHEET/COVER	A-601	SCHEDULES AND DOOR TYPES
A-101	FIRST FLOOR PLAN	A-701	FIRST FLOOR FURNITURE PLAN
A-102	SECOND FLOOR PLAN	A-702	SECOND FLOOR FURNITURE PLAN
A-201	FIRST FLOOR RCP	A-801	FIRST FLOOR FINISH PLAN
A-202	SECOND FLOOR RCP	A-802	SECOND FLOOR FINISH PLAN
A-301	BUILDING SECTIONS AND EXTERIOR DETAILS	A-901	ISOMETRICS, PERSPECTIVES, AND PHOTOGRAPHS
A-401	ELEVATIONS AND ENLARGED VIEWS		
A-501	DETAILS		

Numbering Conventions

The National CAD Standard (NCS) was established to combine multiple competing construction document-numbering conventions. The NCS combines The American Institute of Architects' (AIA) CAD Layer Guidelines, the Construction Specification Institute's (CSI) Uniform Drawing System, and the National Institute of Building Sciences' (NIBS) Plotting Guidelines.

Many design firms develop numbering standards based on the NCS or CSI standards. The example above is provided to illustrate one possible sheet sequence for construction documents.

Ă-103

A-103

A-103

A-412

- The **FIRST LETTER** of the sheet number refers to the discipline. In this example, the **A** refers to **A**rchitecture. Other disciplines include **M**echanical, **E**lectrical, **P**lumbing, and **S**tructural.
- The first **NUMBER** refers to the architectural drawing type. In this example, the **1** refers to **FLOOR PLANS**.
- For floor plans and RCPs, the second two **NUMBERS** refer to the level in the building. In this example, the **03** refers to the **THIRD FLOOR PLAN**.
- The second two **NUMBERS** can also reference additional sheets in the drawing category. For example, sheet **A-412** is sheet **12** in the **A-400** series (elevations).

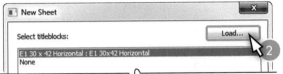

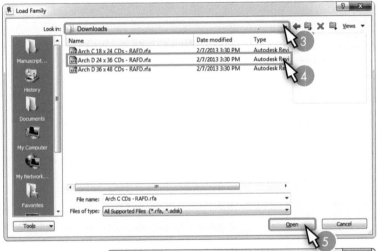

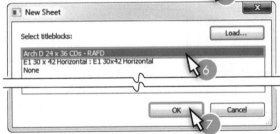

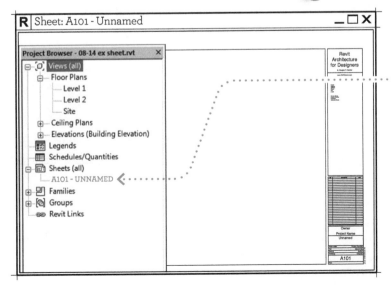

Adding the First Sheet

- *Step 1:* **CLICK** the **SHEET** button in the **VIEW** tab. This opens the **NEW SHEET** dialog box. Because this is the first sheet you are adding to the Revit project, you will need to load a title block family.
- *Step 2:* **CLICK** the **LOAD** button.

- *Step 3:* In the **LOAD FAMILY** file browser, navigate to the folder where you downloaded the textbook companion title blocks.
- *Step 4:* **SELECT** the following title block: **ARCH D 24 X 36 CDS - RAFD.RFA**

  The SI equivalent title block is:
  A1 594x841mm CDS - RAFD.RFA

- *Step 5:* **CLICK** the **OPEN** button. After loading the title block, it will be visible as an option in the **NEW SHEET** dialog box.

- *Step 6:* **SELECT** the **ARCH D 24 X 36 CDS - RAFD** title block.
- *Step 7:* **CLICK** the **OK** button to create a new sheet with the selected title block.

- Revit creates sheet **A101 - UNNAMED** in the Revit project as shown in this example. The sheet is also added to the **PROJECT BROWSER**. The default number and name given to new sheets in Revit is **A101 - UNNAMED**. We will change this later in the chapter.

CREATING SHEETS (continued)

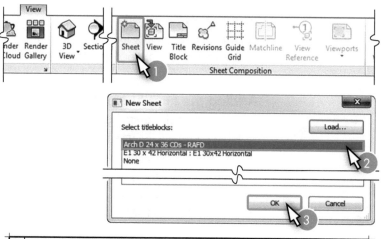

Adding Additional Sheets

- *Step 1*: **CLICK** the **SHEET** button in the **VIEW** tab. This opens the **NEW SHEET** dialog box.

- *Step 2*: **SELECT** the **ARCH D 24 X 36 CDS - RAFD** title block.

  The SI equivalent title block is:
  A1 594x841mm CDS - RAFD.RFA

- *Step 3*: **CLICK** the **OK** button to create a new sheet with the selected title block.

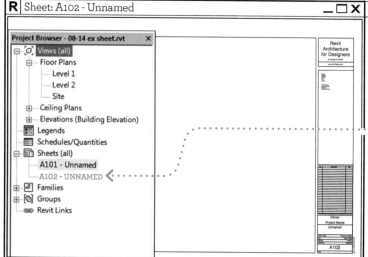

- Revit creates sheet **A102 - UNNAMED** in the Revit project as shown in this example. The sheet is also added to the **PROJECT BROWSER**.

Renaming Sheets

When you create the first sheet in a project, Revit names it A101 - Unnamed. Additional views are named A102, A103, and A104. It does not take very long before the Project Browser is filled with sheets, making it difficult to find a specific drawing.

As you create sheets, rename each sheet with an appropriate number and descriptive title.

- *Step 4*: **RIGHT-CLICK** on the **VIEW** in the **PROJECT BROWSER**.
- *Step 5*: **SELECT RENAME** from the context menu.
- *Step 6*: **TYPE** an appropriate **SHEET NUMBER** and **SHEET NAME** in the dialog box.
- *Step 7*: **CLICK** the **OK** button.

Following these steps, **RENAME** sheet **A102** to **A-201 - FIRST FLOOR RCP**.

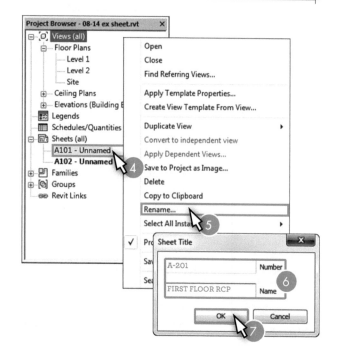

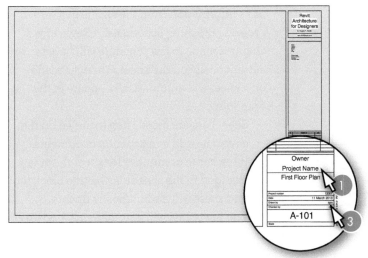

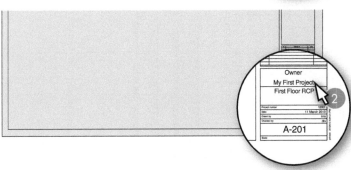

Title Block Variables

One of the innovations BIM brings to title blocks is the way in which Revit can automatically adjust the text labels on sheets in a project. Text labels on a sheet are either project variables or sheet variables.

Project Variables

When a project variable is updated on one sheet, the remaining sheets in the project are automatically updated. Two examples are the Owner and Project Name variables.

- *Step 1*: In sheet **A-101**, **DOUBLE-CLICK** on the **PROJECT NAME** variable. Change it to **MY FIRST PROJECT** and **PRESS ENTER.**
- *Step 2*: Notice that the project name on sheet **A-201** is automatically updated.

Sheet Variables

When a sheet variable is updated on one sheet, the remaining sheets in the project are not updated. Two examples are the Drawn By and the Sheet Name variables.

- *Step 3*: In sheet **A-101**, **DOUBLE-CLICK** on the **DRAWN BY** variable. Change it to **YOUR NAME** and **PRESS ENTER.** Note the **DRAWN BY** variable on sheet **A-201** is not updated.

Adding the Guide Grid

The Guide Grid helps align elements on sheets. It can also help align elements across multiple sheets.

- *Step 1 (not shown)*: **OPEN** the **A-101** sheet from the **PROJECT BROWSER.**
- *Step 2*: **CLICK** the **GUIDE GRID** in the **VIEW** tab. This opens the **ASSIGN GUIDE GRID** dialog box.
- *Step 3*: **TYPE ARCH D GUIDE GRID** in the **CREATE NEW** portion of the dialog box.
- *Step 4*: **CLICK** the **OK** button to assign the new grid to sheet **A-101.**
- *Step 5 (not shown)*: **OPEN** sheet **A-201** and assign the **ARCH D GUIDE GRID.**

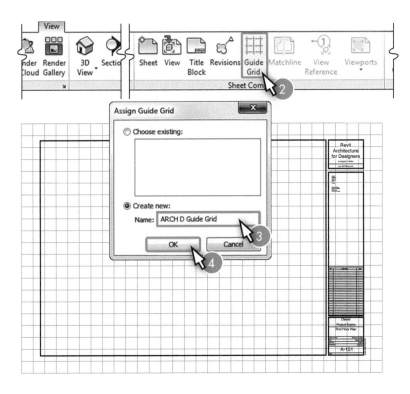

The Sheet List is a dynamic schedule that sorts information from the sheets in a project. Like other schedules in Revit, any changes made in the schedule will update automatically on the sheet. Changes made on a sheet will automatically update in the schedule.

- Sheet lists are most often included on the cover sheet in construction documents.
- If the name or number for sheet A-501 is changed in the schedule, the title block for that sheet will automatically update.
- The Sheet List will automatically update as you add or remove sheets from the project.

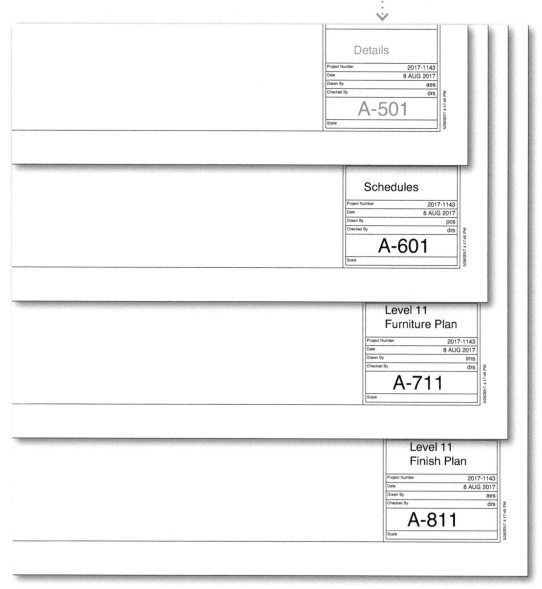

Sheet List	
Sheet Number	**Sheet Name**
A-000	Cover Sheet
A-111	Level 11 Construction Plan
A-211	Level 11 RCP
A-401	Interior Elevations
A-501	Details
A-601	Schedules
A-711	Level 11 Furniture Plan
A-811	Level 11 Finish Plan

Details

Project Number	2017-1143
Date	8 AUG 2017
Drawn By	aes
Checked By	drs

A-501

| Scale | |

Schedules

Project Number	2017-1143
Date	8 AUG 2017
Drawn By	pcs
Checked By	drs

A-601

| Scale | |

Level 11
Furniture Plan

Project Number	2017-1143
Date	8 AUG 2017
Drawn By	ims
Checked By	drs

A-711

| Scale | |

Level 11
Finish Plan

Project Number	2017-1143
Date	8 AUG 2017
Drawn By	aes
Checked By	drs

A-811

| Scale | |

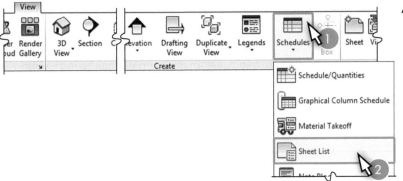

Adding the Sheet Lists

- *Step 1*: **CLICK** the **SCHEDULES DROP-DOWN ARROW** in the **VIEW** tab.
- *Step 2*: **CLICK** the **SHEET LIST** option in the Drop-down menu.

Adding Fields

The Fields tab determines which columns appear in the sheet list.

- *Step 1*: **CLICK ONCE** on the **SHEET NUMBER** field in the **FIELDS** tab.
- *Step 2*: **CLICK** the **ADD** button.

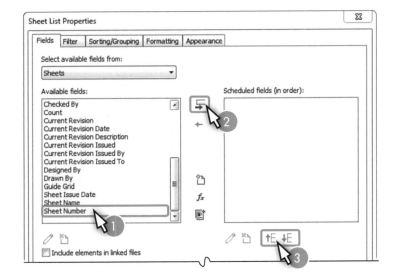

Repeat *Steps 1* and *2* to add the following fields to the schedule (in this order):

- **SHEET NUMBER**
- **SHEET NAME**

- *Step 3*: Use the **MOVE UP** and **MOVE DOWN** buttons to change the order of the fields in the schedule to match the order listed above.

Sorting the List

Use the Sorting/Grouping tab to tell Revit how to sort the sheet list.

- *Step 1*: **SET** the **SORT BY** parameter to **SHEET NUMBER**.
- *Step 2*: **CLICK** the **OK** button to close the **SHEET LIST PROPERTIES** dialog box and open the sheet list.

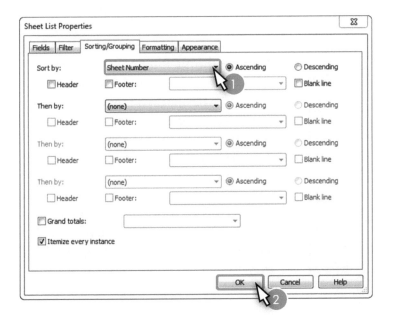

Sheet names and numbers are automatically added to this list as you add sheets in the current project.

Drag the sheet list from the **PROJECT BROWSER** to the cover sheet in the current project.

Adding views to sheets is a relatively easy process in Revit because all of the views and sheets live within a single project. Before you begin, set an appropriate architecture scale for the view and create a sheet with the correct title block.

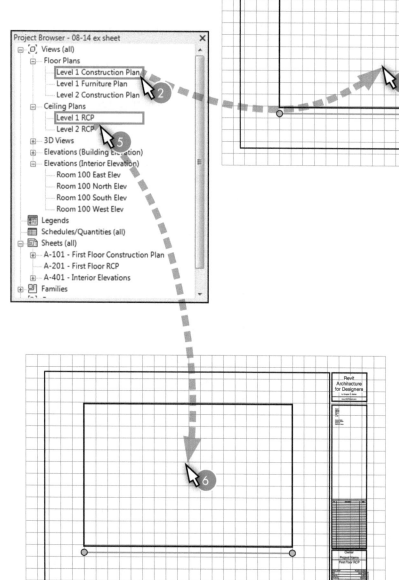

Adding the Floor Plan to A-101

- *Step 1 (not shown)*: **OPEN** sheet **A-101**.
- *Step 2*: **DRAG** the **LEVEL 1 FLOOR PLAN** view from the **PROJECT BROWSER** to the **A-101** sheet view.
- *Step 3*: When the **LEVEL 1 PLAN** view is centered on the sheet, drop it on the sheet by **RELEASING** the mouse button.

Adding the RCP to A-201

- *Step 4 (not shown)*: **OPEN** sheet **A-201**.
- *Step 5*: **DRAG** the **LEVEL 1 RCP** view from the **PROJECT BROWSER** to the **A-201** sheet view.
- *Step 6*: When the **LEVEL 1 RCP** view is centered on the sheet, drop it on the sheet by **RELEASING** the mouse button.

Views can be added to only one sheet in a project. Changes made to a view are automatically updated on the corresponding sheet view.

Coordinating Drawing Symbols

When drawing by hand or in AutoCAD, designers would manually coordinate drawing symbols between plan and elevation drawings. Revit does this automatically.

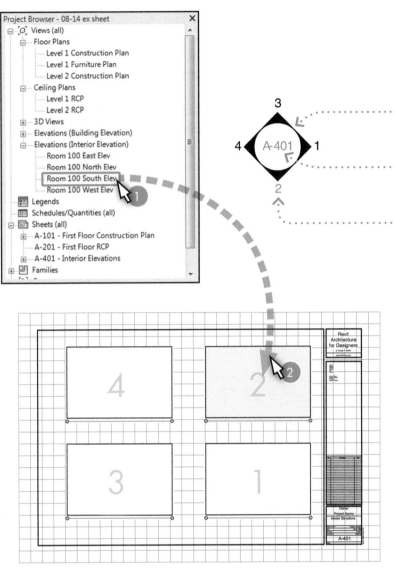

- The **INTERIOR ELEVATION** symbol is automatically added to floor plan views as you create interior elevation views.
- In this example, the **A-401** indicates that the interior elevations are located on sheet A-401.
- **ARROW 2** (the south elevation) is **DRAWING 2** on sheet **A-401**.

- *Steps 1–2*: When you add an elevation view to a sheet, Revit updates the symbol with the elevation's sheet and detail number.

Detail Numbering Schemes

When there is more than one drawing on a sheet, the numbering and arrangement of drawings is very important.

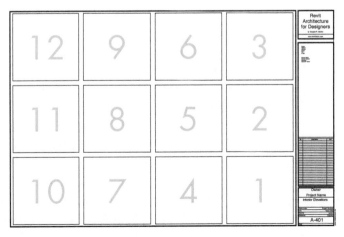

In this example, detail 1 is located at the bottom-right corner of the sheet. Many offices use this standard for detail numbering and detail arrangement.

CUSTOMIZING TITLE BLOCKS

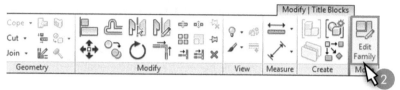

It is possible that you will want to customize the title blocks that ship with this book or with Revit. The best place to start is by loading a title sheet into your Revit project.

- *Step 1 (not shown):* **OPEN** a **SHEET VIEW** and **CLICK ONCE** on the **TITLE BLOCK**.
- *Step 2:* **CLICK** the **EDIT FAMILY** button in the **MODIFY | TITLE BLOCKS** tab. This opens the title block in Revit's **FAMILY EDITOR**.

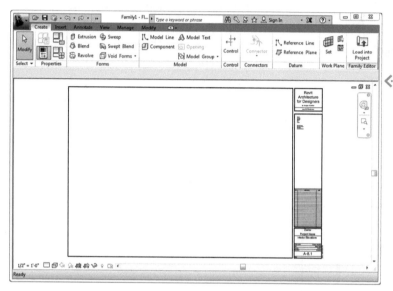

- The **FAMILY EDITOR** looks very similar to Revit's project interface. Notice the tabs in the Family Editor ribbon are different from the tabs in the Project ribbon.

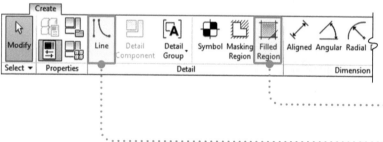

The Create Tab
The **CREATE** tab includes commands that add new items to the title block.

- **CLICK** the **FILLED REGION** button to add hatches to the title block.
- **CLICK** the **LINE** button to add new lines to the title block.

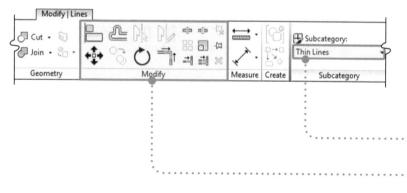

The Modify | Lines Tab
Lines in the title block can be modified with the same tools used to modify walls in a Revit project.

- *Step 1 (not shown):* **CLICK** any **LINE** in the title block to activate the **MODIFY | LINES** tab.
- **CHANGE** the line's **SUBCATEGORY** to adjust the line weight of the selected line.
- **USE** the **MODIFY** tools to adjust the selected line. Tools include Align, Offset, Move, Rotate, Trim to Corner, and Trim/Extend.

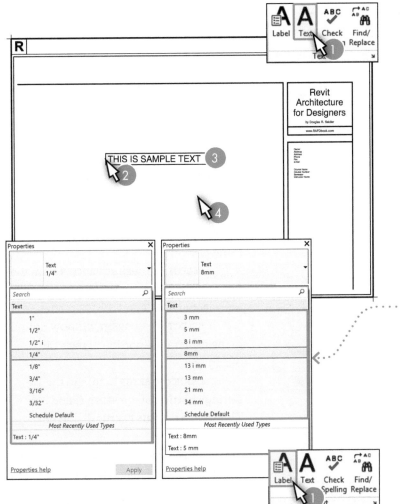

Adding Text to a Title Block

Text added to a title block cannot be edited within the Revit project. In title blocks, text is commonly used for elements that do not change from project to project, such as a design firm's name or contact information.

- *Step 1:* **CLICK** the **TEXT** button in the **CREATE** tab to add text to the title block.
- *Step 2:* **CLICK** in the title block where you want to place the text or **DRAG** a rectangle to create wrapping text.
- *Step 3:* **TYPE** the text you wish to add.
- *Step 4:* **CLICK** anywhere in the view to finish the Text command.

> Standard SI text sizes for construction documents are provided on page 303

- To change the size of the text, **CLICK ONCE** on the **TEXT** and then **SELECT** a different **FAMILY TYPE** in the **PROPERTIES** dialog box.

Adding Text Labels to a Title Block

Labels are intelligent text placeholders that display a family property variable or a project property variable. In title blocks, labels can be edited on a sheet-by-sheet basis in a project. Labels can also automatically populate with information about a sheet, like the sheet number or sheet name.

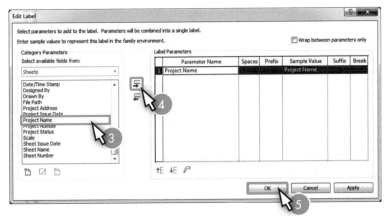

- *Step 1:* **CLICK** the **LABEL** button in the **CREATE** tab to add text to the title block.
- *Step 2 (not shown):* **CLICK** in the title block where you want to place the label. This opens the **EDIT LABEL** dialog box.
- *Step 3:* **SELECT** the **CATEGORY PARAMETERS**. In this example we picked the **PROJECT NAME** parameter.
- *Step 4:* **CLICK** the **ADD TO LABEL** button.
- *Step 5:* **CLICK** the **OK** button.

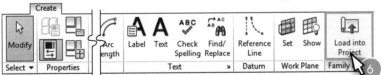

- *Step 6:* When you have completed the title block edits, **CLICK** the **LOAD INTO PROJECT** button in the **CREATE** tab. This replaces the title block in your project with the title block edits made in the family editor.

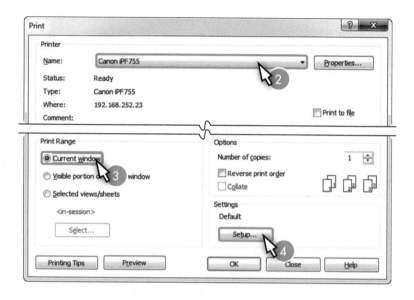

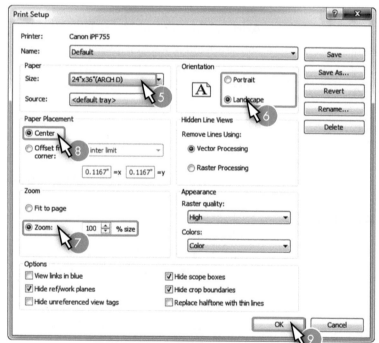

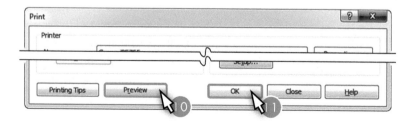

Printing in Revit is vastly improved when compared to configuring paper space, viewports, and printing in AutoCAD.

The architectural scale of drawings is set in each view. While viewports still exist in Revit, they are automatically configured with a simple drag and drop interface.

Printing the Current Window

- *Step 1 (not shown):* **OPEN** the **VIEW** or **SHEET** that you want to print. On the keyboard, **PRESS** the **CTRL** key and the letter **P** at the same time.
- *Step 2:* **SELECT** the desired **PRINTER** from the printer Drop-down menu. In this example we selected the Canon iPF755 plotter.
- *Step 3:* **SELECT** the **CURRENT WINDOW** option in the print range portion of the print dialog box.
- *Step 4:* **CLICK** the **SETUP** button in the settings portion of the **PRINT** dialog box. This opens the **PRINT SETUP** dialog box.

- *Step 5:* **SELECT** the proper **PAPER SIZE**. (The paper size should match the title block size when printing sheets.)
- *Step 6:* **SELECT** the paper **ORIENTATION**.
- *Step 7:* **CHANGE** the **ZOOM** setting to **ZOOM: 100% SIZE**. When you change the zoom setting, the **PAPER PLACEMENT** is automatically changed from **CENTER** to **OFFSET FROM CORNER**.
- *Step 8:* **CHANGE** the **PAPER PLACEMENT** setting back to **CENTER**.
- *Step 9:* **CLICK** the **OK** button. This closes the **PRINT SETUP** dialog box and returns to the **PRINT** dialog box.

- *Step 10:* **CLICK** the **PREVIEW** button to see a preview of the print.
- *Step 11:* In the **PRINT** dialog box, **CLICK** the **OK** button to send the current view to the printer.

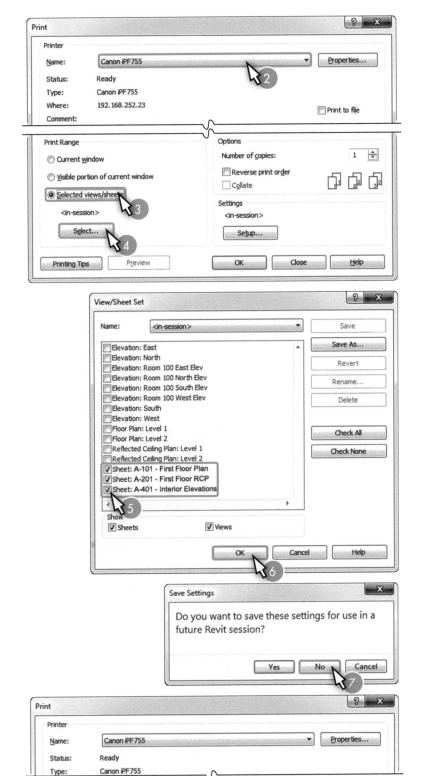

Printing Multiple Views/Sheets

- *Step 1 (not shown):* On the keyboard, **PRESS** the **CTRL** key and the letter **P**.
- *Step 2:* **SELECT** the **DESIRED PRINTER** from the printer Drop-down menu. In this example, we selected the Canon iPF755 plotter.

- *Step 3:* **SELECT** the **SELECTED VIEWS/SHEETS** option in the **PRINT RANGE** portion of the **PRINT** dialog box.
- *Step 4:* **CLICK** the **SELECT** button to select the views/sheets to print. This opens the **VIEW/SHEET SET** dialog box.

- *Step 5:* **CHECK** each **VIEW/SHEET** to include in the print job. In this example, sheets **A-101**, **A-201**, and **A-401** are selected.
- *Step 6:* **CLICK** the **OK** button to close the **VIEW/SHEET SET** dialog box.

You may be prompted to save the view/sheet settings. Clicking Yes allows you to save the sheet selection for a future print. Clicking No will not save the selected sheets, requiring you to pick them again in future prints.

- *Step 7:* **CLICK** the **NO** button.

- *Step 8:* **CLICK** the **SETUP** button in the **PRINT** dialog box.
- *Step 9 (not shown):* In the **PRINT SETUP** dialog box, verify the **PAPER SIZE** and the paper **ORIENTATION**. **CHANGE** the **ZOOM** setting to **ZOOM: 100% SIZE** and the **PAPER PLACEMENT** to **CENTER**. **CLICK** the **OK** button to return to the **PRINT** dialog box.
- *Step 10:* **CLICK** the **OK** button to send the selected views to the printer.

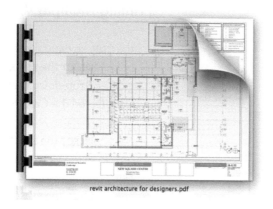

revit architecture for designers.pdf

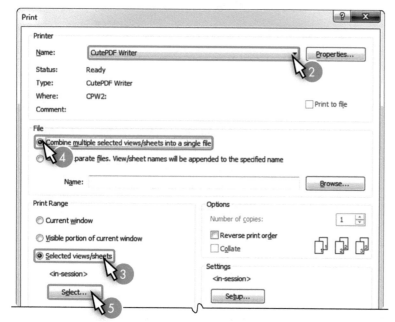

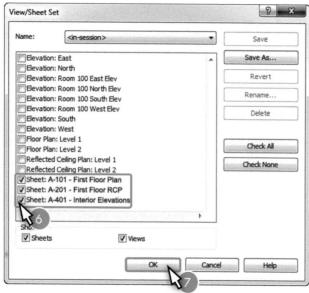

PDF Creation Software

PDF is the standard digital document format used in the architectural industry. Because Revit does not include a PDF writer, you will need to install a special program to create PDFs of your Revit drawings. Two PDF writers include Adobe's Acrobat Pro and CutePDF Writer. Both PDF writers create PDFs from any program through the print dialog box.

Acrobat Pro is included with the Adobe Creative Suite, which you may have installed on your computer.

CutePDF Writer is a popular, free PDF writer.

Tip: To continue the PDF print instruction in this chapter, download and install a PDF writer from **WWW.RAFDBOOK.COM/DOWNLOADS.**

Printing a Multi-View PDF

- *Step 1 (not shown)*: **OPEN** the **VIEW** or **SHEET** that you want to print. On the keyboard, **PRESS** the **CTRL** key and the letter **P**.
- *Step 2*: **SELECT** a **PDF PRINTER** from the printer Drop-down menu. In this example, we selected the **CUTEPDF WRITER.**
- *Step 3*: **SELECT** the **SELECTED VIEWS/SHEETS** option in the **PRINT RANGE** portion of the **PRINT** dialog box.
- *Step 4*: **CLICK** the **COMBINE MULTIPLE SELECTED VIEWS** button.
- *Step 5*: **CLICK** the **SELECT** button to select the views/sheets to print.

- *Step 6*: **CHECK** each **VIEW/SHEET** to include in the print job. In this example, sheets **A-101**, **A-201**, and **A-401** are selected.
- *Step 7*: **CLICK** the **OK** button to close the **VIEW/SHEET SET** dialog box.

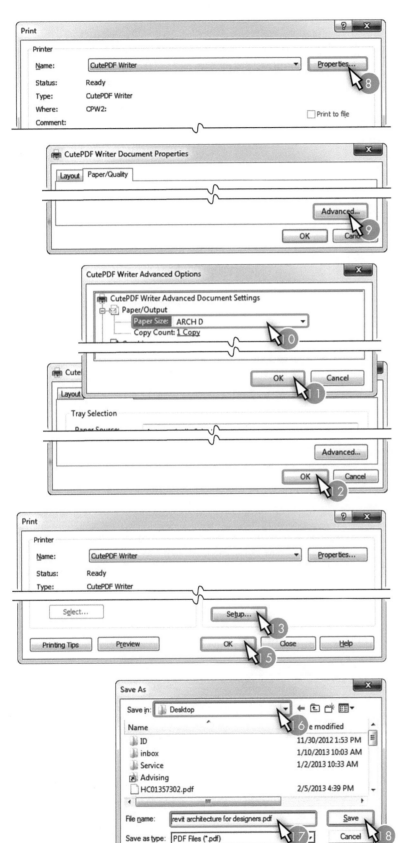

Printing a Multi-View PDF (continued)

- *Step 8*: **CLICK** the **PROPERTIES** button in the **PRINT** dialog box.

- *Step 9*: **CLICK** the **ADVANCED** button in the **CUTEPDF WRITER DOCUMENT PROPERTIES** dialog box.

- *Step 10*: **SELECT** the proper **PAPER SIZE**. (The paper size should match the title block size when printing sheets.)
- *Step 11*: **CLICK** the **OK** button to close the **CUTEPDF WRITER ADVANCED OPTIONS** dialog box.

- *Step 12*: **CLICK** the **OK** button to close the **CUTEPDF WRITER DOCUMENT PROPERTIES** dialog box.

- *Step 13*: **CLICK** the **SETUP** button in the **PRINT** dialog box.
- *Step 14 (not shown)*: In the **PRINT SETUP** dialog box, verify the **PAPER SIZE** and the paper **ORIENTATION**. **CHANGE** the **ZOOM** setting to **ZOOM: 100% SIZE** and the **PAPER PLACEMENT** to **CENTER**. **CLICK** the **OK** button to return to the **PRINT** dialog box.
- *Step 15*: **CLICK** the **OK** button to send the selected views to the PDF writer.

The PDF writer will present a pop-up window requesting the **SAVE AS** information for the PDF.

- *Step 16*: **SELECT DESKTOP** or an alternate location to save the PDF.
- *Step 17*: **TYPE** a **FILENAME** for the PDF.
- *Step 18*: **CLICK** the **SAVE** button to send the PDF to the desktop.

LEARNING EXERCISES

Learning Exercises

These exercises are intended to help you improve your understanding of setting up sheets in Revit.

Learning Exercise 14.1: Sheets

To begin this exercise, open the Revit project completed in Learning Exercises 13.3 at the end of Chapter 13. You can download a sample solution for this exercise at **WWW.RAFDBOOK.COM/DOWNLOADS.**

Follow the step-by-step exercises in the chapter to create the following sheets using the companion Revit project. For each sheet, add the appropriate view or views.

- **A-000** - Cover Sheet with Index
- **A-111** - Level 11 Construction Plan
- **A-211** - Level 11 RCP
- **A-401** - Interior Elevations
- **A-501** - Interior Details
- **A-601** - Door, furniture, finish, and lighting schedules
- **A-711** - Level 11 Furniture Plan
- **A-811** - Level 11 Finish Plan

Learning Exercise 14.2: Custom Title Block

In addition to setting up the sheets above, complete the following:

- Customize the **TITLE BLOCK** using the family editor.
- Print a PDF of the entire drawing set.

Application Exercises

Using an assignment from your instructor or a previously completed studio project, set up the appropriate sheets.

- Customize the **TITLE BLOCK** using the family editor.
- Print a PDF of the entire drawing set.

INDEX

C

Distance

English	Metric
1 inch	2.54 centimeters
1 foot	0.3048 meter/30.48 centimeters
1 yard	0.9144 meter
Metric	**English**
1 centimeter	0.3937 inch
1 meter	3.280 feet

Weight

English	Metric
1 ounce	28.35 grams
1 pound	0.45 kilogram
Metric	**English**
1 gram	0.035 ounce
1 kilogram	2.2 pounds

General Formulas for Converting Units

Number of Units × Conversion Number = New Number of Units

Distance Formulas

To convert **INCHES** to **CENTIMETERS**:

[number of inches] × 2.54 = [number of centimeters]

To convert **CENTIMETERS** to **INCHES**:

[number of centimeters] × 0.3937 = [number of inches]

To convert **FEET** to **METERS**:

[number of feet] × 0.3048 = [number of meters]

To convert **METERS** to **FEET**:

[number of meters] × 3.280 = [number of feet]

To convert **YARDS** to **METERS**:

[number of yards] × 0.9144 = [number of meters]

Weight Formulas

To convert **OUNCES** to **GRAMS**:

[number of ounces] × 28.35 = [number of grams]

To convert **GRAMS** to **OUNCES**:

[number of grams] × 0.035 = [number of ounces]

To convert **POUNDS** to **KILOGRAMS**:

[number of pounds] × 0.45 = [number of kilograms]

To convert **KILOGRAMS** to **POUNDS**:

[number of kilograms] × 2.2 = [number of pounds]

STANDARD ARCHITECTURAL SCALES

Imperial and SI Architectural Scales

Imperial Architectural Scale	Imperial Scale Factor	SI Architectural Scale	SI Scale Factor
3″ = 1′-0″	4	1:5	5
1 1/2″ = 1′-0″	8		
1″ = 1′-0″	12	1:10	10
3/4″ = 1′-0″	16		
1/2″ = 1′-0″	24	1:20	20
3/8″ = 1′-0″	32		
1/4″ = 1′-0″	48	1:50	50
3/16″ = 1′-0″	64		
1/8″ = 1′-0″	96	1:100	100
3/32″ = 1′-0″	128		
1/16″ = 1′-0″	192	1:200	200
1/32″ = 1′-0″	384		
		1:500	500

Plan Drawing Architectural Scales

Drawing Type	Imperial Scale	SI Scale
Site Plans	1/16″ = 1′-0″	1:200
	1/32″ = 1′-0″	1:500
Floor Plans	1/8″ = 1′-0″	1:100
Reflected Ceiling Plans	1/8″ = 1′-0″	1:100
Enlarged Plans	1/4″ = 1′-0″	1:50

Elevation Drawing Architectural Scales

Drawing Type	Imperial Scale	SI Scale
Building Elevations	1/8″ = 1′-0″	1:100
Interior Elevations	1/4″ = 1′-0″	1:50
Casework Elevations	1/4″ = 1′-0″	1:50
	1/2″ = 1′-0″	1:25

Details & Sections Architectural Scales

Drawing Type	Imperial Scale	SI Scale
Building Sections	1/8″ = 1′-0″	1:100
Details	1″ = 1′-0″	1:10
	1 1/2″ = 1′-0″	
	3″ = 1′-0″	1:5

STANDARD PAPER SIZES

Standard Architectural Text Sizes

ISO Paper Size	Height (Imperial)	Height (SI)
Standard Text Height (Dimensions, notes, etc.)	3/32"	2.5mm
Secondary Titles (Schedule & Table Titles)	1/8"	3.5mm
Primary Titles (Drawing names)	3/16"	5mm
Sheet Name & Sheet Number	1/4"	7mm
Sheet Name & Sheet Number	3/8"	8mm
Large Text on Title Sheets	1/2"	13mm
Extra Large Text on Title Sheets	1"	21mm

North American Paper Sizes

US Paper Size	Imperial Size	SI Size	Closest ISO Size
ANSI A (Letter)	8.5" x 11"	216 x 279mm	A4
ANSI B (Tabloid)	11" x 17"	279 x 432mm	A3
ANSI C	17" x 22"	432 x 559mm	A2
ANSI D	22" x 34"	559 x 864mm	A1
ANSI E	34" x 44"	864 x 1118mm	A0
ARCH C	18" x 24"		A2
ARCH D	24" x 36"		A1
ARCH E	36" x 48"		A0
ARCH E1	30" x 42"		

Standard International (ISO) Paper Sizes

ISO Paper Size	SI Size	Imperial Size	Closest US Size
A0	841 x 1188	33-1/8" x 46-13/16"	ANSI E or ARCH E
A1	594 x 841	23-3/8" x 33-1/8"	ANSI D or ARCH D
A2	420 x 594	16-1/2" x 23-3/8"	ANSI C or ARCH C
A3	297 x 420	11-3/4" x 16-1/2"	ANSI B (Tabloid)
A4	210 x 297	8-1/4" x 11-3/4"	ANSI A (Letter)
A5	148 x 210	5-7/8" x 8-1/4"	
A6	105 x 148	4-1/8" x 5-7/8"	
A7	74 x 105	2-15/16" x 4-1/8"	
A8	52 x 74	2-1/16" x 2-15/16"	

KEYBOARD SHORTCUTS

Build

Door	**DR**
Level	**LL**
Model Line	**LI**
Room	**RM**
Wall	**WA**
Window	**WN**

Modify

Align	**AL**
Copy	**CO** or **CC**
Create Similar	**CS**
Delete	**DE**
Match Type Properties	**MA**
Mirror: Draw Axis	**DM**
Mirror: Pick Axis	**MM**
Move	**MV**
Offset	**OF**
Paint	**PT**
Repeat Last Command	**RC**
Rotate	**RO**
Scale	**RE**
Select All Instances: In Entire Project	**SA**
Trim/Extend to Corner	**TR**

Annotate

Aligned Dimension	**DI**
Detail Line	**DL**
Tag by Category	**TG**
Tag Room	**RT**
Text	**TX**

Navigate

Zoom All to Fit	**ZA**
Zoom in Region	**ZR** or **ZZ**
Zoom Out (2x)	**ZO** or **ZV**
Zoom Sheet Size	**ZS**
Zoom to Fit	**ZE** or **ZX**

View Settings

Hide Category	**HC**
Hide Element	**HH**
Hide in View: Hide Category	**VH**
Hide in View: Hide Elements	**EH**
Hidden Line	**HL**
Render	**RR**
Render Gallery	**RG**
Render in Cloud	**RD**
Reveal Hidden Elements Mode (toggle)	**RH**
Thin Lines (toggle)	**TL**
Unhide Category	**VU**
Unhide Element	**EU**
View Range	**VR**
Visibility/Graphics	**VG** or **VV**
Wireframe	**WF**

User Interface Settings

Cancel	**CG**
Cascade Windows	**WC**
Close	**SZ**
Properties Palette (toggle)	**PP**
Tile Windows	**WT**